Philosophy throug Computer Scienc

What do philosophy and computer science have in common? It turns out, quite a lot!

In providing an introduction to computer science (using Python), Daniel Lim presents in this book key philosophical issues, ranging from external world skepticism to the existence of God to the problem of induction. These issues, and others, are introduced through the use of critical computational concepts, ranging from image manipulation to recursive programming to elementary machine learning techniques. In illuminating some of the overlapping conceptual spaces of computer science and philosophy, Lim teaches readers fundamental programming skills and allows them to develop the critical thinking skills essential for examining some of the enduring questions of philosophy.

Key Features

- Teaches readers actual computer programming, not merely ideas about computers
- Includes fun programming projects (like digital image manipulation and Game of Life simulation), allowing the reader to develop the ability to write larger computer programs that require decomposition, abstraction, and algorithmic thinking
- Uses computational concepts to introduce, clarify, and develop a variety of philosophical issues
- Covers various aspects of machine learning and relates them to philosophical issues involving science and induction as well as to ethical issues
- Provides a framework to critically analyze arguments in classic and contemporary philosophical debates

Daniel Lim is an Associate Professor of Philosophy at Duke Kunshan University and a Research Fellow at the Center for Philosophy and Cognitive Science at Renmin University of China. He works in philosophy of mind, philosophy of religion, experimental philosophy, and the intersection of philosophy and computation. He is the author of *God and Mental Causation* (2015).

Philosophy through Computer Science

An Introduction

Daniel Lim

Routledge
Taylor & Francis Group

NEW YORK AND LONDON

First published 2023
by Routledge
605 Third Avenue, New York, NY 10158

and by Routledge
4 Park Square, Milton Park, Abingdon, Oxon, OX14 4RN

*Routledge is an imprint of the Taylor & Francis Group, an
informa business*

© 2023 Taylor & Francis

ISBN: 978-1-032-22137-3 (hbk)
ISBN: 978-1-032-22136-6 (pbk)
ISBN: 978-1-003-27128-4 (ebk)

DOI: 10.4324/9781003271284

Typeset in Bembo
by codeMantra

For IJ—can't believe you're here!

Contents

Preface

I studied computer science back in the 1990s. After completing graduate school, I worked as a web-database programmer for several years. During this time, I developed a growing obsession with philosophical issues borne out of personal struggles. In particular, the existence of God and the nature of mind. So I did what any sensible person would do. I quit my job (to the utter dismay of my father) and went back to school. With a lot of perseverance, support, and luck, I finished my doctorate in philosophy and began working as an assistant professor at Renmin University of China.

After six productive years, I moved to Duke Kunshan University near Shanghai as an associate professor. Due to the disproportionate student demand for computer and data science classes, I was given the chance to teach COMPSCI 101: Introduction to Computer Science. As a result, I had the unique opportunity to teach both philosophy and computer science classes over the last four years. It quickly became evident to me that the conceptual spaces of these two disciplines overlapped in a number of interesting ways. Naturally, I asked, "wouldn't it be great to teach the two together?" I spent time developing the idea of teaching philosophy through computer science by publishing a couple of papers in pedagogy journals. This culminated in my developing a new class, PHIL 109: Philosophy through Computer Science. I offered it for the first time during the Spring 2020 semester and had a fantastic group of students who helped me see what worked and what didn't.

These encouraging results prompted me to begin writing this book. Parts of this book draw from previously published materials. Chapters 1, 7, 9, and 13 include material from "Philosophy through Computer Science" *Teaching Philosophy* 42 (2): 141–153. Chapters 15 and 16 include material from "Philosophy through Machine Learning" *Teaching Philosophy* 43 (1): 29–46.

I am indebted to so many people. Jiaxin Wu, an educational consultant at my institution, worked with me to evaluate the effectiveness of my class. Not only did she help me reflect on and improve the structure of my class, but we also co-authored "Teaching Some Philosophical Problems through

Computer Science" *American Philosophical Association Newsletter: Teaching Philosophy* 20 (2): 2–9. William Rapaport gave me valuable feedback on an initial draft. Corey Maley carefully reviewed all aspects of this book. His painstaking comments and questions greatly improved the material presented here. All remaining errors, of course, are mine.

The pandemic has made things difficult these past couple of years. I would not have been able to do anything without the help of my family. My parents have been steadfast supporters. My sister-in-law, Lila Lee, patiently handled all the graphics in my book. My in-laws tirelessly helped with my twin boys. And my wife did everything to give me the space and time to complete this project. Sora, how did we survive two years as new parents? You are my greatest supporter and best friend. I promise no more books.

Chapter 1

Philosophy and Computer Science

In 1959, Charles Percy Snow delivered the Rede Lecture at Cambridge University titled "The Two Cultures." In it, he lamented the chasm that existed between the sciences and the humanities and the growing inability of scholars in these domains to effectively communicate (let alone collaborate) across the divide. In particular, Snow was concerned that the humanities were being emphasized at the expense of the sciences within the British education system and that sustained division would pose problems for the nation's ability to successfully address world problems.[1]

It's safe to say that the opposite concern exists today: across different universities all over the world, many in the humanities are concerned that the sciences are being emphasized at the expense of the humanities. Today's standard wisdom for directionless undergraduates is: "if you're not sure what to major in, go into science, technology, engineering, and math (STEM)." Whatever you do, avoid the humanities!

This wisdom seems to be reflected in student enrollment numbers. The American Academy of Arts and Sciences reports:

> After 10 consecutive years of declines, the humanities' share of all new bachelor's degrees fell below 12% in 2015 for the first time since a complete accounting of humanities degree completions became possible in 1987.
>
> (AAAS, 2015)

> The Humanities Indicators released eight updates on recent trends in humanities degrees… demonstrating continued declines in humanities bachelor's, master's, and doctoral degrees in the years before the pandemic.
>
> (AAAS, 2021)

Against this backdrop, it's no wonder that proponents of the humanities are forced to regularly justify the value of their degrees to students.

DOI: 10.4324/9781003271284-1

Discussion: What are your thoughts on the sciences and the humanities? Is one domain more important than the other? How are the domains related?

In line with Snow, I believe that more bridge-building between the sciences and humanities is needed. After all, what is on offer from both domains is critical for fluid movement through our rapidly changing societies. I hope to contribute to building across the science-humanities divide by juxtaposing the learning of computer science with the learning of philosophy.

This book is for those who have an interest in both computer science and philosophy but little to no background in either. If you've been intimidated by one (or both) of these disciplines but always wanted to learn more about them, then this book is for you. Part of my goal is to demystify the disciplines so that you'll have the confidence to explore one (or both) further. While the book periodically dips into more challenging conceptual territories, it is always meant to be accessibly presented. Moreover, what is unique about this book is that it intends to bring the disciplines *pedagogically* together. That's why this book is titled "Philosophy *through* Computer Science." It is unlike other books at the intersection of philosophy and computer science that deal almost exclusively with the philosophy *of* computer science.[2] Unlike these other books (and almost any other book that is not focused purely on computer science), this book teaches you to actually program computers (in Python). In the end, you'll be able to write some fairly sophisticated and, what I think are, very interesting computer programs. Moreover, this book will introduce and explore 'classic' philosophical issues that long predate computers, rather than only those philosophical issues that involve 20th-century notions concerning computation. Finally, these 'classic' philosophical issues will be introduced *through* key computational concepts so that your exposure to philosophy will occur in a novel way.

Why computer science and philosophy? There no question that basic computational thinking is necessary for life in an increasingly computer-saturated and computer-mediated world. But the skills developed through studying philosophy, which include critical thinking and openness to diverse viewpoints, are equally necessary. According to a report of the Association of American Colleges and Universities (2013), nearly all surveyed employers were looking for applicants who have a demonstrated capacity "to think critically, communicate clearly, and solve complex problems." Moreover, they believed that these capacities were "more important than their undergraduate major." According to a BBC article (2019), employers also value the ability to understand others' viewpoints that is critical for fostering collaborative environments—"empathy is usually the biggest skill… [it's] an ability to understand the needs and wants of a diverse group of people." In a nutshell, being good at science isn't all that matters—critical yet empathetic thinking is needed too. Philosophy is uniquely situated to help with the development of just such a skill set.

Philosophical Thinking

Many people have no idea what philosophy is about. They simply assume it's an extremely difficult discipline to enter and that its elusive rewards are available only to the gifted few.

Discussion: How do you characterize what philosophy is?

While it's true that philosophy has been preoccupied with answering questions that most people don't care to think about, it's far from true that philosophy involves useless skills. To see this, consider a classic philosophical question: "can we know anything about the world?" Most people have an immediate, real-world response: "of course, we can!"

But what do philosophers do with such questions and answers? Here's a helpful passage from *The Norton Introduction to Philosophy*:

> In philosophy, we pause over these answers and subject them to exacting scrutiny. Such scrutiny can be unsettling, making what was once familiar seem puzzling. As confident understanding gives way to perplexity, a tempting response is to turn away from the questioning that gives rise to it. In philosophy, we make it our business to face the perplexity head-on, and ask whether and how our basic assumptions about knowledge, existence, and morality can be defended.
> (Rosen, Byrne, Cohen, Harman, & Shiffrin, 2018, p. xvii)

I want to say a bit more about some of the things covered in this passage. What might Rosen et al. mean by 'exacting scrutiny'? The authors packed a lot into this idea. At least a part of what is meant by this is that philosophers try to be very careful with their words. They want to get the clearest sense of what words mean so that they can be precise in how they evaluate various claims. For example, when philosophers ask whether we can know anything about the world, a lot of what this question boils down to depends on what is meant by the word 'know.' We might think the answer is obvious, but closer examination reveals that this may not be the case. Can you give a good definition of 'know'? At any rate, philosophers have tried to treat this word with care. In fact, an entire branch of philosophy, known as epistemology, is dedicated (among other things) to the understanding of the word 'know' and its cognates. We might refer to this care with words as **conceptual analysis**.

Rosen et al. also make reference to the questioning of 'basic assumptions.' This is an important skill to develop as a philosopher. Earlier, I quoted a BBC article on the value of the humanities that, among other things, highlighted empathy as an important job skill. Part of what makes a person empathetic is the ability to suspend belief in one's assumptions. Disagreement and division often arise because of an inability to see things from another person's perspective. When people get into heated arguments over sensitive topics, they simply can't understand how others are unable to see things 'correctly' (which often means, they can't understand why others don't see things *their* way). By turning the questioning of assumptions into a practiced skill, philosophical thinking can become an essential part of developing empathy.

Finally, the passage ends with reference to how assumptions might be 'defended.' This involves the marshaling of evidence for or against various claims. The critical assessment of attempts to provide evidence for claims lies squarely in the area of philosophy known as logic. Many simply refer to this as 'critical thinking,' but we will call it **logical analysis**.

So, it seems learning how to do philosophy well will help one become a critical empathetic thinker. In this book, we endeavor to develop such skills by examining some classic issues in philosophy.

Computational Thinking

On February 23, 2001, *This American Life*, a weekly public radio program, featured a story titled 'Superpowers' where they explored, among other things, which superpower people thought was better: flight or invisibility.

Discussion: If you could choose a superpower to have for yourself, which of these two would it be? And why?

The key to exploiting a superpower, like flight, is to know what possibilities it opens for you. But this may not always be a straightforward task. On the one hand, your imagination may be incorrectly constrained in certain ways. You might think that you can only use your superpower for several minutes a day. This may prevent you from entertaining all the amazing possibilities that are available to you—like flying to another city or even across the ocean. On the other hand, your imagination may be incorrectly *un*constrained in certain ways. You might think you can use your superpower to fly to the moon. This may encourage you to believe in fanciful possibilities that are in fact impossible—like flying without the need to breathe oxygen. It would be helpful in this regard if we could clearly demarcate what is and is not possible with our newly acquired superpowers.

Turning to computers, we can easily think of computers as providing us with several distinct superpowers. In order to exploit these potential powers, however, one requires clear knowledge of what these powers make possible.

Discussion: What are computers good at doing? What are humans good at doing? How do these tasks differ?

While there are a variety of ways we might think about the superpowers computers offer (Wing, 2006), we will limit ourselves to three. They are the powers of: (i) logic, (ii) memory, and (iii) speed. You might think—but we already have these powers! Indeed, we have excellent logic, memory, and speed. But how do our powers in these domains compare with the powers of computers? In terms of logic, do humans ever make mistakes? A computer (in some sense) never makes mistakes. In terms of memory, how many numbers can a human remember? Maybe a hundred or even a thousand? A computer can remember billions. In terms of speed, how quickly can humans calculate a million arithmetic operations? Maybe a couple of weeks of continuous work without any sleep or breaks? A computer can do it in less than a second.

These are amazing feats that, when compared to the deliverances of human powers, are truly super. To exploit these superpowers of logic, memory, and speed, however, we must learn how to get computers to do what we want them to do. This is no easy task because computers are brittle. Unless we provide computers with extremely precise instructions that follow strict syntax and grammar, they will not do what we want them to do. Moreover, the kinds of instructions computers require are often much more fine-grained than the kinds of instructions we're used to giving to other humans. We might, for example, simply tell a human to add up the first million positive integers starting from one and a human would know exactly what to do. In order to get a computer to do this, we'd have to break down the task into many, more detailed instructions.

This brings us to what many call 'computational thinking.' Once we identify a task that we believe computers can solve well, applying the techniques of computational thinking in an iterative but non-linear fashion will often prove critical in making progress. Because there is no universal definition of computational thinking, I'll stick with Jeannette Wing's (2014) definition to get started:

> Computational thinking is the thought processes involved in formulating a problem and expressing its solution(s) in such a way that a computer—human[3] or machine—can effectively carry it out.

We can break computational thinking down into the following four categories: decomposition, pattern recognition, data representation, and algorithm formulation.

Decomposition is breaking down a complex problem into simpler, more manageable sub-problems. The idea is that once these sub-problems are solved, their solutions can effectively be combined to solve the original complex problem. For example, a task that often benefits from decomposition is writing an essay. It's probably best to start with an outline. By doing this, it's possible to break down the complex task of writing an essay into simpler, more manageable parts. Instead of trying to write everything at once, decomposition allows one to selectively focus on the introduction, body, or conclusion. Once each of these more manageable parts is completed, one can simply put the parts together.

Pattern Recognition is looking for similarities among diverse problems. If similarities (or patterns) are found, it may be possible to use a single method for solving all of these problems with minor variations. So, for example, consider the task of manufacturing cars. Since we know that all cars share certain similarities such as an engine, a body, and wheels, to manufacture *any* car we simply need to manufacture each of these parts. That is, there is a single generalizable method for manufacturing cars. Though each car will differ in various ways, based on differences in their parts (engine type, body design, wheel size, etc.), manufacturing the overall car will remain structurally constant.

Data Representation is a kind of abstraction—focusing only on the relevant information and filtering out the irrelevant information. Maps serve as great examples of this kind of abstraction. Every map requires choices about what information to include and what information to exclude. A map of the solar system, for example, will rarely represent the actual distances between the sun and the planets (more often than not this would require far too much space—if the earth had a 1-inch radius, its distance to the sun would be about 2,000 feet!). Consequently, this information is often excluded. What matters, in most cases, is that the map conveys the proper *order* of the planets in terms of their relative distances from the sun. The map only has to represent, for example, the fact that Mercury is closer to the Sun than Earth. The actual distance from the Sun to Mercury is irrelevant.

Finally, **Algorithm Formulation** is creating a step-by-step recipe for solving a problem. Though you may not think of it as an algorithm, whenever you change lanes while driving you are following an implicit algorithm. First, you check to see if the lane you'd like to enter is open. Then you turn on the signal so other drivers are aware of your intention. You check the mirrors and blind spots and, if it's safe, smoothly move into the center of the desired lane. Once in, you turn off the signal and continue on your way. Clearly articulating the steps in this way not only allows you to accomplish a task, but it makes it possible for you to instruct others in accomplishing this same task.

At a very high level, what I hope you get out of this book (in addition to an introduction to philosophy *through* an introduction to computer science) are skills that are useful for pursuing work in the sciences, the humanities, and the burgeoning intersection of these domains. Because no book can be about all the skills relevant to the sciences and the humanities, I've been selective and focused on philosophy and computer science. I refer to some of the essential skills in these domains as philosophical and computational thinking. While we will definitely spend time learning more about these skills on a conceptual level, the bulk of this book will take a more practical approach. In order to develop philosophical thinking skills, we'll read about specific philosophical issues and try to do some actual philosophical thinking to understand some of the debates surrounding these issues. In order to pick up computational thinking skills, we'll work with the Python programming language and try to do some actual computational thinking to define tasks and write programs that carry out these tasks.

Looking Ahead

We'll begin in the next chapter by installing a Python development environment, interacting with the computer through Python, and familiarizing ourselves with the built-in text editor. The remainder of the book, as a quick perusal of the table of contents shows, is organized as a series of topics that alternate between computer science and philosophy. First, computational concepts will be introduced. Then, these computational concepts will be used to introduce and explore philosophical issues. Algorithms in computer science will be paired with logical analysis in philosophy, graphical image manipulation will be paired with external world skepticism, functions will be paired with the functionalist theory of mind, the so-called Game of Life will be paired with free will and determinism, recursive programming will be paired with the existence of God, and basic machine learning techniques will be paired with the problem of induction. And the final chapter will focus on the ethics of issues arising out of recent applications of computer technologies.

This book is only meant to get you started, not to make you an expert. Philosophical and computational thinking are topics that you can spend a lifetime mastering. And though we will spend a lot of time 'doing philosophy' and writing computer programs, I hope you will also try to keep the higher-level objectives in mind. More than remembering specific points about certain philosophical debates, I hope you develop a structured way of assessing debates in general by using philosophical thinking techniques: conceptual analysis, logical analysis, and the questioning of assumptions. More than remembering the exact Python syntax needed to carry out certain programming tasks, I hope you develop a structured way of assessing and addressing tasks (especially ones that computers are well suited to carry out) through computational thinking techniques: decomposition, pattern recognition, data representation, and algorithm formulation.

Notes

1   Snow was concerned, among other things, that England would be unable to help close the gap between the rich and poor nations of the world.

2   See, for example, Rapaport (2021) and Turner (2018). Texts like these focus on the ontology of programs, the epistemology of program correctness, the intentionality of specification, and the nature of computational abstraction, among other things. While these topics are interesting, because they are often discussed within a narrow area of philosophy, they will not be covered here. Instead, focus will be given to topics that are addressed in *introductory* philosophy textbooks.

3   Though the term 'computer' is almost exclusively used today to refer to machines, they were once used to refer to humans who perform mathematical calculations.

References

AAAS. (2015). *Bachelor's Degrees in the Humanities*. Retrieved from American Academy of Arts and Sciences: https://www.amacad.org/humanities-indicators/higher-education/bachelors-degrees-humanities

AAAS. (2021, June 14). *Humanities Degrees Declining Worldwide Except at Community Colleges*. Retrieved from American Academy of Arts and Sciences: https://www.amacad.org/news/humanities-degrees-declining-worldwide-except-community-colleges

AACU. (2013). *It Takes More Than a Major*. Retrieved from Association of American Colleges & Universities: https://www.aacu.org/sites/default/files/files/LEAP/2013_EmployerSurvey.pdf

BBC. (2019, April 2). *Why 'Worthless' Humanities Degrees May Set You Up for Life*. Retrieved from BBC: https://www.bbc.com/worklife/article/20190401-why-worthless-humanities-degrees-may-set-you-up-for-life

Rapaport, W. (2021, August 30). *Philosophy of Computer Science*. Retrieved from UB CSE Department: William J. Rapaport: https://cse.buffalo.edu/~rapaport/Papers/phics.pdf

Rosen, G., Byrne, A., Cohen, J., Harman, E., & Shiffrin, S. (2018). *The Norton Introduction to Philosophy*. New York: W.W. Norton & Company.

Turner, R. (2018). *Computational Artifacts: Towards a Philosophy of Computer Science*. Berlin: Springer.

Wing, J. (2006). Computational Thinking. *Communications of the ACM, 49*(3), 33–35.

Wing, J. (2014, January 10). *Computational Thinking Benefits Society*. Retrieved from Social Issues in Computing: http://socialissues.cs.toronto.edu/index.html%3Fp=279.html

Chapter 2

Python

Some people fail to understand what a computer can do because they are limited to the fixed applications they regularly use—applications like web browsers and word processors. A critical feature of a computer, however, is that it's **programmable**.[1] Most machines are built to perform a specific task. A calculator, for example, is built to help us perform basic arithmetic calculations. A radio is built to help us extract information from the airwaves and translate it into sound. These machines are limited to the specific tasks they were designed to perform—they cannot do anything else. The only way to get a calculator to perform the tasks of a radio would be, in essence, to take it apart and turn it into a *different* machine. That is, disassemble it and reassemble it into a radio.

The key breakthrough with computers is that, because they are programmable, a single machine, without being disassembled and reassembled, is capable of performing *any* computable task that *any* other machine can do. This is why, on a *single* machine (like my laptop), I can perform operations that a traditional calculator performs, but I can also run databases to store and analyze datasets or write essays (like the chapters of this book) that include text, fancy fonts, and images. The calculator, the database, and the word processor are all different programs that harness the power of the computer so that different combinations of operations can be run for different purposes. If I knew how, I could write a *new* program that runs on my laptop that could perform a combination of operations for a purpose that never existed before.

So, how can we harness this amazing power that is latent in every computer? How can we make it do what we want? The answer is through programming languages. In this book, we will be using the **Python** programming language to introduce computer programming. It is important to remember, however, that this is *not* a book about Python. There are many other books that provide a more comprehensive and detailed introduction to Python. Here, it is used as a tool to get a handle on the basics of writing programs and the general skills involved in computational thinking. The hope is that you will develop a sense for how to deal with and

DOI: 10.4324/9781003271284-2

program computers—a transferrable skill that can be deployed through the application of any other programming language. Moreover, we want to use the computational concepts acquired in this process to introduce (and explore) some classic philosophical issues. So, don't expect this book to cover *every* feature of the Python programming language—plenty will be left out!

There are at least two reasons why Python was chosen for this book. First, it is relatively easy to understand and the learning curve is lower than other languages like Java or C++. Second, it is arguably the most popular programming language in the world. In 2021, the Institute of Electrical and Electronics Engineers rated Python as the most popular language[2] (out of 55 possible languages). Though the popularity of any given language is bound to change, it's safe to say that Python will remain prominent throughout the remainder of this decade.

Installing Python

To get started, you must first install Python on your computer. You can do this by going to the official website: http://python.org. If you hover your mouse over the 'Downloads' tab, you should be presented with a button that links to the latest release (which at the time of my writing is Python 3.10.1 on December 16, 2021). If the latest release doesn't work on your computer because your operating system (e.g., Windows 7) is too old, then you'll have to delve a little deeper into the website. Assuming you are using a computer running recent versions of Windows or macOS, you can click on the relevant link in the 'Downloads' dropdown menu. This should present you with a variety of options. If you're running Windows, you should probably download the 'Windows installer' (either 32-bit or 64-bit depending on your computer) since you're probably most familiar with installing programs through installers. For more information about downloading and installing Python, the official website recommends going to https://wiki.python.org/moin/BeginnersGuide/Download.

If you simply stick with the default settings when installing Python, you will install the Integrated Development and Learning Environment (IDLE). This is useful for directly interacting with Python by issuing single-line statements, but it also makes it easy to create, modify, save, and execute Python programs with an arbitrary number of statements through its built-in text editor (more on this later in this chapter).

Objects and Types

As we begin our journey into the world of Python programming, it may be helpful to be reminded that Python is a programming *language*. Like any new language, learning to 'speak' in Python requires a lot of patience and practice. The early stages of language acquisition can be especially frustrating because *everything* is foreign. Not only is the spelling and pronunciation of individual words difficult, but trying to figure out how these words fit into the bigger grammatical picture can initially be downright impenetrable. Don't worry if all the new terminology doesn't make sense or you feel overwhelmed by the conceptual overload. This is completely normal. Trust the process and take things one step at a time.

Python is called an **interpreter**[3] because you can think of Python as a real-time human–machine translator. While a human–human translator helps us talk with other humans who don't share our language, a human–machine translator helps us talk with computers. The difference with Python is that it does not understand normal human languages like English. Python understands machine language on the one hand and the Python programming language on the other. So, it's up to us to learn the Python programming language so that we can use the Python interpreter to tell the computer what we want it to do. When we write code in Python, the Python interpreter immediately translates our code into machine language and communicates it to the computer. The computer executes this code and the Python interpreter communicates the computer's response back to us.

To see this in action, let's begin by opening IDLE. This should begin a session with the Python interpreter where you will see the following characters: '>>>' on the screen. The '>>>' is a prompt the Python interpreter uses to signal that it is waiting for a statement from you, the programmer.

Try typing a number into the Python interpreter and press <Enter> (or <Return>). You should see something like this:

```
>>> 12345
12345
```

Almost everything in Python is an **object**.[4] So, the number you just typed, 12345, is an object in Python. All objects in Python also have a **type** (or kind). The number 12345 is of type **int** (or integer).

There are four *atomic* types in Python—'atomic' because objects of these types are *not* divisible into further parts. They have no decomposable structure. Here are the four types:

- **int**: integer (e.g., -3, 20).
- **float**: real number with decimal points (e.g., -3.0, 3.14).
- **bool**: logical value—there are two: True or False.
- **NoneType**: 'nothing'—it only has a single value: None.

A *structured* type that can be used for representing text is of type **str** (or string). These objects are enclosed in quotation marks—single or double quotes are both acceptable, so long as they are used consistently (don't begin a string with a single quote and end it with a double quote or vice versa).

- **str**: text (e.g., 'hi', "Ironman").

Strings are considered structured objects because they are divisible into parts. The string "Ironman is cool" is composed of 15 characters (including the two spaces), and each character is individually accessible.

Before going on, try typing in your own examples of each of these five object types to get comfortable interacting with the Python interpreter.

```
>>> 100
100
>>> 100.0
100.0
>>> True
True
>>> None
>>> 'Hello World'
'Hello World'
```

There are a couple of things to note here. The spelling and capitalization of True (and False) are critical because everything you communicate to Python is **case-sensitive**. If you typed true (with a lowercase t), you should have received an error message because Python doesn't know what true is.

Moreover, notice that None receives no response from the Python interpreter. This is because None literally means nothing (why something like None is important will be addressed, at least partly, in a later chapter). Finally, even though true yields an error, 'true' (with quotes) does not yield an error because 'true' is considered a string. It follows that while both are valid statements, True and 'True' are very different objects. The former is a bool, while the latter is a str.

You can check the type of any object in Python by using the **type** function. To use a function, you simply use the *name* of the function followed by the object in question enclosed in parentheses. Because we want to use the type function, this can be done as follows:

```
>>> type(12345)
<class 'int'>
```

The example above returns <class 'int'>, which stands for the integer type (or class).

Exercise 2.1: Try using the type function on all five different types of objects and make sure you can properly identify what kinds of objects belong to each type.

Finally, it is possible to convert (some) objects of one type into objects of a different type by using the name of the type as a function. This is sometimes called casting. It's best to simply look at some examples to see how this works.

```
>>> int(3.14)
3
>>> float(3)
3.0
>>> str(3.14)
'3.14'
>>> int('5')
5
>>> int('hi')
Error
```

In order, the first statement converts 3.14 (a float) into 3 (an integer). Notice that the decimal portion of the float is simply removed to create an integer. The second statement converts 3 (an integer) into 3.0 (a float) by adding a 0 decimal value. The third statement converts 3.14 (a float) into '3.14' (a string), and the fourth statement converts '5' (a string) into 5 (an integer). The third and fourth conversions both work because the symbolic notation of each object in their respective pairs is identical. The fifth statement attempts to convert 'hi' (a string) into an integer, but this generates an error because the symbols 'h' and 'i' have no numerical counterparts.

Expressions

Now we are ready to explore one of the computer's superpowers: **logic**—the ability to follow directions and execute operations, in some sense, without mistakes (a superpower computers share with calculators). While humans are prone to error for a variety of reasons (e.g., lack of attention, fatigue), computers never lose focus or grow tired. They have the superhuman ability to do exactly what they are told! In this section, we will consider some of the operations computers can carry out with god-like perfection.

First, let's consider arithmetic operations. Objects can be combined with other objects through the use of operators to form **expressions**. The + operator, for example, can be used to add two numbers.[5]

```
>>> 2 + 3.5
5.5
```

The evaluation of an expression will result in an object of some type. 2 + 3.5, for example, will evaluate to an object of type float, 5.5. You can verify this by using the type function on this expression.

```
>>> type(2 + 3.5)
<class 'float'>
```

Other basic **arithmetic operators** include: -, *, /, %, //, and **:

- x - y   subtraction operator returns x subtracted by y.
- x * y   multiplication operator returns x multiplied by y.
- x / y   division operator returns x divided by y.
- x % y   remainder operator returns the remainder of x divided by y.
- x // y   integer division operator returns the quotient of x divided by y.
- x ** y   exponent operator returns x raised to the power y.

These operators can be used in conjunction with each other and can be nested with parentheses. The *order* of operation is as you'd expect it to be. The exponent operator, for example, takes precedence over (and is therefore executed before) the multiplication and division operators, which in turn take precedence over the addition and subtraction operators. This order can be overridden with parentheses. In this example, multiplication is carried out first, and then addition.

```
>>> 5 + 2 * 4
13
```

In this example, because of the parentheses, addition is carried out first, and then multiplication.

```
>>> (5 + 2) * 4
28
```

Exercise 2.2: Be sure to familiarize yourself with the arithmetic operators and get comfortable writing expressions. Write an expression that calculates the number of centimeters that are in ten miles (where there are 5,280 feet in a mile and 3.28084 feet in a meter).

Now let's consider **comparison operators**. Expressions formed with comparison operators result in objects of type bool (that is, True or False).

- x == y   equality operator returns True if x equals y (False otherwise).
- x != y   inequality operator returns True if x does not equal y (False otherwise).

- x < y   less-than operator returns `True` if x is less than y (`False` otherwise).
- x > y   greater-than operator returns `True` if x is greater than y (`False` otherwise).
- x <= y   at-most operator returns `True` if x is at most y (`False` otherwise).
- x >= y   at-least operator returns `True` if x is at least y (`False` otherwise).

You can test these operators out for yourself:

```
>>> 1 == 1
True
>>> 1 != 1
False
>>> type(1 == 1)
<class 'bool'>
>>> type(False)
<class 'bool'>
```

Exercise 2.3: Write an expression using comparison operators to check whether the following statement is true: there are more hours in a year than there are seconds in a day.

Variables

Now we are ready to learn about another computer superpower: **memory**. The introduction of **variables** allows us to name and perfectly remember objects. Variables can be created (and subsequently reassigned new values) by using the **assignment operator**, =. Here, we create a variable called x and assign 5 to it. Any object of any type can be assigned to a variable. In this example, we happen to assign an integer to x.

```
>>> x = 5
```

Notice, unlike the operators we've been introduced to so far, nothing is displayed on the screen in response to an assignment operation. Moreover, the assignment operator should not be confused with the *equality* comparison operator. The former consists of a single equal sign (=), while the latter consists of two equal signs (==). The assignment operator, in the example above, is *making* x equal to 5. But the equality comparison operator is *checking* to see if x is equal to 5.

```
>>> x == 5
True
```

When values are assigned to variables, it is easiest to think of the variables as names. So when we assign 5 to x, we can think of x as being another name for (and therefore another way of referring to) 5. We might use Figure 2.1 to visualize what the assignment operator does.

Now we can use x wherever we once used 5 since x acts as another way of referring to 5. If we simply type x, Python will evaluate this to be the object that was assigned to it, namely 5.

```
>>> x
5
```

Furthermore, we can use existing variables as values to be used in assignment operations for other variables.

```
>>> y = x
```

Notice what happens here. As visualized in Figure 2.2, it is the object assigned to x that is assigned to the variable y. It is not the variable x itself that is assigned to the variable y. If this were the case, then changing the object assigned to x would change the object assigned to y. But this is not what happens. Subsequent assignments to x do not affect what y refers to. Below, x is assigned to a new integer, 10. Despite this, y continues to refer to 5.

```
>>> y
5
>>> x = 10
>>> x
10
>>> y
5
```

Figure 2.1 5 is assigned to x.

Figure 2.2 5 is assigned to both x and y.

We might use Figure 2.3 to visualize the situation after a new object is assigned to x.

The order of evaluation is also important to keep in mind. The right side of the assignment operator is always evaluated first. This is what makes the following assignment possible.

```
>>> x = x + 1
```

The right side of the assignment operator, x + 1, is evaluated first. The value of x (prior to the assignment operation) is 10 so the resulting value, after evaluating the expression, is 11. This object is then assigned to the variable on the left side of the operator, which (again) is x. The resulting situation might look something like Figure 2.4.

Variable names can be composed of any combination of alphabet letters, numbers, and the underscore character (_). Uppercase and lowercase letters are different so variables with all the same letters but different capitalization will be considered different variables. The only constraint is that you must begin a variable name with a letter from the alphabet.

You also want to be careful of the names you choose. Earlier, you learned about the type function that comes built-in to the Python programming language. With the assignment operator, you can create a variable with the same name (type) and thereby change what type refers to. This is a very bad idea since you will lose the built-in ability of the original type function!

```
>>> type(1)
<class 'int'>
>>> type = 1
>>> type
1
```

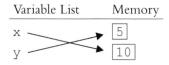

Figure 2.3 10 is assigned to x, 5 remains assigned to y.

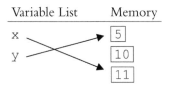

Figure 2.4 11 is assigned to x.

```
>>> type(1)
Error
```

This sequence of statements results in an error. Because `type` no longer refers to the *function* that returns the type of an object and instead refers to the integer 1, the final statement is tantamount to executing the following (which is nonsense in Python):

```
>>> 1(1)
```

While you could no longer use `type` as a function, what you could do is add numbers to `type` without any complaints from Python, since `type` now refers to a number.

```
>>> type + 1
2
```

This would be considered bad programming style and should be avoided—do not use variable names that already exist and refer to objects in Python!

Moreover, there are some names that are off-limits. These are the **reserved words**. They include `and`, `not`, and `or` (logical operators to be covered in the next chapter), among others. Any attempts to assign values to reserved words like these will result in an error.

Finally, it's good practice to come up with variable names that are meaningful. Consider the following several lines of code:

```
>>> likujyh = 10
>>> awsedrf = 3.14
>>> zsxdcfv = awsedrf * likujyh ** 2
```

You may or may not be able to decipher what is being calculated here, let alone be confident that you're typing the variable names correctly without carefully paying attention to each character. The following several lines of code, though carrying out the same calculation, are much easier to understand.

```
>>> radius = 10
>>> pi = 3.14
>>> area = pi * radius ** 2
```

For Python, of course, it really doesn't matter how variables are named. Both sets of statements are just as easy for Python to work with. The key is that well-written code will be easier for *humans* to understand. This is especially important in cases where code needs to be reused or revised by different people (even later versions of yourself!). Martin Fowler, a prominent software developer, summarizes this nicely:

> Any fool can write code that a computer can understand. Good programmers write code that humans can understand.
>
> (Fowler, 2019, p. 15)

So, it's a good idea to be thoughtful about variable names—a habit well worth developing.

Exercise 2.4: Create variables to calculate how much money you will earn in 25 years (assuming there are 52 weeks in a year) if you make $30 per hour and work 40 hours per week.

Text Editor

When trying to execute multiple lines of code, you may find it cumbersome to type all the statements into the interpreter correctly. Moreover, it's impossible to go back and make (even minor) changes to what you've already typed without having to type everything all over again. This can be extremely frustrating. It would be nice, therefore, to use a text editor to manipulate code in a more manageable way.

There are many excellent text editors that can serve this purpose. Some popular options include Atom, Sublime, Vim, and VS Code. Thankfully, the distribution of Python that you already installed, by default, includes a text editor.

To use the text editor in IDLE, you simply need to create a new file. The 'New File' option can be found under the 'File' tab of your IDLE window. This should open a new window where you can write out as many Python statements as you like.

```
x = 10
y = 'Hello World'
z = True
```

Once you're finished typing your statements, you must save the file and choose the 'Run Module' option under the 'Run' tab. This will send your code to the Python interpreter. If you typed everything in correctly, your code should have executed without any errors. It may be odd that nothing is reported back to you in the Python interpreter. This is because you are no longer *interacting* with the Python interpreter one line at a time. When executing a file, nothing will be displayed on the screen unless Python is explicitly told to do so. Nevertheless, the variables x, y, and z were created and assigned the relevant values.

In order to explicitly display things in the Python window, the **print** function must be used. It works the same way the type function does: type in the name of the function followed by an object (or expression) enclosed in parentheses.

```
>>> print(3.14 * 10 ** 2)
314.0
>>> area = 3.14 * 10 ** 2
>>> print(area)
314.0
```

Unlike the type function, however, you can give the print function multiple objects to be displayed so long as they are separated by commas.

```
>>> print("The area of a circle with radius", radius,
"is", area)
The area of a circle with radius 10 is 314.0
```

In this example, the print function is given four objects. The first and third are strings, the second is an integer, and the fourth is a float. Notice that spaces are automatically added between each object. This is why there is a space between the word 'radius' and the integer 10, 10 and the word 'is,' and 'is' and the float 314.0.

There is one final thing to note about executing statements through a file. You'll notice that the following appears in the Python interpreter:

```
==== RESTART: C:\test.py ===
```

As the first word suggests, the Python interpreter is restarted before executing the file. This means all previous work done in the interpreter will be destroyed. So, for example, if the variables x, y, and z were created prior to executing the file, these would be removed.

Exercise 2.5: Create a new file in the IDLE text editor and write code that will calculate the volume of a circle with a specified radius. Then display the radius and volume of the circle using the print function.

Key Points

- Installation of the IDLE Python environment.
- Basic types in Python: int, float, bool, NoneType, and str.
- Arithmetic and Comparison operators.
- Variables and the Assignment operator.
- The IDLE text editor.

Notes

1   While virtually all modern computers are programmable, there were plenty of non-programmable computers in the past including Konrad Zuse's machines and Alan Turing's Bombe.
2   https://spectrum.ieee.org/top-programming-languages-2021
3   In contrast to *compiler*-based languages (e.g. Java and C/C++), which translate code into executable programs that then need to be explicitly executed, *interpreter*-based languages translate code and execute the resulting programs immediately.
4   This may sound mysterious. After all, what is an object? Simply put, an object is a collection of data and methods that act on that data. There is a lot more to be said about this, but perhaps the best way forward is to simply look at examples and develop an understanding for what an object is.
5   Though there are spaces that separate the numbers and the + operator in the examples below, these spaces are not necessary. In fact, the numbers and the + operator can be separated by an arbitrary number of spaces (zero or more). Feel free to experiment as you code. You will see that different programmers develop differing syntactic styles.

Reference

Fowler, M. (2019). *Refactoring: Improving the Design of Existing Code.* New York: Addison-Wesley.

Chapter 3

Algorithms

Counterfeit Coin Problem[1]

You are given three coins. One (and no more than one) of these coins *may* be a counterfeit. All genuine coins have exactly the same weight, but a counterfeit will be slightly heavier or slightly lighter than a genuine coin. This slight difference is undetectable to the unaided human senses. The only way the difference can be discerned is by using an extremely sensitive balance scale. Balance scales consist of two plates (or bowls) suspended at equal distances from a fulcrum. This will never disclose the *absolute* weight of any object, it will only provide information about the *relative* weights of the objects being compared.

Assuming we use the names coin1, coin2, and coin3 for these three coins, can you come up with a method using a balance scale that will determine whether one of these coins is a counterfeit? And if there is a counterfeit, your method should be able to pick out the counterfeit coin and determine whether it is heavier or lighter than a genuine coin.

Discussion: Take a moment to think through your own solution to this problem before proceeding.

How might we apply some of the techniques of computational thinking to this problem? The first technique that might come to mind is **decomposition**. How can we decompose this problem into smaller, more manageable, sub-problems?

We can begin with the observation that for any given use of the scale, there are three possible outcomes: (1) the objects on both sides have the exact same weight; (2) the object (or objects) on the right is heavier than the object (or objects) on the left; and (3) the object (or objects) on the left is heavier than the object (or objects) on the right. Given this, we can begin by comparing two coins: coin1 and coin2 (it really doesn't matter which two coins we pick for this). And instead of trying to solve the entire problem at once, we can selectively focus on one of the three possible outcomes. Once each possible outcome is handled, the overall problem will be solved.

DOI: 10.4324/9781003271284-3

Before moving on to the solution discussed below, consider what each possible outcome means. What would it mean if we weigh two of the three coins, and those two have the same weight? On the other hand, what would it mean if two of the three coins do not have the same weight?

OUTCOME 1: `coin1 == coin2`

If `coin1` and `coin2` have the same weight, we know that they are both genuine. This means `coin3` *may* be a counterfeit. To test this, we compare either `coin1` or `coin2` (it doesn't matter which, since both are genuine) with `coin3`. Here, again, we are faced with three possible outcomes. In case they have the same weight, we know that there are no counterfeits. However, if the scale doesn't balance, we know that `coin3` must be a counterfeit and, depending on which way the scale tips, we will know whether `coin3` is heavier or lighter. If the scale tips in favor of `coin1` or `coin2`, then we know that `coin3` is lighter. If the scale tips in favor of `coin3`, then we know that `coin3` is heavier.

OUTCOME 2: `coin1 > coin2`

If `coin1` is heavier than `coin2`, then we know that one of these coins is a counterfeit, which means `coin3` *must* be genuine. Either `coin1` or `coin2` can then be compared with `coin3`. If `coin1` is compared with `coin3` and the scale is balanced, then we know that `coin2` is a counterfeit and that it is lighter. If `coin1` is compared with `coin3` and the scale does not balance, we know it must tip in favor of `coin1` (pause for a moment and make sure you can see that the scale can never tip in favor of `coin3` in this case). So `coin1` is a counterfeit and it is heavier.

OUTCOME 3: `coin1 < coin2`

If `coin1` is lighter than `coin2`, then again we know that one of these coins is a counterfeit, and `coin3` is genuine. Either `coin1` or `coin2` can then be compared with `coin3`. If `coin1` is compared with `coin3` and the scale is balanced, then we know that `coin2` is a counterfeit and that it is heavier. If `coin1` is compared with `coin3` and the scale does not balance, we know it must tip in favor of `coin3`. So, `coin1` is a counterfeit and it is lighter.

This, then, is a foolproof method for solving the counterfeit coin problem since we account for all possible outcomes. Decomposition played a critical role in simplifying the problem so that we could systematically attack each sub-problem.

Discussion: It may be easier, however, to understand this method by visualizing the logic (Figure 3.1). Can you fill in the remaining possibilities?

What has just been described is an **algorithm**—a step-by-step procedure for solving a well-defined problem. Another human can easily carry out

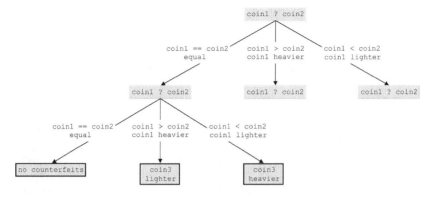

Figure 3.1 A decomposition of the Counterfeit Coin Problem.

these steps. The human doesn't even have to understand the problem being solved. She simply has to 'follow the directions'—for example, she simply has to put `coin1` and `coin2` on the scale and act accordingly. Mindlessly following the directions will inevitably lead to the correct solution.

But can this algorithm easily be carried out by a properly functioning computer? When the logic behind an algorithm is relatively simple and clearly laid out, chances are translating it into code will be a straightforward task. To do this, however, we'll need to add more functionality to our growing knowledge of Python. So far, all the code we've looked at has been organized in a way that the execution of statements is linear: statements are executed one after another without any break in order. What we need now is the ability to selectively execute statements based on certain conditions.

Conditionals

The **conditional** allows us to control which statements are executed based on certain conditions. The basic structure can be seen in Figure 3.2.

The first blank must be filled in with a condition: a `bool` object or an expression that evaluates to a `bool` object. If this condition evaluates to `True`, then the block of code in the `if` clause will get executed. Here, 'block of code' simply refers to at least one line of code (a block of code can include an indefinite number of statements). If the condition evaluates to `False`, then the block of code is entirely skipped and Python continues to execute code that comes after the `if` statement.

Note that the block of code is **indented**. This is critical because it tells Python what code belongs inside the `if` clause and what doesn't.

```
if _____ :     ◄——————————— Boolean expression
   _____       ◄——————————— block of code
```

Figure 3.2 **The basic structure of a conditional.**

Finally, don't forget that the first line of the conditional must end with a colon (:).

To see how this works, let's take a look at an example.

```
>>> if x < 10:
        print('small')
```

The condition is the Boolean expression x < 10. If x < 10 evaluates to True, then print('small') will be executed. If x < 10 is False, then print('small') is skipped. So, if x is less than 10, the string 'small' will be displayed on the screen. If x is not less than 10, then print('small') will be skipped and nothing happens.

You may have noticed that handling indentations correctly can be quite cumbersome in the Python interpreter. I suggest you do everything in the IDLE text editor from now on because we will be dealing with multiple lines of code with varying levels of indentation. To reflect the difference between using the Python interpreter directly and using the IDLE text editor, the '>>>' prompt will be omitted when using the IDLE text editor.

Since a block of code—not just one line of code—can be placed within the if clause there is no limit to the number of statements that can be included. Above, the if clause is composed of a single statement, print('small'), but an indefinite number of statements can be placed here. Consider the following code.

```
if x < 10:
    print('small')
    print(x)
    print(x == 10)
```

If the condition is True, then the three print statements will all be executed. If the condition is False, nothing will be displayed—the block of code in the if clause will simply be skipped.

To illustrate the importance of indentation, consider the following code. Though it is composed of the same statements, its behavior will be very different.

```
if x < 10:
```

```
    print('small')
print(x)
print(x == 10)
```

Question: Because the indentation differs from the code above, this code behaves differently. Can you predict what will happen?

The second and third `print` statements will be executed regardless of the truth or falsity of the `if` condition. Only the first `print` statement is part of the `if` clause, so whether it gets executed depends on whether or not x is less than 10.

Exercise 3.1: Write code that checks whether the variable x is even. If it is, then display the string `'It is even!.'` (Hint: use the `%` operator to check the remainder of x divided by 2. What must the remainder be if x is even?)

In case you ran into some problems with the previous exercise, here are a couple of things to remember. First, to check for the evenness of x, you will probably need to use the equality operator (`==`). It is easy, however, to confuse this with the assignment operator (`=`) because they both use equal signs. Don't forget that the equality operator requires *two* equal signs. Second, to actually test your code, x must already exist and be assigned a numerical value. If it does not already exist, even if your solution is correct, your code will generate the following error:

```
NameError: name 'x' is not defined
```

An optional `else` clause can be added to the `if` statement to provide an additional layer of logic.

```
if x < 10:
    print('small')
else:
    print('big')
```

The `else` clause specifies a block of code that will be executed if the condition is `False`. This construction guarantees that one (and only one) of these two blocks of code will be executed. If the condition is `True`, the block of code in the `if` clause will be executed and the block of the code in the `else` clause skipped. If the condition is `False`, the block of code in the `else` clause will be executed and the block of code in the `if` clause skipped. Either way, one (and only one) of these two blocks of code will be executed.

Multi-Clause and Nested Conditionals

This same kind of logic can be extended to an indefinite number of mutually exclusive blocks of code using `elif` (short for 'else if') clauses. This structure ensures that one (and only one) of the blocks of code will be executed in a multi-clause conditional. Below is an example:

```
if x < 10:
    print('small')
elif x < 20:
    print('medium')
elif x < 30:
    print('large')
else:
    print('x-large')
```

This conditional has four separate blocks of code. Note that this is a *single* conditional statement with four clauses. This will display `'small'` if x is less than 10, display `'medium'` if x is greater than or equal to 10 and less than 20, display `'large'` if x is greater than or equal to 20 and less than 30, and display `'x-large'` if x is greater than or equal to 30. Note, again, that all the blocks of code are mutually exclusive—only *one* of the four blocks of code will be executed. Moreover, one of the four blocks of code must be executed.

The following code is the same as the code above, but the `elif` clauses are replaced with `if` clauses. That means there are now *three* independent conditional statements. The first two conditionals each have a single clause (an `if` clause), while the third has two clauses (an `if` clause and an `else` clause). The critical difference is that now it's possible that more than one of the four blocks of code can be executed.

```
if x < 10:
    print('small')
if x < 20:
    print('medium')
if x < 30:
    print('large')
else:
    print ('x-large')
```

Exercise 3.2: It's possible for the first three blocks of code to *all* be executed. What value must x be in order for this to happen?

More complex Boolean expressions can be constructed by using the following **logical operators**.

- x and y: and operator returns `True` only if x and y are both `True` (`False` otherwise).

- x or y: or operator returns True if x or y (or both) is True (False otherwise).
- not x: negation operator returns True if x is False (False otherwise).

The following Boolean expression will be True if x is an even number *and* it is less than 10.

```
x % 2 == 0 and x < 10
```

Exercise 3.3: Write an expression that evaluates to True if x is odd or y is even.

Conditionals can also be nested within each other. If 10 is assigned to the variable x what will happen when the following code is executed?

```
if x < 10:
    print('small')
    if x % 2 == 0:
        print('even')
    else:
        print('odd')
else:
    print('large')
    if x % 2 == 0:
        print('even')
    else:
        print('odd')
```

Since x refers to 10, the condition (x < 10) in the main if clause evaluates to False. So, the entire first block of code (which includes a nested conditional) is skipped. The second block of code in the else clause must be executed. First, the string 'large' is displayed on the screen. Then the nested conditional is executed. The condition of the nested if clause is True (since the remainder of 10 divided by 2 is 0) so the string 'even' is displayed on the screen. Finally, because the condition is True, the block of code in the nested else clause is skipped.

Exercise 3.4: Write code that displays 'foo' if x is even and is divisible by 10, displays 'bar' if x is even and divisible by 7, and displays 'baz' if x is odd. (Hint: the first two conditions share the requirement that x is even. Using nested conditionals will allow you to check for x's evenness only once.)

Counterfeit Coin Implementation

We are now in a position to turn the algorithm for solving the counterfeit coin problem into code. Assuming there are three variables called coin1, coin2, and coin3 that are assigned the weights of the three coins in question, we can write out the logical framework of the algorithm as depicted in Figure 3.1 as follows:

```
if coin1 == coin2:
    if coin1 == coin3:
        print('there are no counterfeit coins')
    elif coin1 > coin3:
        print('coin3 is counterfeit and lighter')
    else:
        print('coin3 is counterfeit and heavier')
elif coin1 > coin2:
    _____

else:
    _____
```

Exercise 3.5: Can you replace the blanks with code so that the proper information will be displayed on the screen?

To test your code, you will need to create the variables coin1, coin2, and coin3 and explicitly assign them values (of your choosing). It would be a good exercise to execute your code with different value assignments to ensure that every possible outcome is accounted for. So, for example, at least one of your value assignments should give coin1, coin2, and coin3 all the same value. This should cause your code to display 'there are no counterfeits' on the screen.

Key Points

- An algorithm is a step-by-step procedure for solving a well-defined problem.
- Conditionals are a means of controlling statement execution.
- Multi-clause and nested conditionals.
- Logical operators.

Note

1   This is the easiest version of the so-called 'Balance Puzzle' (or 'Weighing Puzzle') which is a logic puzzle based on balancing items to discern which among a set of items has a different weight. This puzzle was used by Ferragina and Luccio (2018) as a way of introducing algorithms and I found it engaging and helpful so the idea is used here as well.

Reference

Ferragina, P., & Luccio, F. (2018). *Computational Thinking: First Algorithms, Then Code*. Cham, Switzerland: Springer.

Chapter 4

Logic

In the previous chapter, we developed an algorithm to solve the Counterfeit Coin Problem and then implemented this algorithm in Python using conditionals. These concepts lead naturally to a foundational area of philosophy known as **logic**. While there is no consensus on what should be included in its domain, for the purposes of this book, we will limit the definition of logic to the analysis and evaluation of **arguments**. In the rest of this chapter, we will focus on the **logical analysis** of arguments as a way of developing our overall ability to think philosophically.

The term 'argument' has a technical definition within logic and should not be confused with a heated exchange of different opinions and views. An argument is a set of statements, called **premises**, that provide evidence (or reason) to affirm the truth of another statement, called the **conclusion**. A **statement** is a sentence that is either true or false. Not all sentences are statements, so be careful that you only include statements in your arguments. The sentence "go to bed," for example, is not a statement. It would be odd to say that it is true or false: it's a command (I often give to my kids).

Consider the following argument:

Argument A₁

1. If Obama is American, then Obama is human.
2. Obama is American.
3. Therefore, Obama is human.

The premises are statements 1 and 2 and the conclusion is statement 3. Notice that each of the statements in this argument is capable of being true or false. As it happens, both premises are true and so is the conclusion. This is an excellent argument. Not only are the premises true, but the premises also guarantee the truth of the conclusion. So the conclusion must be true if the premises are, too.

DOI: 10.4324/9781003271284-4

Let's take a moment to connect what's going on in this argument with what we saw in the previous chapter concerning the conditional if operator. We can begin by using variables, obama_american and obama_human, to represent the statements "Obama is American" and "Obama is human," respectively.

We can assign None to obama_human:

```
obama_human = None
```

This represents that it is an open question whether "Obama is human" is true. Because this is the conclusion, it is what the argument on offer is meant to convince us of.

We might then represent premise 2 in code as follows:

```
obama_american = True
```

This would be claiming that the statement "Obama is American" is true. Next, we can represent premise 1 in code as follows:

```
if obama_american == True:
    obama_human = True
```

This would be claiming that if the statement "Obama is American" is true then the statement "Obama is human" must also be true. Note the difference between the equality operator (that has two equal signs) in the condition of the if statement and the assignment operator (that has a single equal sign) within the block of code of the if statement (refer back to the section on Conditionals in Chapter 3 if this isn't clear). Putting this together, the entire argument might be translated into Python in the following way:

```
obama_human = None
  obama_american = True

  if obama_american == True:
    obama_human = True
```

So, in a very natural sense, Argument A_1 can be represented as a conditional if statement along with a couple of assignment statements. It can be seen as a way of moving from one statement to another in a logically understandable manner. You might even think of an argument as an algorithm to reach a certain conclusion. So, as we proceed, keep the possibility of translating arguments into code in the back of your mind and, where possible, make an attempt to do the translation.[1]

Truth & Validity

How can we assess whether Argument A₁ is a good argument or not? Generally, there are two features to look for: (1) whether the premises are true and (2) whether the premises entail the conclusion. That is, we want to assess the **truth** of the premises and the **validity** of the inference from the premises to the conclusion.

First, are the premises true? Let's look at premise 1. It is a conditional statement. Philosophers like to give names to everything, so they've given names to the two parts of conditional statements. The first part (the if clause), "Obama is American," is called the **antecedent**. The second part (the then clause), "Obama is human," is called the **consequent**. Because we're dealing with a conditional statement, it is important to remember that it is making a **hypothetical** claim. It is not making the claim that the antecedent is true, namely that Obama is, in fact, American. Nor is it making the claim that the consequent is true, namely that Obama is, in fact, a human. It is the hypothetical claim about what would be the case *if* Obama were American. Put in this way, Obama's actual citizenship is irrelevant to the truth of premise 1. What matters for the truth of premise 1 is an underlying claim about the *relationship* between Obama's being American (the antecedent) and Obama's being human (the consequent). Put in this way it's almost true by definition because we assume that all Americans are humans. Being human can be seen as a necessary condition for being American: it's impossible to be American without also being human. So, premise 1 seems to be a straightforward fact.

How about premise 2? Though there have been some conspiracy theories about Obama's not being a natural-born US citizen, premise 2 is nonetheless true—it's a simple, well-attested fact.

Second, do the premises entail the conclusion? The word '**entail**' in logic has a very specific meaning. What it means for the premises to entail the conclusion is that it is *impossible* for the premises to be true and the conclusion to be false. It must be emphasized that 'impossible' in this context is not merely an adjective to accentuate that something is not likely to happen. For example, someone might say, it's impossible to win the lottery. In this sense, 'impossible' doesn't literally mean that winning the lottery is impossible. Rather it's a hyperbolic way of saying that the chances of winning are extremely small. In a technical philosophical setting, however, this would, strictly speaking, be false. It is *not* impossible to win the lottery—there is always a possibility (no matter how small). What we are concerned with in logic is absolute necessity. So, to claim that the premises entail the conclusion is an extremely strong claim—it is the claim that there are no possibilities (no matter how small) that the premises are true and the conclusion false.

Regarding Argument A₁, it seems that the premises do entail the conclusion. If it's the case that premise 2 is true (i.e., Obama is in fact American) and if it's the case that premise 1 is true (i.e., Obama's being American guarantees Obama's being human), then it is *im*possible in the strict logical sense for the conclusion (i.e., Obama's being human) to be false. So, the truth of the premises absolutely guarantees the truth of the conclusion. When this is achieved, we say that the argument is **valid**. That is, the inference (or reasoning) that moved us from the premises to the conclusion is good.

Given that validity is a feature of arguments, it would be incorrect to say that a single premise is valid (or invalid). Premises are either true or false. It is the entire argument that can be valid or invalid. Similarly, it would be incorrect to say that the argument is true or false. We should say that the argument is either valid or invalid.

Note also that the word 'if' is being used in a technical sense in Argument A_1. When we use this word in colloquial contexts, it usually doesn't carry the same guarantees. If I were to tell you that I will not leave the house *if* it's raining, this is not usually understood in the logical sense of entailment—where rain absolutely guarantees my not leaving the house. There are some obvious exceptions to this conditional. If my child is badly injured and needs immediate medical attention, I will leave the house even if it's raining.

In this sense, it's helpful to think of the word 'if' in the way the if statement works in Python. There are no exceptions in the way Python executes conditionals. If the condition is True, then the block of code in the if clause will be executed. This is absolutely guaranteed, and there are no exceptions. There is something mechanical and robotic about the way these statements are handled in Python. We should operate similarly when using the word 'if' in conditional statements in the context of logic.

According to these two features, then, we can see that Argument A_1 does very well. Its premises are true, and it is valid: the premises entail the conclusion. When these two features are *both* achieved, we say that the argument is **sound**. If one or both of these features is missing, we say that the argument is **unsound**.

To get a better handle on these features, let's look at some variations on Argument A_1.

Argument A_2

1.   If Obama is Chinese, then Obama is human.
2.   Obama is Chinese.
3.   Therefore, Obama is human.

What should we make of Argument A_2?

First, are the premises true? Premise 1 is true since we know that all Chinese people are human. Remember premise 1, being a conditional, is a hypothetical claim. It is not the claim that Obama is, in fact, Chinese. It's the claim that *if* Obama were Chinese, then Obama would be human. Put this way, premise 1 is clearly true. Premise 2, however, is clearly false. It is not the case that Obama is, in fact, Chinese. On this basis alone, we know that Argument A_2 is unsound since one of its premises is false.

The analysis, however, is incomplete. We still want to know whether the premises entail the conclusion. That is, we want to know whether the argument is valid. The argument is indeed valid because it is impossible for the premises to be true and the conclusion false. Of course, not all the premises are true, but the question here is: *if* the premises were true, then it surely seems that the conclusion could not fail to be true as well. In other words, the inference (or reasoning) from the premises to the conclusion is good. An advocate of Argument A_2, who confidently believed in the truth of the two premises, would be reasoning perfectly in concluding that Obama is human. That is, there is nothing wrong with the person's logic. Where this person goes wrong is in believing something, namely premise 2, that is not actually true. So, we should say that though Argument A_2 is unsound, it is nevertheless valid—the reasoning embedded in it is perfect.

Let's consider another variation on Argument A_1:

Argument B_1

1. If Obama is American, then Obama is human.
2. Obama is human.
3. Therefore, Obama is American.

What should we make of Argument B_1?

First, are the premises true? Premise 1 is true since we know that being human is a necessary condition for being American. Premise 2 is also true since we know that Obama is, in fact, human. So, both premises are true.

But, do the premises entail the conclusion? No. This may not be obvious because you might have been influenced by the obvious truth of the conclusion—Obama is clearly American. Indeed, *all* the statements in this argument (the premises and the conclusion) are true. Nevertheless, the inference from the premises to the conclusion is invalid.

If we limited our knowledge only to the premises (and did not know whether or not Obama was American), we would not be able to draw the conclusion that Obama is American based on the premises alone. If all we knew was that Obama is human, then we would not be able to conclude that Obama is American. This is because there are many different ways of being a human (e.g., being Chinese) and there is no guarantee that being human leads to one's being American.

We should say that Argument B_1 is unsound *and* invalid, even though the premises and conclusion are all true. Though the proponent of this argument would have no false beliefs, she would nevertheless be engaging in faulty reasoning—her logic is bad.

Exercise 4.1: Consider the following two arguments. Can you classify them in terms of validity and soundness?

Argument E₁

1. If Isaac wins the lottery, then Joshua will have a happy life.
2. Isaac wins the lottery.
3. Therefore, Joshua will have a happy life.

Argument E₂

1. If Abraham Lincoln was assassinated, then Abraham Lincoln died.
2. Abraham Lincoln died.
3. Therefore, Abraham Lincoln was assassinated.

Counterexamples & Formal Structure

Let's think a bit more about why Argument B₁ is invalid. To do this, consider a variation on this argument where we replace Obama with Xi Jinping.

Argument B₂

1. If Xi Jinping is American, then Xi Jinping is human.
2. Xi Jinping is human.
3. Therefore, Xi Jinping is American.

In this case, we can easily see that the premises are true and the conclusion is false. So, we know that Argument B₂ must be invalid—we can *plainly* see that the premises are true and the conclusion is false. This is precisely what would not be possible for a valid argument since true premises guarantee the truth of the conclusion in a valid argument.

But, what does Argument B₂'s invalidity have to do with Argument B₁'s invalidity?

The answer is that validity is only concerned with the **formal structure** of the argument. The actual content of the argument, whether it's about Obama or Xi Jinping (or someone else altogether), is irrelevant. Notice that Arguments B₁ and B₂, despite having different content, share the exact same formal (or logical) structure.

Argument B₁	Argument B₂
1. If **Obama is American**, then <u>Obama is human</u>.	1. If **Xi Jingping is American**, then <u>Xi Jingping is human</u>.
2. <u>Obama is human</u>.	2. <u>Xi Jingping is human</u>.
3. Therefore, **Obama is American**.	3. Therefore, **Xi Jingping is American**.

In Argument B$_1$, if we replace the statement "Obama is American" with the variable p and we replace the statement "Obama is human" with the variable q, then we get the following argument.

Argument B$_X$

1. If p then q.
2. q.
3. Therefore, p.

Argument B$_X$ captures the formal structure of Argument B$_1$. The content concerning Obama, being American, and being human, is eliminated. Now the logical reasoning underlying the argument is laid bare. We can see that the first premise is a conditional involving p and q and the second premise is the claim that q is true.

Notice that in Argument B$_2$, if we replace the statement "Xi Jinping is American" with p and the statement "Xi Jinping is human" with q, it also becomes Argument B$_X$. Consequently, we can see that Argument B$_X$ captures the formal structure of Argument B$_2$ as well. It is in this sense, then, that we can say that Arguments B$_1$ and B$_2$ have the exact same formal structure. And it is in this sense that we can use Argument B$_2$ to show that Argument B$_1$ is invalid. We might say that Argument B$_2$, or more specifically Xi Jinping, serves as a **counterexample** to Argument B$_1$. Replacing Obama with Xi Jinping changes nothing about the formal structure. It is now obvious, however, that the argument (namely Argument B$_2$) is invalid because the premises are true and the conclusion is false. By replicating the exact logic in Argument B$_1$, Argument B$_2$ demonstrates that an obviously false conclusion can be inferred from obviously true premises. So, Argument B$_2$ clearly exposes the faulty reasoning embedded in Argument B$_1$.

The key to a good counterexample, then, is making sure the exact logic of the argument under consideration is replicated while devising premises that are obviously true and a conclusion that is obviously false. With this in mind, let's revisit Arguments A$_1$ and A$_2$.

Question: Can you extract the formal structure of these two arguments?

Argument A$_1$	Argument A$_2$
1. If Obama is American, then Obama is human.	1. If Obama is Chinese, then Obama is human.
2. Obama is American.	2. Obama is Chinese.
3. Therefore, Obama is human.	3. Therefore, Obama is human.

Replacing the statements "Obama is American" and "Obama is human" with the variables p and q, respectively, in Argument A$_1$, we can settle on the following argument.

Argument A_X

1. If p then q.
2. p.
3. Therefore, q.

Argument A_X captures the formal structure of Argument A_1.

Discussion: Can you see that it also captures the formal structure of A_2? Convince yourself of this before proceeding.

We can see that A_X is valid since the truth of the premises entails the conclusion. It is impossible for the premises to be true and the conclusion false. This way of reasoning is sometimes called ***modus ponens*** (from the Latin *modus ponendo ponens*, meaning "method where affirming affirms") and is *always* a logically valid way of reasoning.

Because Argument A_X is valid and validity has nothing to do with the content, it turns out that we can replace p and q with *any* statement we want while preserving the validity of the resulting argument. For example, if we replace p with "Obama is Korean" and q with "Obama is Russian," we get the following argument.

Argument A_3

1. If Obama is Korean, then Obama is Russian.
2. Obama is Korean.
3. Therefore, Obama is Russian.

Both premises and the conclusion are false. Obama's being Korean does not entail Obama's being Russian, so premise 1 is false. And Obama is clearly not Korean nor Russian so premise 2 and the conclusion are also false. Nevertheless, I hope it is evident to you that the reasoning is flawless. If it were the case that Obama's being Korean entailed Obama's being Russian and Obama was, in fact, Korean, then it would be impossible for Obama not to be Russian! So, despite the ridiculousness of the statements in Argument A_3, it is clearly a valid argument.

From these examples, we can see that validity has nothing to do with the content of an argument. It is focused purely on the formal inferential connection between the premises and the conclusion.

Question: Extract the formal structure of the following argument. How would you evaluate it? If it is invalid, can you provide a counterexample?

Argument C_1

1. If Obama is American, then Obama is human.

2.   It is false that Obama is human.
3.   Therefore, it is false that Obama is American.

The formal structure of Argument C$_1$ can be distilled by replacing the statement "Obama is American" with the variable p and the statement "Obama is human" with the variable q. This yields the following argument.

Argument C$_X$

1.   If p then q.
2.   Not q.
3.   Therefore, not p.

Here, the term 'not' is used as shorthand for the phrase "it is false that." The conditional in premise 1 implies that q is a necessary condition for p. That is, it is impossible for p to be true without q also being true. So, if q is false, then p must also be false. Based on this, we can see that this is a valid argument and all arguments with this formal structure will be valid as well. This way of reasoning is sometimes called **modus tollens** (from the Latin *modus tollendo tollens*, meaning "method where denying denies") and is *always* a logically valid way of reasoning.

Now consider an argument with a very similar formal structure that is *in*valid.

Argument D$_1$

1.   If Obama is Chinese, then Obama is Asian.
2.   It is false that Obama is Chinese.
3.   Therefore, it is false that Obama is Asian.

What do you make of this argument? Its formal structure can be extracted by replacing the statement "Obama is Chinese" with the variable p and the statement "Obama is Asian" with the variable q. This yields the following argument.

Argument D$_X$

1.   If p then q.
2.   Not p.
3.   Therefore, not q.

Despite its similarity with Argument C$_X$, this argument is invalid. This, again, may be surprising because the premises and the conclusion are all true in Argument D$_1$. But, we can come up with a *counterexample* by devising a different argument that has: (i) the same formal structure and (ii) premises that are obviously true and a conclusion that is obviously false. Consider the following argument.

Valid Formal Structures	Invalid Formal Structures
Argument A_{IFS} (modus ponens) 1 If p then q. 2 p. 3 Therefore, q. Argument C_{IFS} (modus tollens) 1 If p then q. 2 Not q. 3 Therefore, not p.	Argument B_{IFS} (affirming the consequent) 1 If p then q. 2 q. 3 Therefore, p. Argument D_{IFS} (denying the antecedent) 1 If p then q. 2 Not p. 3 Therefore, not q.

Argument D_2

1. If Obama is Chinese then Obama is human.
2. It is false that Obama is Chinese.
3. Therefore, it is false that Obama is human.

Arguments D_1 and D_2 have the same formal structure which is captured in Argument D_X. Nevertheless, with Argument D_2, the premises are true and the conclusion is false. So, we know that Argument D_2 is invalid. Since Arguments D_1 and D_2 have the same formal structure, it follows that Argument D_1 must be invalid as well. Despite the truth of all its statements, Argument D_1 is a poor argument because the reasoning is flawed.

We've discussed four different formal structures of arguments that utilize conditionals. Two are valid and two are invalid. Here, they are summarized.

Deductive and Inductive Arguments

So far, we've only been examining arguments that *aspire* to be valid. Validity, however, is a concept that deals with arguments that depend on logically guaranteed inferences. Not all arguments depend on logically guaranteed inferences. There are also arguments that deal with probabilities (not certainties). Consider the following argument.

Argument E_1

1. If the first 100 marbles drawn from a bag are red, then the 101st marble to be drawn will also be red.
2. The first 100 marbles drawn from a bag are red.
3. Therefore, the 101st marble to be drawn will also be red.

Here, the truth of the premises does not absolutely guarantee the truth of the conclusion. It is *possible* for the premises to be true and the conclusion to be false. Moreover, it's arguable that this argument was never intended to provide absolute certainty—it never aspired to be valid. Perhaps, it was offered simply to provide a good (but not conclusive) reason for believing the conclusion.

These two kinds of arguments can be classified as **deductive** and **inductive** argument types. Deductive arguments are ones that aspire to be valid—ones where the truth of the premises is meant to absolutely guarantee the truth of the conclusion. Inductive arguments are ones that do not aspire to the high standard of validity. They merely aspire to provide good (but not conclusive) support for their conclusions.

When an inductive argument has premises that provide good support for its conclusions, we can classify it as a **strong** argument. That is, the inferential connection between the premises and the conclusion is strong. If the inferential connection between the premises and the conclusion is not strong, we can classify it as a **weak** argument. Note that the notions of inductive strength and weakness depend on the context. There is no strict threshold of probability that would make an inductive inference strong in all circumstances. It's probably safe to infer, for example, that a student who averages more than 90% on her exams is a good student. But, in baseball, it's probably safe to infer that a player who manages to successfully get a hit 30% of the time is a good batter.

If an inductive argument is strong and has premises that are true, then we can classify the argument as a **cogent** argument. If an inductive argument is not strong or one (or more) of its premises is false, then we can classify it as an **uncogent** argument. We can think of strength and cogency as the inductive counterparts for validity and soundness in deductive arguments.

	Deductive *argument*	**Inductive** *argument*
Inferential connection	**Valid**: *if the premises are true, the conclusion must be true.* **Invalid**: *if the premises are true, the conclusion may be false.*	**Strong**: *if the premises are true, the conclusion is likely to be true.* **Weak**: *if the premises are true, the conclusion is not likely to be true.*
Truth	**Sound**: all premises are true, and the argument is valid. **Unsound**: at least one premise is false, or the argument is invalid (or both).	**Cogent**: all premises are true, and the argument is strong. **Uncogent**: at least one premise is false, or the argument is weak (or both).

There is, of course, a lot more to be said—entire books have been written about logic![2] But, we have enough of the necessary tools to be able to logically analyze the arguments that will be presented later in this book.

Reconstructing Arguments

An important skill all philosophers need to develop is the ability to reconstruct arguments embedded in what other people write or say. Indeed, this is an important skill for *anyone* to develop. We are constantly inundated with information and advice from a myriad of voices, so it is vital that we are able to understand the core reasoning behind these recommendations and critically assess their merits. The process of reconstructing another person's argument, however, is not always an easy task. Moreover, there is no strict formula or method that we can follow in order to do this well. It is a skill that must be developed with practice.

Let's consider an opinion piece sent as a letter to the editor of the May 31, 2020, issue of the *Dallas Morning News*. This letter was written in light of the Texas government's rejection of a proposal for mail-in voting due to the COVID-19 pandemic. Can you reconstruct the argument that is implicitly embedded in this piece?

> I think the biggest issue here is containing the spread of the coronavirus. It seems to me apparent, from the advice of experts, that voting in person will inevitably cost lives. It is incredible to me that there is anyone arguing otherwise.
>
> – Charlotte Connelly

How would you reconstruct Charlotte's argument in premise–conclusion form? A useful place to start is to get a handle on what you think is the conclusion of her argument. The conclusion, while obvious, is not explicitly contained in the actual letter. Her conclusion is implied: the Texas government's rejecting mail-in voting is wrong.

How does she marshal support for her conclusion? She primarily rests her claims on expertise. To reach the conclusion, then, we might interpret Charlotte's logic as being contained in two conditionals.

Argument CC$_1$

1. If experts advise against voting in person, then we should not vote in person.
2. If we should not vote in person, then it is wrong to block the mail-in voting expansion.
3. Experts advise against voting in person.
4. Therefore, it is wrong to block the mail-in voting expansion.

Once a reconstruction is complete, the first and perhaps most important question to ask is: what would the author think of this reconstruction? That is, what would Charlotte say? Assuming we deem Charlotte's perspective on this matter to be important (since it's *her* argument), we want to make sure that we interpret her reasoning in the best possible light. That is, we want to practice the principle of **charity**. It would be counterproductive to reconstruct her argument in a way that deliberately makes her reasoning look foolish. This wouldn't help anyone make progress in the debate because we'd be responding to a 'straw man' representation (i.e., a cheap imitation easy to attack) of Charlotte's reasoning, rather than Charlotte's *actual* reasoning.

Once we're reasonably satisfied with the reconstruction, we can move on to assessing its merits. First, we can be confident that the argument is valid. It is set up with two conditionals that behave the way a series of conditionals might behave in Python. The code might look something like this:

```
wrong_to_block = None
not_vote_in_person = None
expert_advice = True

if expert_advice == True:
    not_vote_in_person = True

if not_vote_in_person == True:
    wrong_to_block = True
```

Here, the variables could be used to represent the various statements in Argument CC$_1$. expert_advice stands for "experts advise against voting in person," not_vote_in_person stands for "we should not vote in person," and wrong_to_block stands for "it is wrong to block the mail-in voting expansion."

Let's now consider the truth or falsity of each of the three premises. Concerning premise 1, is it true that if experts advise against voting in person, then we should not vote in person? Perhaps it depends on the *kind* of experts we're dealing with. While the argument suggests that the experts would be public health experts, there is nothing explicitly stated. If the experts are experts in voter behavior (and not public health) then perhaps there is a reason for dismissing premise 1. We might conclude that its truth is contingent on the kind of expertise that is being referenced.

Premise 2 seems harder to reject. But upon closer inspection, perhaps, there is a weakness here as well. It depends on what is meant by "should not be done." Some things should not be done because they would be illegal, but not morally wrong (such as jaywalking). Some things should not be done because they would be irrational, but not morally wrong (such as playing a bad move in chess). And some things should not be done because they are morally wrong (such as stealing). There are many other examples, but clearly "should not be done" does not imply "morally wrong." So, if "should not be done" is understood in a broad sense (rather than the strictly moral sense), then it would not follow that blocking mail-in voting is morally wrong.

Finally, premise 3 seems to be a straightforward matter of fact checking. Did experts really advise against voting in person? Here, perhaps, we'd like to see evidence for this claim. Is there an official statement that was given by a body of experts? Or is this more anecdotal? Even if we have an official statement, is the statement amenable to different interpretations?

There is, no doubt, much more that can be said about Argument CC$_1$. But at least we went through an initial pass of the process of critically analyzing an argument. We first produced a charitable reconstruction of Charlotte's implicit argument. Because it was valid, we then inspected each of the premises to determine whether each is true.

Question: Reconstruct another letter from the *Dallas Morning News* on the same topic—mail-in voting as a response to the COVID-19 pandemic.

> If it would be a great threat to public health and safety to go to the polls and stand in line, then using the same logic, all of the retailers, beaches, parks, malls and restaurants should close immediately. Our citizens think nothing of standing in line to get into a store but standing in line to vote is dangerous? Therein lies my confusion. You simply cannot have it both ways. If one is safe then all are safe and vice versa. Don't you think that the local officials will do everything they can to make sure voting is safe? I do. Saying voting is dangerous but going to Walmart is OK is hypocritical on many levels. If we all go vote in person and wear a mask and gloves and they clean the machines, everything will work just fine. If you are afraid to go vote, then you must be just as afraid to go the store.
>
> – David Keene

Here is a possible reconstruction of David's argument:

Argument DK$_1$

1. In-person voting and the opening of retailers, parks, and restaurants present the same level of threat to public safety.
2. If in-person voting and the opening of retailers, parks, and restaurants present the same level of threat to public safety, then it is hypocritical to support the opening of retailers, parks, and restaurants, but reject in-person voting.
3. It is hypocritical to support the opening of retailers, parks, and restaurants, but reject in-person voting.

Discussion: Is this similar to your own reconstruction? What would David think of this reconstruction? Is it missing anything? Is this argument valid? Can you find weaknesses in any of the premises?

Key Points

- Logic is the analysis of arguments.
- Good arguments require both truth and validity.
- Validity is a formal feature of arguments that abstracts away from the content.
- Deductive and Inductive arguments differ in the kind of inferences they aspire to present.
- Reconstructing others' arguments must be done charitably.

Notes

1 No attempt will be made to provide readers with the tools to evaluate the properties of programs. The primary use of the conditional if statement in this chapter is to emphasize the strictness of the relationship between the antecedent and the consequent. More on this will be covered later in this chapter.
2 See Hurley (2017) for a recent and accessible book-length introduction to logic. See Quine (1982) for a classic introduction to logic from one of the 20th-century experts of logic.

References

Hurley, P. (2017). *A Concise Introduction to Logic*. Boston, MA: Cengage.
Quine, W. V. (1982). *Methods of Logic*. Cambridge, MA: Harvard University Press.

Chapter 5

Iteration

While Loops

We'll now get a sense for the computer's superpower of **speed**. Computers are extremely good at doing repetitive tasks and doing them extremely quickly. To get a computer to exhibit this speed, we now turn to **iteration** (or the use of loops). There are two main ways of handling iteration in Python. Let's begin with the **while** loop. Similar to a conditional, a while loop begins with the evaluation of a condition followed by a block of code. The basic structure of a while loop is given in Figure 5.1.

If the Boolean expression evaluates to True, then the block of code is executed. Once the block of code is finished executing, the Boolean expression is evaluated again. If it remains True, then the block of code is executed again. This process repeats itself until the Boolean expression evaluates to False. In a nutshell, the block of code in a while loop is repeatedly executed so long as the condition is satisfied. Here is an example:

```
x = 1
while x <= 10:
    print(x)
    print(x+1)
```

Assuming 1 is assigned to the variable x, the Boolean expression, x <= 10, evaluates to True. Since the condition is satisfied, the block of code is executed. The print statement displays 1. The next print statement displays 2. Then the process is repeated. The Boolean expression is evaluated a second time. Since x hasn't changed, the Boolean expression remains True. Since the condition remains satisfied, the block of code is executed

```
while _____ :  ◄——————— Boolean expression
       _____     ◄——————— block of code
```

Figure 5.1 The basic structure of a while loop.

DOI: 10.4324/9781003271284-5

a second time and another 1 and 2 are displayed. Try executing this code for yourself. You will immediately see how quickly 1s and 2s are displayed on the screen. On my computer, more than a hundred 1s and 2s were displayed in a split second.

Executing this code will also make it immediately evident that this loop will *not* terminate because the condition will always remain satisfied. This is what we call an **infinite** loop, and it will continue to display 1s and 2s until the Python interpreter is forcefully stopped. You can stop the iteration by pressing <CTRL>+C. This is useful to know because, chances are, you will have your share of unintentionally written infinite loops as you develop your programming skills. Sometimes, of course, an infinite loop is what you want, so you shouldn't think that an infinite loop is always bad.

If we want to avoid infinite loops when designing while loops, we must always remember that *something* involved in the condition must change for the evaluation of the Boolean expression to change at some point in the iteration. Otherwise, as seen above, while loops can easily turn into infinite loops. A simple modification to the code above will avoid the infinite loop. The value of x can be incremented on each iteration. This will result in integers from 1 to 10 being displayed on the screen:

```
x = 1

while x <= 10:
    print(x)
    x = x + 1
```

Since x begins with the value 1, the while loop condition is initially satisfied. The block of code is executed, so 1 will be displayed on the screen, and then x will be incremented to 2. We return to the beginning of the loop and find that the condition remains satisfied. The block of code is executed, so 2 will be displayed on the screen, and then x will be incremented to 3. This cycle will repeat until 10 is displayed on the screen and x is incremented to 11. At this point, when we return to the beginning of the loop, the condition will no longer be satisfied, x is no longer less than or equal to 10, and the loop will terminate.

A shorthand way of incrementing the value of a variable is by using the += operator:

```
x += 1
```

This adds whatever is on the right side of the += operator to the variable that is on the left side of the operator. It is shorthand for x = x + 1.

Exercise 5.1: Write code using a `while` loop that displays the first ten multiples of 3. In order to do this you can make a small modification to the code for displaying the first ten positive integers given above—simply multiply x by 3.

Exercise 5.2: Write code that will display all the integers between `1000` and `2000` (inclusive) that are divisible by `11`. You can do something similar here by assigning `1000` to x prior to the execution of the loop. Then you simply add a conditional that displays x only when it is divisible by `11` (remember to use the % operator for remainder division).

To stop the iteration in the middle of the block of code within a loop, the break statement can be used.

```
x = 1
while x <= 10:
    print(x)
    if x == 5:
        break
    x += 1
```

This is the same code as above, except an `if` statement has been added to the block of code within the `while` loop. Since the condition of the `if` statement evaluates to `True` on the fifth iteration of the `while` loop, the break statement will execute and cause the loop to terminate. The x += 1 statement after the `if` statement within the `while` loop will be skipped entirely and Python will continue working through statements (if any) that exist immediately outside the loop.

A companion statement is `continue`. Unlike `break`, this statement does not terminate the loop. It will skip any statements remaining in the loop and immediately jump back to the beginning. If the condition governing the loop still evaluates to `True`, the block of code in the loop will be executed again.

```
x = 1
while x <= 10:
    print(x)
    if x == 5:
        continue
    x += 1
```

In this version of the code, the `break` statement is replaced with continue. In this case, when the `continue` statement is executed, the x += 1 statement is skipped, and Python will return to the beginning of the loop. This will then display an endless series of 5s.

It is important to note that some `while` loops may never even get started. If the condition is not satisfied, to begin with, the block of code within the loop will never be executed.

Strings

Unlike 'atomic' objects (like those of type `int`, `float`, or `bool`), **strings** are *structured*—they have parts. Strings are written using quotation marks (single or double quotes are both fine as long as they are used consistently) and are aptly named since they 'string' together zero or more characters.

```
>>> name1 = 'George Boole'
>>> name2 = "George Boole"
```

Though we have two different variables, `name1` and `name2`, the strings they refer to are equivalent—the single and double quotes make no difference. You can verify that they are the same by checking for equality:

```
>>> name1 == name2
True
```

Because strings have a structure, there are ways of extracting the different characters in a string by their locations in the string. An individual character in a string can be extracted through **indexing** via brackets (`[]`).

```
>>> name1[0]
'G'
>>> 'George Boole'[0]
'G'
```

These statements extract the first character from the variable `name1` and the string `'George Boole,'` which both evaluate to `'G.'` Indexing begins with `0` and works its way up in increments of `1` until the last character of the string is reached. Notice that the space (`' '`) counts as a character. It is the seventh character in `name1` located at index `6`.

G	e	o	r	c	e		B	o	o	l	e
0	1	2	3	4	5	6	7	8	9	10	11

Indexing can also work in reverse using negative numbers. The last character in a string can be accessed by indexing the string at `-1`. This

works its way down in decrements of 1 until the first character of the
string is reached.

G	e	o	r	g	e		B	o	o	l	e
-12	-11	-10	-9	-8	-7	-6	-5	-4	-3	-2	-1

So, the first character of name1 can also be indexed using -12:

```
>>> name1[-12]
'G'
```

Though structured, strings are **immutable**. This means that once a string
is created, its constituent parts can't be modified. So, for example, we
wouldn't be able to replace a given character within name1. The following
assignment operation will generate an error.

```
>>> name1[0] = '-'
TypeError: 'str' object does not support item assignment
```

If we wanted to replace a character within name1 (e.g., 'B' to 'C'), we
could take the different parts of name1 that we want to keep, construct
a *new* string with the character replaced, and assign this new string to
name1. Notice, the original string, 'George Boole,' would not have
changed. Instead, a new string, 'George Coole,' would have been created and then assigned to name1.

To do this, we'll need to be able to select contiguous sections of a string
through **slicing**. Slicing is accomplished via brackets and colons (:).

```
>>> name1[0:6]
'George'
```

This statement extracts the first six characters of name1, which is
'George.' The first number specifies the beginning index of the sliced
substring. The second number specifies the index where the sliced substring ends. Notice that the sliced substring ends at and does *not* include
the character at index 6. In other words, the space is not included in the
resulting string.

We will also need the + operator. This can be used, not only to add
numerical values but to combine distinct strings into new ones.

```
>>> name1[0:6] + ' is the creator of Boolean Logic'
'George is the creator of Boolean Logic'
```

This statement combines two strings: the string referred to by `name1[0:6]` and the string, `' is the creator of Boolean Logic.'` Now we have the tools to replace a character in a given string through the use of slicing and the + operator. Here is one way we might replace the `'B'` in `name1` with `'C'`:

```
>>> name1[0:7] + 'C' + name1[8:12]
'George Coole'
```

Note that the second index (12) in the slice `name1[8:12]` is an index that doesn't exist in `name1`. The last positive index in `name1` is 11. Remember, slicing always extracts a substring that ends at but does not include the character at the specified index. Slicing to the index of the last character will result in a substring that excludes the last character.

```
>>> name1[7:11]
'Bool'
```

This means that a number greater than the index of the last character must be used in order to ensure that the entirety of the rest of the string will be captured. In this case, we use 12 (but any integer greater than 11 will do).

Slicing can also be done while leaving one or both indices out. By leaving the first index out, the slice will begin at the first character of the string. By leaving the second index out, the slice will end at the last character of the string (and include the last character). By leaving both indices out, the slice will generate a copy of the entire string. You can see this at work here:

```
>>> 'George Boole'[:6]
'George'
>>> 'George Boole'[7:]
'Boole'
>>> 'George Boole'[:]
'George Boole'
```

Finally, a useful function for ascertaining the number of characters that exist in a string is the **len** function. It can be used as follows:

```
>>> len(name1)
12
>>> len('George Boole')
12
>>> name1[:len(name1)]
'George Boole'
```

Exercise 5.3: Create a new string by slicing the first name out of name1, adding 'Mr. ' to the front and a greeting to the end. Make sure there are spaces in the right locations!

Having come this far, it may have become evident to you that while loops can be used to iterate over and process (in some way) the characters in a given string. We can do this by taking advantage of the fact that the indices of the characters in a string range from 0 to one less than the length of the string. We've already generated loops that print out integers from 1 to 10, so it will take a slight modification to handle looping from 0 to one less than the length of the string. For the string assigned to name1, we'd like to loop from index 0 to index 11 (since the length of name1 is 12).

```
x = 0

while x < len(name1):
    print(x)
    x += 1
```

Hopefully, you can trace the execution of this code and see that it will display integers from 0 to 11. Now we can use the changing value of x to work our way through every index of the string assigned to name1.

```
x = 0

while x < len(name1):
    print(name1[x])
    x += 1
```

This will print out every character of 'George Boole' on a separate line. The way each character is 'processed' is by being displayed on the screen. But we can process the characters in any number of ways. We may want, for example, to count the number of times a given letter, say the character 'o,' appears in a string. To do this, we need to create a variable, say number_of_os, prior to the execution of the loop that will store the number of times this character is processed. When iterating over every character we can use a conditional to check if the character is equal to 'o.' If so, number_of_os can be incremented. When the loop finishes, number_of_os will have the number of times 'o' occurs in name1. This information can then be displayed on the screen.

```
x = 0
number_of_os = 0
while x < len(name1):
    if name1[x] == 'o':
        number_of_os += 1
```

```
    x += 1
print('There are', number_of_os, 'os')
```

What if we wanted to count the number of upper case *and* lower case 'o's in a string? We would simply need to change the Boolean expression in the conditional embedded in the `while` loop. One way to do this would be to use the `or` operator.

```
if name1[x] == 'O' or name1[x] == 'o':
```

Now, the condition will be true if the character being processed is either an 'O' or an 'o.'

Another way of doing this is to use the **in** operator. The `in` operator checks to see if one string is 'in' another. That is if one string is a substring of another.

```
>>> 'a' in 'Ezra'
True
>>> 'a' in 'John'
False
>>> 'bcd' in 'abcde'
True
>>> 'bcd' in 'dcb'
False
```

Using the `in` operator, we could also have written the condition above as follows:

```
if name1[x] in 'Oo':
```

Exercise 5.4: Write code that will count the number of vowels (upper case and lower case) that occurs in `name1`.

Lists

Let's now revisit the computer's superpower of **memory**. Earlier, we introduced this superpower through the use of variables. Although you might have thought that this allows computers to remember things, it doesn't really show us how computers can remember *a lot* of things. To introduce the computer's power to remember a lot of things, we now turn to lists.

Like strings, **lists** are structured objects. Unlike strings, lists are **mutable**. That is, the constituent parts of a list can be modified. Moreover, while all the elements in a string must be characters, the elements in a list can be of *any* type.

A list can be created using brackets ([]) and comma-separated objects as follows:

```
>>> L1 = [1, 'hi', 3.14, False, [1, 2, 3]]
```

This statement creates a list with five objects and assigns this list to the variable L1. Like strings, each object in a list is indexed. Notice that the fifth element in L1 is another list.

1	'hi'	3.14	False	[1,2,3]
0	1	2	3	4

Also like strings, lists can be sliced and used as an input to the len function. Lists can even be combined with other lists to form new lists using the + operator.

```
>>> L1[1]
'hi'
>>> L1[2:4]
[3.14, False]
>>> len(L1)
5
>>> L1 + ['there',100]
[1, 'hi', 3.14, False, [1, 2, 3], 'there', 100]
```

Because lists are mutable—they can be modified after they are created. Lists can be modified in at least two ways. One way is to use an assignment operator to change the object located at a specific index.

```
>>> L1[0] = 'abc'
```

This replaces the first object stored in L1 (the integer 1) with the string 'abc.' So, L1 will now be:

```
>>> L1
['abc', 'hi', 3.14, False, [1, 2, 3]]
```

Another way of modifying an existing list is to use the append function. It is used the way functions like print are used, but it must be prefixed with a '.' and the list to be modified. This will take whatever is supplied in the parentheses and append it to the end of the list.

```
>>> L1.append(12)
```

This statement adds the integer 12 to the end of L1 so it is now:

```
>>> L1
['abc', 'hi', 3.14, False, [1, 2, 3], 12]
```

Lists are useful for storing a lot of data. Using what we've learned so far, we can use a loop to create a list of integers from 1 to 1000. To do this, we can first create an empty list called nums. Then using a while loop that iterates on x, we can append each successive value of x to nums. The following code will, in an extremely short time, create and remember a list of the first thousand positive integers.

```
nums = []
x = 1
while x <= 1000:
    nums.append(x)
    x += 1
```

Exercise 5.5: Write code that creates a list called result that contains the first ten powers of 2.

Making a small change to the condition of the while loop allows us to create and remember a ridiculously large amount of integers. By changing the 1000 to 1000000, we can create a list, almost instantaneously, of the first million positive integers. The use of iteration and lists allows us to exploit the computer's superpowers of memory and speed simultaneously.

For Loops

Another way of handling iteration is through the **for** loop (sometimes referred to as a count loop). The for loop doesn't use a Boolean expression that regulates whether the block of code in its body is executed. Rather, it uses a variable that is iterated over a sequence of objects. Strings and lists can be considered different kinds of sequences. What matters is that a sequence is an ordered set of objects. This is why for loops are sometimes called *definite* loops. They have a pre-set number of iterations (based on the number of objects in the sequence) that they will run through.

The general form of the for loop is as follows:

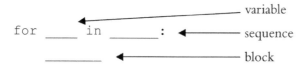

Figure 5.2 The basic structure of a for loop.

   The first object in the sequence is assigned to the variable; then the block of code is executed. Then the second object in the sequence is assigned to the variable and the block of code is executed a second time. This continues until all the objects in the sequence are successively assigned to the variable, and the block of code is executed.

   One way of creating a sequence is to use the range function. It can be used with one or two integer inputs. If two integers are given, then range creates a sequence of integers from the first integer up to, but not including, the second integer. The following statement creates a sequence of integers from 1 to 10.

```
>>> range(1,11)
range(1,11)
```

If one integer is given, then it creates a sequence of integers from 0 up to, but not including, the given integer. The following statement creates a sequence of integers from 0 to 10.

```
>>> range(11)
range(0,11)
```

Though there are differences, it may be useful to think of this range as a *list* of integers from 0 to 10.

0	1	2	3	4	5	6	7	8	9	10
0	1	2	3	4	5	6	7	8	9	10

   Elements from this range can be indexed just like strings and lists.

```
>>> range(11)[3]
3
```

So, the range function can be used as the sequence in a for loop as follows:

```
for number in range(1,11):
    print(number)
```

The range function is evaluated first and a sequence of integers from 1 to 10 is created. Then the variable number is assigned to the first object in this sequence. So, 1 is assigned to number. Then the block of code is executed. This results in a 1 being displayed on the screen. Then the next object in the sequence, 2, is assigned to number. Then the block of code is executed a second time. This continues until the last object in the sequence, 10, is assigned to number, the block of code is executed and the loop terminates.

Exercise 5.6: Write code using a for loop that displays the first ten multiples of 3.

Since strings and lists are also sequences, we can iterate over them using the for loop by swapping out the range function with an existing string or list. We can then, for example, print out all the elements of the sequence with very little code. Let's try rewriting the code we wrote earlier to display all the characters in a string using a while loop. Here is the code.

```
x = 0

while x < len(name1):
    print(name1[x])
    x += 1
```

Compare this with the code needed to do the same thing with a for loop.

```
for x in name1:
    print(x)
```

While both pieces of code do the same thing, there are a couple of important differences. First, the for loop is more compact and arguably more readable. Second, the for loop is missing information that is readily available in the while loop. The for loop does not give us access to the indices of the elements we are processing. In the while loop, we know what index every character is located at since the variable x stores this value. We could, of course, use the for loop in a way that preserves information about the indices as follows:

```
for x in range(len(name1)):
    print(name1[x])
```

This, however, would come at the expense of the compactness and readability of the code. Third, depending on what is done in the blocks of code within each loop, the behaviors of the loops can change radically. For example, what do you think would happen if we assigned a new string to name1 in the block of code within the loop?

```
x = 0

while x < len(name1):
    print(name1[x])
    name1 = 'Alan Turing'
    x += 1
```

When this while loop begins, it will operate under the original value of name1, which is the string 'George Boole.' So, the block of code will display the character at index 0 of name1—the character 'G.' Then name1 will be assigned to 'Alan Turing' and x will be incremented. In the next iteration, the code will display the character at index 1 of name1 (with its newly assigned content)—'l.' Then name1 will be assigned (again) to 'Alan Turing' and x will be incremented. This will go on until all the characters of name1 are displayed. The result of this loop is that 'G' will be displayed then each of the characters in 'lan Turing' will be displayed.

What if we changed what name1 refers to in the body of the for loop?

```
for x in name1:
    print(x)
    name1 = 'Alan Turing'
```

Perhaps surprisingly, this will display all the characters in the original value of name1 (i.e., 'George Boole'). Assigning a new string to name1 seems to do nothing. This is because a for loop is a *definite* loop. The execution of the first line of a for loop sets the value of the sequence at the start. This sequence is not altered once the loop begins. So, even if name1 is changed so that it refers to a new string, this changes nothing in terms of the sequence that was established at the onset of the for loop.

Though both while and for loops deal with iteration, you may find, with practice, that you have a preference for one. In many cases, it may not matter which style of iteration you choose. In some cases, where you want an indefinite loop, only the while loop will do. In other cases, where the number of iterations is fixed, code built on for loops may be much easier to manage.

Simple Programs

We've added quite a bit to our growing repertoire of Python abilities. Before going on, it's very important to put all of this together and work on writing more substantive pieces of code.

Let's start with code that will add up all the integers in a list called L2 and store the result in a variable called sum. One way to do this is to create the variable sum up front and assign it to the integer 0. This represents the sum of all the integers in the list that have been *processed so far*. Since we haven't begun working our way through L2, sum is initially set to 0. Now we simply increment sum based on each integer we process in the iteration. This can be done using a for loop.

```
L2 = [1,2,3,4,5]
sum = 0
for x in L2:
    sum += x
```

Given what we have covered so far, this should be straightforward. The nice thing about computers, again, is that they can work with extremely large amounts of data. While summing up a list of five integers might not be impressive, imagine if L2 contained a thousand integers. Or a million integers. This would make little difference to the computer—both lists would be processed in less than a second!

Exercise 5.7: Write code that does the same thing (calculates the sum of the integers in L2) using a while loop. (Hint: don't forget that the len function also works on lists).

What if we now wanted to find the smallest integer in L2? Again, this may seem like a trivial task given a list of five integers, but what if we had a thousand (or a million) integers? How would you go about devising an algorithm to figure this out?

One thing we know is that we'll have to examine every integer in the list. One strategy might be to keep track of the smallest integer that has been *processed so far*. To do this, we can create a variable called small_est_so_far and assign it the first integer in L2. Then, when iterating over L2, we simply have to compare each integer with smallest_so_far. If the integer is less than smallest_so_far, we can assign this integer to smallest_so_far. If not, we can simply move on to the next integer in the list and leave smallest_so_far as is. By the time we are finished processing all the integers, smallest_so_far will be the smallest integer in L2. Here is what the code might look like using a while loop.

```
x = 1
smallest_so_far = L2[0]
while x < len(L2):
    if L2[x] < smallest_so_far:
        smallest_so_far = L2[x]
    x += 1
```

Make sure you understand exactly what is happening in this code. The details are very important and building up a level of comfort in writing these kinds of loops is critical to developing your programming skills.

Exercise 5.8: Write code that finds the *largest* integer in L2 using a for loop.

Let's end this chapter by writing a slightly more complex program—one that checks whether a given integer is prime. A number is prime if it is greater than one and is not evenly divisible by a positive integer that is greater than one and less than itself. So, five is prime because it is greater than one and there is no positive integer greater than one and less than five that evenly divides it. Six, on the other hand, is *not* prime because it is greater than one and it is evenly divisible by a positive integer greater than one and less than six (two and three both evenly divide six). There are no even numbers that are prime except two—it's the only prime even number.

How can we write a program that checks whether a given variable x is assigned to a prime number? A natural solution would be to transform the logic implicit in the definition of primality into code. Here's how it might look:

```
prime = True

if x <= 1:
    prime = False
else:
    divisor = 2
    while divisor < x:
        if x % divisor == 0:
            prime = False
            break
        divisor += 1
```

First, we create a variable `prime` and assign it to `True`. This means that we are assuming x is prime unless proven otherwise. Next, we check for the two necessary and sufficient conditions of primality. If x is less than or equal to 1, we know that it cannot be prime, so we set `prime` to `False` and we're finished. If x is greater than 1, then we have to make sure there are no numbers greater than 1 and less than x that evenly divide x. In order to check this, we create another variable `divisor` and assign it to 2 (the smallest integer greater than 1). We will use `divisor` to check every integer in the range of integers from 2 to x-1 to see if x is divisible by any of these integers. This is why the Boolean expression in the `while` loop is: `divisor < x` (meaning, keep looping until `divisor` is no longer strictly less than x). Within the loop, we check to see if `divisor` evenly divides x using the remainder operator (`%`). If there is an integer that evenly divides x, then we know that x cannot be prime. So, we set `prime` to `False` and terminate the loop. Otherwise, `divisor` is incremented, and the loop repeats. If the loop completes because `divisor` is no longer less than x, then we know that all the integers from 2 to x-1 have been checked. Since none of the integers in this range evenly divide x, nothing needs to be done since prime was set to True at the outset.

Exercise 5.9: Rewrite the program to check whether x is prime by using a for loop instead of a while loop.

Don't worry if you feel like you wouldn't have been able to write the code to check for primality on your own. Remember that programming is an art. There is no single 'right' way to write a program. It takes a lot of practice, and you will eventually develop your own style. For now, just make sure you understand how the program works.

Key Points

- A string is a structured, immutable data type that can be indexed and sliced.
- A list is a structured, mutable data type that can be indexed and sliced.
- while loops are indefinite loops that are useful for iteration.
- for loops (or count loops) are definite loops that are useful for iteration.

Chapter 6

Image Manipulation

Two-Dimensional Lists and Nested Loops

Before jumping into image manipulation, we need to add the important concept of **nested loops** to our programming toolkit. In the previous chapter, we were introduced to two kinds of looping statements, the while loop and the for loop. In this chapter, we will look at nesting a loop inside another loop. With a single loop, we saw how it was possible to iterate over sequences of objects. These sequences, however, were **one-dimensional**. That is, they were ordered according to a single sequence of indices. The value of nested loops is that it allows us to iterate over **two-dimensional** sequences—ones that are ordered according to two sequences of indices.

The natural way to implement two-dimensional sequences in Python is through the use of **nested lists**. We saw in the previous chapter that lists are structured objects that can store objects of any type—even other lists. So, we can make a two-dimensional sequence by embedding equal-sized lists in another list. Here is an example.

```
>>> grid = [[1,2,3],[4,5,6],[7,8,9]]
```

This is a list with three elements, each of which is a list of three elements. We can see this by using the len function.

```
>>> len(grid)
3
```

We can access each list inside grid by using a bracketed index. The following statement will extract the first list in grid.

```
>>> grid[0]
[1,2,3]
```

DOI: 10.4324/9781003271284-6

We can add a second bracketed index to extract a given element within this sub-list. If we wanted to extract the 2, we could use the following statement.

```
>>> grid[0][1]
2
```

It might be useful to visualize the two-dimensional list as follows. This makes it easy to see why grid[0][1] extracts 2. It is like asking for the element at row 0 and column 1.

Exercise 6.1: Write a statement that displays the last row in grid.

	Column 0	Column 1	Column 2
Row 0	1	2	3
Row 1	4	5	6
Row 2	7	8	9

Exercise 6.2: Write statements that display the numbers 3, 4, and 8 by locating them in grid.

Discussion: Before going on, it might be useful to think through an important aspect of computational thinking—**data representation**. What do you think grid can be used to represent?

If you are familiar with the game called Tic-Tac-Toe (or Xs and Os, or noughts and crosses, or whatever name you might have used), the 3x3 two-dimensional list introduced above can be a natural way of representing the Tic-Tac-Toe board. If you are not familiar, Tic-Tac-Toe is a two-player game where players take turns marking the spaces (one player with Xs and the other player with Os) in a 3x3 grid. If a player succeeds in placing three of their marks in a row (horizontally, vertically, or diagonally), this player wins. If neither player succeeds, then the game ends in a draw.

Instead of filling the two-dimensional list with integers, we could fill it with 'X's and 'O's like this:

```
[['X','O','O'],['X','O','X'],['X','X','O']]
```

This can more easily be visualized as a Tic-Tac-Toe board if presented with each sub-list occupying a distinct row:

```
[['X','O','O'],
 ['X','O','X'],
 ['X','X','O']]
```

There is, of course, much more to be said about how a two-dimensional Python list can be used to model the game of Tic-Tac-Toe, but what you should see is that grid can be used to represent things that may, at first glance, seem to be far removed from Python lists.

It turns out that two-dimensional lists can be used to represent many different kinds of data. They can be used to represent binary relationships (relationships between two entities). Since binary relationships are ubiquitous, this representation can be used in a variety of applications. Consider, for example, the relationships on a social networking website like Facebook. Here, there is an entire web of *friend* relationships between users. If Elijah is friends with Jeremiah and Timothy but Jeremiah and Timothy are not friends with each other, this can be modeled using a two-dimensional list that is often referred to as an **adjacency matrix**. The name, however, is not important. What is critical is the representational power that two-dimensional lists have.

```
>>> adj_matrix = [[0,1,1], [1,0,0], [1,0,0]]
```

This can be presented in a more intuitive way (like the Tic-Tac-Toe grid above) as follows:

```
[[0,1,1],
 [1,0,0],
 [1,0,0]]
```

How does this represent the binary friend relationships between Elijah, Jeremiah, and Timothy? If we use index 0 to represent Elijah, index 1 to represent Jeremiah, and index 2 to represent Timothy, then each number in adj_matrix can be used to represent the kind of relationship that is shared between any two of these three people adj_matrix might be visualized as the table given below.

	0 (Elijah)	1 (Jeremiah)	2 (Timothy)
0 (Elijah)	0	1	1
1 (Jeremiah)	1	0	0
2 (Timothy)	1	0	0

The numbers in adj_matrix are limited to 0s and 1s (because this is the standard way adjacency matrices are used). A 0 represents there is no friendship relation and a 1 represents there is a friendship. We can see that adj_matrix[0][1] is a 1 and can be interpreted as saying that Elijah is Jeremiah's friend. We can also see that adj_matrix[1][2] is a 0 and can be interpreted as saying that Jeremiah is *not* Timothy's friend. Hopefully, you get the idea and can see how this way of using two-dimensional lists can be applied to other domains that contain binary relationships.

Discussion: Can you think of other ways two-dimensional lists might be used to represent real-world data?

Getting comfortable with data representation is critical for exploiting the powers of a computer. It is, for example, what allows Facebook to model the friendship relationships that exist in its network. Developing techniques for representing real-world data is critical for leveraging the powers of a computer in processing this data.

Now, let's think about how we might iterate over all the data in a two-dimensional list like grid. Here is where the idea of nested loops comes into play. We might think of iterating over all the elements in grid based on rows and columns. In the 'outer' loop, we can iterate over all the rows. And in the 'inner' loop, we can iterate over all the columns in a given row. Let's start with the outer loop. The code might look as follows.

```
for row in range(3):
    print(grid[row])
```

This will simply iterate over each sub-list in grid and display each on the screen.

```
[1,2,3]
[4,5,6]
[7,8,9]
```

To iterate over *each* integer within each row, we need to do a bit more processing with each row in this loop. We will now nest an *inner* loop within the body of the *outer* loop so that every column in each row can be processed.

```
for row in range(3):
    for column in range(3):
        print(grid[row][column])
1
2
3
4
5
6
7
8
9
```

This will display each integer from 1 to 9 on the screen. Embed the structure of this nested loop in your mind because it will be a useful way of iterating over two-dimensional lists in a variety of other contexts.

Exercise 6.3: Write code that displays every integer in the two-dimensional list data. Note that data has two rows and four columns.

```
data = [[1,2,3,4], [5,6,7,8]]
```

Image Data Representation

What matters for us in the present chapter is how a two-dimensional list can be used as a way of representing visual data. Below is a 7x7 two-dimensional list that is assigned to the variable face. We can imagine, for now, that each of the elements in this list is a representation of a color. We can call each element a **pixel**. Pixels are the smallest units of color that can be manipulated in a digital image. Your computer screen, for example, can be thought of as a digital image. It too is composed of pixels. My laptop is currently displaying a screen with a 1366x768 grid of pixels. That is, the screen is divided up into 1,366 pixels from left to right (columns) and 768 pixels from top to bottom (rows). This yields a total of 1,049,088 pixels. That's a lot of data to deal with!

Let's take a closer look at the 7x7 two-dimensional list assigned to the variable face.

```
face = [[gray,gray,gray,gray,gray,gray,gray],
        [gray,gray,black,gray,black,gray,gray],
        [gray,gray,gray,gray,gray,gray,gray],
        [gray,gray,gray,black,gray,gray,gray],
        ...
        [gray,gray,gray,gray,gray,gray,gray]]
```

The values in each sub-list of face are the color values: gray and black. We might visualize this two-dimensional list as follows.

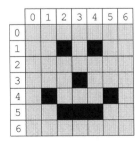

Figure 6.1 A colored representation of the 7x7 two-dimensional list assigned to face.

The problem is that the terms gray and black do not represent anything in Python. If you type gray into the Python interpreter, it will give you an error (unless you already created a variable with that name).

How are we supposed to represent colors in Python? We can't come up with a different name (e.g., gray and black) for every possible color that can be displayed on a screen. Can you imagine trying to come up with a name for every shade of red?

One way colors are represented in a digital image is through the RGB format. The letters R, G, and B stand for red, green, and blue. The intensity of each of these three colors can be represented as an integer value ranging from 0 to 255, where 0 represents no intensity (as in the absence of the color) and 255 represents the maximum level of intensity. So, for example, a pixel with the values (255,0,0) would represent a pure red color because red has value 255, green has value 0, and blue has value 0. Similarly, (0,255,0) would represent a pure green color, and (0,0,255) would represent a pure blue color. The absence of all colors (0,0,0) yields black and the maximum intensity of all colors (255,255,255) yields white. Varying these intensities gives us access to over 16 million different colors—more than the average human eye can distinguish (which is about 10 million)!

Exercise 6.4: What RGB values would produce a purple color (an equal mix of red and blue)? How about a yellow color (an equal mix of red and green)?

Exercise 6.5: What color would the RGB values (0,255,255) produce?

Armed with the basics of two-dimensional lists and the RGB color format, we are almost ready to start manipulating images in Python. We can now represent images as two-dimensional lists of pixels where each pixel is represented by three integers in the range 0–255.

Graphics

The **tkinter** library is the standard library for handling graphical user interfaces (GUI) in Python. A library is a collection of Python statements and function definitions that we can include in our programs. These statements and function definitions greatly expand the power of what we can do with Python.

The tkinter library, however, may not be that easy to use for a beginning programmer. To help facilitate its use, John Zelle, a professor of computer science at Wartburg University, created a library that acts as a wrapper over the tkinter library.[1] This library is contained in a Python file on his website here: https://mcsp.wartburg.edu/zelle/python/graphics. py. To be able to use this library, simply download this file and add it to the folder (directory) that you are saving your Python files in (if you're having trouble downloading the file see the 'Downloading Files' section in the Appendix for help). Documentation can be found on Zelle's website (https://mcsp.wartburg.edu/zelle/python). I highly encourage you to explore it for yourself.

To get started, let's make sure that the **graphics** library is accessible in your Python files. Create a new Python file in the IDLE text editor and try executing the following import statement.

```
from graphics import *
```

The '*' character in the import statement tells Python to import *everything* in the graphics library.

If everything went well, nothing should happen in the Python interpreter. This means that the library was properly imported. If something does happen, something must have gone wrong. In particular, you may get the following error message:

```
ModuleNotFoundError: No module named 'graphics'
```

If you did, chances are the graphics.py file is *not* in the same folder as your Python file.

Assuming you now have access to the graphics library, we can issue our first statement (assuming you haven't deleted the import statement).

```
window = GraphWin('Image Manipulation',1280,720)
```

GraphWin is a function that takes three inputs: a string and two integers. The string specifies the title of the window and the integers specify its dimensions. The return value of this function is a GUI object that is assigned to the variable window. By creating this object, a 1280×720 pixel window should be displayed on your screen. Moreover, you should see the title, 'Image Manipulation,' written along the top bar of this window.

While there are many things we can do with this library, we will keep things as simple as possible. In this chapter, we will focus solely on the Image object. To do this, we must first have a digital image to work with. You can download the dana_skate_greenscreen.png image from my website (https://danielflim.org/phil-through-cs/resources/). Of course, you can use an image that's already on your computer or download an image through your preferred web browser. The only constraint is that the image should be in either the Portable Pixmap, Graphics Interchange, or Portable Network Graphics format in order to work with the graphics library. That is, the image file name should end with either the .ppm, .gif, or .png suffixes.

To get started, put the digital image in the same directory as your Python file. I am using the dana_skate_greenscreen.png image, so the following code will create a new `Image` object in Python based on this digital image.

```
img = Image(Point(640,360),'dana_skate_greenscreen.png')
img.draw(window)
```

`Image` is a function that creates a new `Image` object. It is given two inputs: a `Point` object that specifies the location where the image will be displayed, and a string that specifies the name of the image file you want to use. The resulting `Image` object is then assigned to the variable `img`. Note that creating the Image object will not display the image. In order to display the image on the screen, the `img.draw` function must be executed.

The `img.draw` function takes a `GraphWin` object, in this case, `window`, as input and displays the image in `window`. The coordinates (640,360) specify the location in `window` where the image will be displayed. Note that 640 is half of 1,280 and 360 is half of 720, so it specifies the location at the center of window. Because the image will be displayed so that the *center* of the image is at (640,360) and both the image and the window have the same dimensions, the entire image will fit perfectly in `window`.[2] Moreover, the dana_skate_greenscreen.png image file, like the graphics.py file, must be in the same folder as the Python file you are currently working with for this statement to work properly.

Alternatively, you can create a new `Image` object that is not tied to any existing image by providing a `Point` object that specifies the location of the image and two integers that represent the width and height of the image (instead of the name of an image file). The pixels in this image will be colored black by default since this is a blank image.

```
new_img = Image(Point(250,250), 500,500)
```

We can extract information about an image's resolution by using the `getWidth` and `getHeight` functions of the `Image` object. These functions can be used as follows.

```
>>> img.getWidth()
1280
>>> new_img.getHeight()
500
```

There are two functions that are essential to manipulating individual pixels in `Image` objects. They are the `getPixel` and `setPixel` functions.

The first function extracts the color information out of a specified pixel in the Image object. The pixel is specified by supplying the function with two integers that signify the x and y coordinates of the pixel. The coordinate system of an image works like a typical Cartesian coordinate system with one difference, the y-axis is positive in the downward direction (not the upward direction). Moreover, the origin (0,0) is located at the top-left corner of the image (not the center).

The new_img object refers to something like the 500×500 pixel box in Figure 6.2. To access the pixel at the specified location, we move 250 pixels along the x-axis and 400 pixels along the y-axis. The getPixel function, when supplied with (250,400) will return a list with three integers that represents the RGB value of the specified pixel's color. If you do this with the new_img object, you should get a black pixel in response (this is because, as mentioned earlier, when creating a new Image object without a pre-existing image, all the pixels default to black).

```
>>> new_img.getPixel(250,400)
[0,0,0]
```

To extract each individual color intensity from the RGB value, you might do the following.

```
>>> rgb = new_img.getPixel(250,400)
>>> r = rgb[0]
>>> g = rgb[1]
>>> b = rgb[2]
```

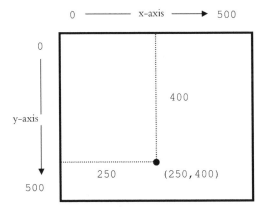

Figure 6.2 The location (250,400) on an image coordinate system.

Alternatively, you could do multiple assignments in a single comma-separated statement.

```
>>> r, g, b = new_img.getPixel(250,400)
```

Now, we are in a position to iterate over every pixel in a given image and process it in some way. An easy way to do this is by deploying a nested for loop.

```
for x in range(500):
    for y in range(500):
        print(new_img.getPixel(x,y))
```

This should print out 250,000 lines of essentially the same list [0,0,0] since every pixel in new_img is black. The important thing is that with this nested loop we can process all 250,000 pixels of color data in new_img.

We can also change the color of any given pixel by using the setPixel function. We can use this function to color the entire image red. Here is code that will carry this out.

```
for x in range(500):
    for y in range(500):
        new_img.setPixel(x,y,color_rgb(255,0,0))
```

Notice the setPixel function takes three inputs. The first two are integers that specify the location of the pixel and the second is the execution of the color_rgb function. This function takes three integers as input that represent the RGB value and returns a string that represents the color as a hexadecimal value (you don't have to understand what this is, what matters is that color_rgb takes three integers as input and returns an object that the computer recognizes as the relevant color). This will make the entire image red.

To see the image, don't forget that you need to use the draw function:

```
>>> new_img.draw(window)
```

The input to this function is the GraphWin object we had initially assigned to the variable window. This is like telling new_img to draw itself in window.

Note that this should take a fair amount of time. The nested loop will have to iterate over 250,000 pixels and assign new RGB values for each. Notice also that the dimensions of new_img and window are not the same. Because window is so much bigger, you should see a lot of empty space.

Finally, you can save the `Image` object to a file by using the `save` function. You simply need to supply it with a string that specifies the name of the file.

```
>>> new_img.save('new_image.gif')
```

A very important part of naming the image file is the suffix. In this example, the suffix of the filename is '.gif.' This tells the `Image` object to save the color information as a GIF (graphics interchange format) file. This is a commonly used format that compresses image data so that file sizes remain small. Alternatively, you could save the image in PNG (portable network graphics) format using the '.png' suffix. This is a lossless format that preserves image data as is—no information is lost. You should also be able to save the image in PPM (portable pixel map) format using the '.ppm' suffix. You can test these formats out for yourself by saving the `Image` object into different formats. You can then compare the quality of the resulting images and their relative file sizes. The tradeoff between quality and file size is one that you can negotiate.

```
>>> new_img.save('new_image.png')
>>> new_img.save('new_image.ppm')
```

This shows you that the *same* color information can be encoded in at least three different ways.

Putting all this code together into a single Python file, we have the following.

```
from graphics import *

window = GraphWin('Image Manipulation',256,256)
img = Image(Point(128,128),256,256)
for x in range(256):
    for y in range(256):
        img.setPixel(x,y,color_rgb(255,0,0))
img.draw(window)

img.save('red.png')
img.save('red.ppm')
img.save('red.gif')
```

After executing this code, you should make sure that the three image files are indeed created in the folder containing your Python file. If your computer doesn't support all three image file formats, don't worry. As long as one of them works, you should have no problem working through the exercises in this book. That being said, it's important to note that not all images you manipulate in Python can be saved in GIF format. Images in this format are limited to a palette of 256 colors. Images that have more than 256 colors cannot easily be saved in GIF format through this library. To be safe, you should use the PNG format because it handles a palette of more than 16 million colors.

Exercise 6.6: Create a 250×250 GraphWin object titled 'Exercise 6.6' and assign it to the variable win. Then create a 250×250 Image object and assign it to the variable img (make sure the location is correctly set so that it will be centered when later displayed in win). Then change all the pixel colors to blue, display img in win, and save the image as a PNG file.

Image Manipulation Tasks

Now we have the tools to carry out some interesting image manipulation tasks. One thing we might try to do is to create an image with a gradient between two colors. This is a fancy way of saying that we want to make one color fade into another. What if we wanted to make a red-green gradient? We would want the left side of the image to start with red (255,0,0) and slowly transition to green (0,255,0). For the red value to move from 255 to 0 smoothly over 500 pixels, we would need to work in increments of 0.512 (which is what we get when we divide 256 into 500 equal parts). So, we want the values for the red color component to steadily decrease in the following sequence: 255, 254.488, 253.976, 253.464, ..., 0. And we want the values for the green color component to steadily increase in the following sequence: 0, 0.512, 1.024, 1.536, ..., 255.

Figure 6.3 shows what the RGB values for the first four pixels should be, along with the final pixel in the first row of the image. The superscripts after each group of RGB values represent the pixel number in the first row.

The problem is that RGB values must be provided as integers, so these decimal values won't do. We can easily extract the integer portion of these

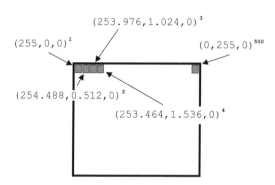

Figure 6.3 A 500x500 red-green gradient image.

decimal values by casting them into integers using the int function. Once this is done, you will get a tidier sequence of integer RGB values that smoothly transitions from (255,0,0) to (0,255,0). The sequence of values should be:

```
(255,0,0), (254,0,0), (253,1,0), (253,1,0), ... (0,255,0)
```

Now, to put all of this together, we have the following code. You should write this in a text editor so that you can ensure that you type all the code correctly and have it available for editing.

```
from graphics import *

new_img = Image(Point(250,250), 500,500)
inc = 256/500
for x in range(500):
    R = int(255-inc*x)
    G = int(inc*x)
    B = 0
    for y in range(500):
        new_img.setPixel(x, y, color_rgb(R, G, B))

new_img.save('red-green-gradient.png')
```

Note that new_img is never displayed since no GraphWin object was ever created for the image to be displayed in.

Everything in this code has already been explained above. The one exception is how the RGB value for each pixel in the nested loop is generated. Notice that the outer loop uses the variable x to iterate over a range of integers from 0 to 499. Multiplying x with 0.512 will give us the sequence: 0, 0.512, 1.024, 1.536, ..., 255. This will give us the sequence of values for the green color component so it moves from low intensity to high intensity. By using the int function on each of these numbers, we simply extract the integer portion of the number and get the following sequence: 0, 0, 1, 1, ..., 255. Taking this same value and subtracting it from 255 will give us the same sequence in reverse order: 255, 254.488, 253.976, 253.464, ..., 0. Applying the int function gives us the sequence: 255, 254, 253, 253, ..., 0. We use this sequence of values for the red color component so that it moves from high intensity to low intensity.

Exercise 6.7: Write code that will generate a green–blue color gradient that runs from top to bottom (not left to right) in an image of resolution 250×250.

Discussion: Another interesting task is to transform a color image into black and white. Before moving on, take a moment to think about how you might solve this problem.

This will require us to open an existing image, extract its resolution, and create a new image with the same resolution. Then for each pixel in the existing image, we have to figure out a way to convert the color information into some value in the black and white spectrum. We've seen that (0,0,0) represents black and (255,255,255) represents white. An important observation is that there are 256 possible values in the black and white spectrum and each component of the RGB value in this spectrum must have the same integer value. One idea would be to take the average of the integer values for every pixel in the existing image and use the integer portion of this average to create a new RGB value in the black and white spectrum. So, a pixel with the RGB values (104,23,217) will be converted to (114,114,114) because the integer portion of the average of 104, 23, and 217 is 114. The following code is one way of implementing this algorithm.

```
from graphics import *

existing_img = Image(Point(0,0),'test.png')
width = existing_img.getWidth()
height = existing_img.getHeight()
new_img = Image(Point(0,0),width,height)
for x in range(width):
    for y in range(height):
        R,G,B = existing_img.getPixel(x,y)
        average = int((R+G+B)/3)
        new_img.setPixel(x,y,color_rgb(average,aver-
age,average))

new_img.save('test-bw.png')
```

Note that the existing image file is named 'test.png.' You should replace this with the name of a color image file that you'd like to make black and white.

The image manipulation tasks in this chapter, as you can see, all revolve around the use of nested loops. Here, the information from every pixel that is processed in the existing image is used to specify the RGB value of every corresponding pixel in the new image. Before moving on, be sure you understand each line of code.

Finally, let's look at the task of adding a background to a green-screen image. This technique is often used in the movie industry and is technically referred to as **chroma key compositing** (or chroma keying). It is a visual effect for layering two images (or video streams) together based on a certain color—in our case, green. The green color range in the foreground image is made transparent by replacing each green color pixel with the

Figure 6.4 Chroma Key Compositing dana_skate_greenscreen.png with cloud_background.png.

corresponding pixel in a background image. You can see how this might work in Figure 6.4.

As a concluding task, try your hand at chroma keying using the dana_skate_greenscreen.png. To do this, you'll also need a background image with the same 1280×720 dimensions. I use the cloud_background.png image available on my website (https://danielflim.org/phil-through-cs/resources/). You will have to figure out a way to detect when a pixel in the skateboarding image is the right shade of green for it to be replaced. This may take a bit of ingenuity because, while it's easy to get most of the green pixels replaced, unless you are careful there will be a residual green glow that surrounds the skateboarder in the resulting composite image.

Once you can detect the right green color, the algorithm for chroma keying is easy. For every pixel in the foreground image that is green, use the color information from the corresponding pixel in the background image to set the color of the corresponding pixel in the composite image. For every pixel in the foreground image that is *not* green, use the color information from this pixel to set the color of the corresponding pixel in the composite image.

There are a variety of image manipulation tasks (e.g., image blurring) that are now available to you through the content covered in this chapter. If you are interested in trying your hand at more advanced techniques, try looking up steganography—good luck!

Key Points

- Nested loops are perfect for iterating over every element in two-dimensional lists.
- Digital images can represent the color of each pixel through the RGB format.
- Color gradients, black and white images, and chroma keying are image manipulation tasks that can be carried out with Zelle's graphics library.

Notes

1   A wrapper is code that translates a library's existing interface into another interface. In this case, Zelle's library is used to provide a simpler interface than that of the tkinter library.

2   If you are not using the dana_skate_greenscreen.png image, your image will likely have different dimensions so the numbers you use for the width and height of the GraphWin object as well as the Image object should be different if you'd like your image to fit perfectly in the window.

Chapter 7

Skepticism

In the previous chapter, we learned how to create images and specify the RGB values of each pixel. Here is code that creates (without displaying) a 256×256 gray Image object and assigns it to img:

```
from graphics import *

img = Image(Point(128,128),256,256)
for x in range(256):
    for y in range(256):
        img.setPixel(x,y,color_rgb(127,127,127))

img.save('gray.png')
img.save('gray.gif')
```

img is then used to generate two different image files that encode the relevant color information in two different formats. Here are visualizations of the PNG and GIF files.

Figure 7.1 Two 256×256 gray images. One is encoded as a GIF and the other is encoded as a PNG.

DOI: 10.4324/9781003271284-7

Can you tell the difference between these two images? I surely can't. In fact, they should be indistinguishable to any normal human being. Despite this, the way the color information underlying these two images are encoded is quite different. This can plainly be seen by inspecting the sizes of the files. The image on the left is a GIF file and it is 398 bytes in size. The image on the right is a PNG file and it is 808 bytes in size—more than twice as large as its GIF counterpart. The size discrepancy is due to the fact that GIF files use a compression algorithm.

Given this, when presented with one of these images, can you be certain whether the image you are looking at is a GIF or a PNG? No, they are visually indistinguishable. What you see *underdetermines* what kind of file underlies the visual image. You might think that what you're looking at is a GIF, but that would amount to little more than a guess since you don't have evidence that reliably helps you decide. Consequently, we can say that you don't have *knowledge* of what kind of file it is that you are looking at.

Epistemology

What exactly do we mean when we say that you don't have knowledge of the file type? This brings us to the branch of philosophy called **epistemology**. This term is derived from ancient Greek (episteme) and it simply means knowledge. One of the tasks of epistemology is to better understand what knowledge is. One way this is done is by breaking the concept of knowledge down into its component parts. For example, we might want to analyze the concept of being a bachelor by breaking it down into its component parts. This is a straightforward task since this concept is defined by combining the concepts of being male and being unmarried.

We can correctly say that a person S is a bachelor if and only if S is male and S is unmarried.[1] The language here is important. To say that S is a bachelor **if** S is male and S is unmarried is to identify *sufficient* conditions for being a bachelor. That is, if S is male and unmarried, then S is a bachelor. This suggests that while there may be other ways of being a bachelor, at least one way this can be accomplished is by being male and unmarried. Here is another example. To say that S is an animal if S is a dog is to identify a sufficient condition for being an animal. Though there are other ways of being an animal (e.g., being a cat), being a dog is at least one way of being an animal and is therefore sufficient for being an animal. It is not, however, a necessary condition for being an animal. It is possible to be an animal without being a dog.

To say that S is a bachelor **only if** S is male and S is unmarried is to identify the *necessary* conditions for being a bachelor. That is, if S is a bachelor, it must be the case that S is male and unmarried. This does not suggest that satisfying these conditions will guarantee that S is a bachelor. It only says that it is impossible for S to be a bachelor if S is not at least male and unmarried. Here is another example. To say that S is a dog only if *S* is an animal is to identify a necessary condition for being a dog. It is impossible to be a dog without also being an animal. It is not, however, a sufficient condition for being a dog. *S*'s being an animal does not guarantee that *S* is a dog since there are many kinds of animals.

Discussion: But what about the concept of knowledge? Before reading on, can you come up with a set of component parts that constitute knowledge? What are the necessary and/or sufficient conditions that must be met for someone to know something?

Conceptual Analysis

Trying to identify the necessary and/or sufficient conditions for the proper application of a concept is what many philosophers call conceptual analysis. Conceptual analysis is one of the critical components of philosophical thinking. Traditionally, it has been thought that there are three necessary and sufficient conditions for knowledge: truth, belief, and justification.

Truth is taken to be an uncontroversial component of knowledge. Consider the statement: grass is purple. It seems odd to say, for example, that Micah *knows* that grass is purple. It may very well be the case that he takes himself to know that grass is purple. It's not difficult to imagine Micah confidently saying, "I know that grass is purple!" But he couldn't have *known* this because it's false. It doesn't seem like you can know something that is false, because there is an element of accuracy involved in our attributions of knowledge. The following principle, therefore, seems reasonable. If a person, *S*, knows *p*, then *p* must be true. That is, truth is a *necessary* condition of knowledge.

Belief is also taken to be an uncontroversial component of knowledge. Beliefs include *anything* that one believes. They are not limited to things that are deeply important to our identities, like our religious and political beliefs. If Micah knows that grass is green, then it would be natural for him to answer, "grass is green" when asked about the color of grass. This is strong evidence that Micah actually believes that grass is green. Indeed, it's hard to think of a statement that a person knows but doesn't believe. The following principle, therefore, seems reasonable. If a person, *S*, knows *p*, then *S* must believe *p*. That is, belief is a *necessary* condition of knowledge.

Discussion: *S*'s believing *p* and *p*'s being true are good candidates for being components of knowledge. If *S* knows *p*, then *S* must believe *p* and *p* must be true. That is, belief and truth are necessary conditions of knowledge. But are they also sufficient conditions? If *S* believes *p* and *p* is true, then does *S* know *p*?

Most philosophers have thought that belief and truth are *necessary* conditions of knowledge, but not *sufficient* ones. Consider the following statement (call it *p*).

There are 1,423,509 rocks on the shore of Waikiki Beach.

Let's say, Liliana, by sheer coincidence and for no apparent reason, forms the belief that p: she just decides to believe that there are 1,423,509 rocks on the shore of Waikiki Beach. Moreover, suppose that it turns out that p is in fact true. So, Liliana believes p and p is true. Does it follow that she *knows* p? According to Plato, an ancient Greek philosopher, she would not know p. She would merely have a correct guess that p. It's a matter of sheer luck that Liliana happened to land on the right number of rocks on the shore of Waikiki Beach.

What's missing, it seems, is a *rationale* for believing p. Liliana has no evidence for believing that there are 1,423,509 rocks. She could just as easily have formed the belief that there are 1,423,508 rocks instead. She never conducted a study and counted the rocks on Waikiki Beach. Therefore, she lacks **justification** for believing in p's truth. This is what philosophers have traditionally taken to be the third *necessary* component of knowledge in addition to truth and belief. Without justification, we should not say that a given person has knowledge.

It seems reasonable to conclude that truth, belief, and justification are all necessary conditions of knowledge. But are these three conditions jointly sufficient? At first glance, it seems quite plausible. After all, counterexamples to this claim are not readily available. Can you think of a true statement p that S believes with justification that nevertheless fails to count as something that S knows? If not, we might offer the following conceptual analysis of what it means for someone to *know* something.

Conceptual Analysis

S knows p if and only if:

(1) S believes p.
(2) p is true.
(3) S is justified in believing p.

This is sometimes referred to as the JTB (justification, truth, and belief) analysis of knowledge and is often credited as being the 'standard' analysis of knowledge.[2] Given this analysis, we are ready to explore one of the perennial preoccupations in epistemology—external world skepticism.

External World Skepticism

Skepticism is the claim that we lack knowledge (in a certain domain). Usually, this does not mean that we don't *believe* anything and it does not mean that the things we typically believe are not *true*. The traditional claim of skepticism is that we don't have *justification* for the things we typically believe. Consequently, if we lack justification for the things we typically believe to be true, we fail to have knowledge of the things we typically take to be true—our beliefs amount to little more than guesses.

A *global* form of skepticism would be the claim that we do not know anything at all. Global forms of skepticism, however, may be self-undermining because the proponent of such views would (presumably) be claiming that she at least knows one thing: that global skepticism is true. A *local* form of skepticism would be the claim that we do not know anything within a given domain. The most discussed domain (in many philosophical contexts) is the **external world**. The term 'external' is used here to make a distinction between what goes on inside our minds and what goes on outside our minds. Things that exist in our minds might include things like beliefs, emotions, sensations, and experiences. Things that exist outside our minds might include things like rocks, chairs, planes, and mountains. So, what is at stake here are our beliefs about things like rocks, chairs, planes, and mountains. I believe, for example, that the chair I'm sitting on is brown. Not only do I believe this, I think that I *know* this. The external world skeptic, however, would claim to the contrary that I do not know this. In fact, it may be that the chair I think I'm currently sitting on doesn't even exist! Indeed, *everything* in the external world might not exist. This threatens practically all of our beliefs about the external world. But how does one come to such a radical conclusion?

René Descartes, a 17th-century French philosopher, gave us a recipe for reaching such a conclusion.

> How often, asleep at night, am I convinced of just such familiar events—that I am here in my dressing-gown, sitting by the fire— when in fact I am lying undressed in bed! Yet at the moment my eyes are certainly wide awake when I look at this piece of paper; I shake my head and it is not asleep; as I stretch out and feel my hand I do so deliberately, and I know what I am doing. All this would not happen with such distinctness to someone asleep. Indeed! As if I did not remember other occasions when I have been tricked by exactly similar thoughts while asleep! As I think about this more carefully, I see plainly that there are never any sure signs by means of which being awake can be distinguished from being asleep.
>
> (Descartes, 2003, pp. 67–68)

Consider what it's like to have a *realistic* dream (one in which you are *not* aware that you are dreaming). The other night I had a dream that I was swimming in the ocean surrounded by tropical fish. One of the many beliefs I had during this dream was that there was an especially colorful tropical fish about five feet in front of me. Let's call this belief B_{dream}. This belief, at the time I was thinking it, was clearly false. Despite my utter confidence in this belief, I was not in the ocean and there were no tropical fish near me. Instead, I was in my room, lying on my bed with my eyes closed. I did not *know* B_{dream} (even though I thought that I did) for the obvious reason that B_{dream} was false.

Now consider the time I really swam in Hanauma Bay surrounded by tropical fish. While swimming near one of the coral reefs, I had a belief that there was an especially colorful tropical fish about five feet in front of me. Let's call this belief B_{real}. I was confident that this belief was true, and it was, in fact, true. It seems natural to say that I did have knowledge of B_{real}: in other words, I knew that there was an especially colorful tropical fish about five feet in front of me.

So how is the dream situation, involving B_{dream}, supposed to undermine my claim to knowledge regarding B_{real}? The key is to focus on the *justification* I had for each of my beliefs. It is safe to say that the *kind* of justification I had for both beliefs was the same. Both beliefs were based on my visual *experiences*. My visual experiences *of* an especially colorful tropical fish about five feet in front of me gave me a reason to believe, in both situations, that there *was* an especially colorful tropical fish about five feet in front of me. But if the visual experiences I had in both situations were the same (and equally believable), then the justification I had in both situations would have been the same as well.

We might say that my justification *underdetermines* which situation I was in—it didn't tell me whether I was in a dream situation or in a real (ocean) situation. Both situations, after all, yield the same kind of visual experiences. So, merely by inspecting the visual experiences in each situation, it was impossible for me to tell which situation I was actually in.

Discussion: Before moving on, can you reconstruct Descartes' argument in premise-conclusion form? Are you persuaded by Descartes' reasoning?

Returning to external world skepticism, the logic behind Descartes' argument might be regimented into a formal argument as follows.

1.   Your visual experiences can come about through a real situation, or your visual experiences can come about through a dream situation.

Figure 7.2 The visual experiences that justify B_{dream} and B_{real} are the same.

2. You have no reason to believe that your visual experiences come about through a real situation rather than a dream situation.
3. If premise 1 and premise 2 are true, then you have no reason to believe that your visual experiences come about through a real situation.
4. If you have no reason to believe that your visual experiences come about through a real situation, then you have no knowledge of the external world.
5. Therefore, you have no knowledge of the external world.

Now that the argument is put into premise-conclusion form using conditionals (as we learned in Chapter 4), it's easy to check for validity. The way the argument has been presented, we can confirm that the argument is valid—it is impossible for the premises to be true and the conclusion false. Here is the argument with only its formal structure.

1. p
2. q
3. If p and q then r.
4. If r then s.
5. Therefore, s.

To take things a bit more slowly, we can see that the first three premises entail r because the first two premises ensure that the antecedent of the third premise is true. Since r is the antecedent of the fourth premise, we can see that s must be true.

Given that the argument is valid, the only remaining way to evaluate this argument is to assess whether the premises are true.

One might argue that premise 2 is the weak link: the visual experiences generated by dream situations and real situations are not the same. The visual experiences we have when we dream are qualitatively different from the visual experiences we have when we are awake. Importantly, we can detect the falsity of our dream visual experiences.

But this may only hold for lucid dreams, in which we already know we're dreaming *in the dream*. This is a highly debatable claim. In defense of premise 2, one might make an appeal to one's own dreams. Surely you've had dreams that seemed so real you were convinced that they were actually happening (and therefore were unaware that you were dreaming).

It turns out, therefore, that this way of arguing for external world skepticism hinges on a critical claim—the claim that the kind of visual experiences we have while having realistic dreams (that are not lucid) are indistinguishable from the kind of visual experiences we have while in real situations. Let's call this the **visual equivalence claim**. The upshot

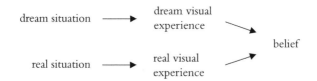

Figure 7.3 Visual experiences when we are awake are different from visual experiences when we are dreaming.

is that the persuasiveness of this argument might fundamentally depend on the persuasiveness of the visual equivalence claim.

At this point, it may be helpful to return to the PNG and GIF example that I began this chapter with. I hope you can see that Descartes' depiction of our relationship with the external world is analogous to our relationship with these image files. In the same way our visual experiences underdetermine their sources (they might be generated by dreams or by the external world) so the colored pixels that are displayed on a screen underdetermine the format of the underlying file (PNG or GIF).

Visual Perception

Many have complained, however, that Descartes' dream scenario is too far-fetched. It would be nice if there were a way to argue for external world skepticism without relying on the visual equivalence claim. A contemporary development of an argument for external world skepticism does exactly this. It does so by focusing not on situations involving the possibility of realistic dreams and the defense of the visual equivalence claim, but on the act of perception itself.

Let's begin with the way we 'naturally' think about the relationship between the external world and the way we perceive the external world to be. I think it's safe to say that most of us think this is a relationship of exact similarity. That is, when we perceive the world, we passively receive an exact copy of the world in our visual experiences (like a photocopier)— what we perceptually experience is what is actually there. Here is how Donald Hoffman, a cognitive scientist, puts it:

> If I'm sober, and don't suspect a prank, I'm inclined to believe that when I see a cherry, there is a real cherry whose shape and color match my experience, and which continues to exist when I look away. This assumption is central to how we think about ourselves and the world.
>
> (Hoffman, 2019)

But is this really how perception works—as a passive photocopier of the external world? First, we should recognize that the relationship between the external world and our *perception* of the world is a **causal** one. External objects, like cherries, in conjunction with the way light is reflected off their surfaces, *cause* certain things to happen in the eyes of humans who happen to be looking. The changes in the human eye, in turn, *cause* electrical signals to be sent to the brain, and these signals *cause* the brain to construct a perceptual experience.

Though the causal process from cherry to perception happens almost instantaneously (a few hundred milliseconds), we must not lose sight of the fact that it is nevertheless a multi-step *process*. A variety of transformations occur at each step in the journey from the cherry to the experience of the cherry.

Here is the critical point: the causes and effects at each stage of this process are *not* related to each other in terms of exact similarity. Contrast the cherry with the electrical signals caused by the cherry, which are then sent from the eye to the brain (caused by the reflected light's stimulating the rod and cone cells in the retina). There are all kinds of differences between the cherry and these electrical signals. The most obvious differences are that the cherry has a shape and a color, but the electrical signals don't. In fact, I'm not even sure what it would mean to say that electrical signals have shapes or colors at all. To attribute such properties to electrical signals would be an example of what philosophers call a category error. It's like saying that the number two is red or democratic governance is spherical. Taken literally, numbers do not have colors, and governance has no geometric shape. Similarly, electrical charge has no color or shape either.

To strengthen this point, we can draw another analogy with what we learned in the previous chapter about digital images. Consider the way digital images are manipulated in Python. Each pixel has an RGB color value, stored as a group of three integers, which controls the color of the pixel. These number values (in conjunction with the computer) can be thought of as the causes of the color of the pixel being displayed in the image. But what relationship is there between (255,0,0) and the color red? Red, for lack of a better description, appears red to us. But do the numbers (255,0,0) appear red to us? Does it even make sense to say that they have any color whatsoever? Clearly, the cause (the RGB value) and the effect (the pixel's color) do not share a relationship of exact similarity. Indeed, it's hard to see any notable or interesting similarities between the two. So, given these examples, we can safely say that there is no guarantee that the relation of exact similarity holds between causes and effects. Why should we then think that the relation of exact similarity holds between the cherry and our perception of the cherry?

Second, the idea that we *passively* perceive the external world or that the external world imprints itself on our visual experiences is almost certainly

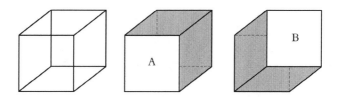

Figure 7.4 Necker Cube.

wrong. The brain, in receiving information about the light reflected off the cherry's surface, actively *constructs* a visual experience. There are many interesting and suggestive examples that support this thesis, but here I'll share two.

The Necker Cube is an optical illusion developed by Louis Albert Necker in the 1800s. It is a wireframe drawing of a cube that has no visual cues regarding its orientation. It can be interpreted in at least two ways: (A) in a downward direction with the lower-left square acting as the front side of the cube or (B) in an upward direction with the upper-right square acting as the front side of the cube.

This can be seen in Figure 7.4. The dashed gray lines in Cubes A and B represent lines that are meant to be hidden from view. As you stare at the left-most cube (i.e., the Necker Cube), with practice, you can flip between Cubes A and B in terms of your interpretation. The point here is that the Necker Cube image never changes—the external object remains static. Yet, your perception of the object changes—the inner visual experience is dynamic. Sometimes you perceive the Necker Cube as Cube A and at other times you perceive it as Cube B. Here's how Hoffman puzzles over this illusion:

> Each time you view the figure you see Cube A or Cube B, but never both at once. When you look away, which cube is there: Cube A or Cube B? Suppose you saw Cube A just before you looked away, and you answer that Cube A is still there. You can check your answer by looking back. If you do this a few times, you'll discover that some-times you see Cube B. When this happens, did Cube A transform into Cube B when you looked away? Or you can check your answer by asking friends to look. You'll find that they often disagree, some saying that they see Cube A, others that they see Cube B. They may all be telling the truth, as you could check with a polygraph. This suggests that neither Cube A nor Cube B is there when no one looks, and that there is no objective cube that exists unobserved, no publicly available cube waiting for all to see. Instead, if you see Cube A while your friend sees Cube B, then in that moment you each see the cube that your visual system *constructs*. There are as many cubes as there are

observers constructing cubes. And when you look away, your cube ceases to be.

(Hoffman, 2019)

Here is a different kind of example. The so-called Checker Shadow Illusion was developed by Edward Adelson in the 1990s. The image consists of a checkerboard with a cylindrical object casting a shadow across its surface. It appears that square A is darker than square B, but the squares, in fact, are the exact same shade and brightness. This can be verified by careful inspection. One way to do this would be to cut out a mask that hides everything but the shades of the two squares. This effectively removes the illusion.

What this demonstrates, again, is that the brain is actively at work in constructing a perception of what is out there. Because we have extensive implicit knowledge of how checkerboards and shadows work, our brain, in a sense, *forces* us to see square A as being darker than square B. Even after we've verified that the squares are the exact same shade and brightness, we can't stop perceiving square A as being darker than square B (this is something called 'cognitive impenetrability' in the philosophy of mind: the fact that we know A and B are the same color makes no difference to how we see them as looking like different colors). The precise information that exists in the image regarding the shade and brightness of the two squares is exactly the same, but our brain, when making sense of these squares in the overall visual context, constructs an experience that makes it extremely difficult not to believe that square A is darker than square B.

There are at least two reasons, then, to question whether the relationship between the external world and our perception of that world is one of

Figure 7.5 Checker Shadow Illusion.

exact similarity. First, perception occurs through a causal process replete with transformations (light to nerves to electricity to brains) where there is no guarantee that the causes and their effects share any obvious similarities (let alone the relationship of exact similarity). Second, the brain does not passively receive impressions from the external world; it is actively at work constructing visual experiences that might or might not be exactly similar to the external world.

Evolution

Some readers might complain that this is all a bit too quick. They might take issue with the rhetorical question asked earlier: "Why should we then think that the relation of exact similarity holds between the cherry and our perception of the cherry?" It seems there is a very reasonable answer to this question. While there might not be any general similarity relation that holds between causes and effects, it seems **evolution**, if it has indeed shaped the way we perceive the external world, must have equipped us with sense organs that provide us with visual experiences that closely resemble the objects in the external world that caused them. Here's how Robert Trivers, an evolutionary theorist, puts this:

> Our sense organs have evolved to give us a marvelously detailed and accurate view of the outside world—we see the world in color and 3-D, in motion, texture, non-randomness, embedded patterns, and a great variety of other features. Likewise for hearing and smell. Together our sensory systems are organized to give us a detailed and accurate view of reality, exactly as we would expect if truth about the outside world helps us to navigate it more effectively.
>
> (Trivers, 2011)

Trivers is not alone in this sentiment—there are a number of other influential cognitive scientists who concur.[3] But does evolution have to work this way?

First, evolution does not require accuracy (in the sense of resemblance and exact similarity) to select traits for the intergenerational transmission of perceptual organs. What matters is not accuracy but behavioral effectiveness. Here is a humorous example given by Alvin Plantinga in discussing the requirements of evolution:

> Perhaps Paul very much likes the idea of being eaten, but when he sees a tiger, always runs off looking for a better prospect, because he thinks it unlikely the tiger he sees will eat him. This will get his body parts in the right place so far as survival is concerned, without involving much by way of true belief.... Or perhaps he thinks the tiger is a large,

friendly, cuddly pussycat and wants to pet it; but he also believes that the best way to pet it is to run away from it.... Clearly there are any number of belief-[and]-desire systems that equally fit a given bit of behavior.

(Plantinga, 1993)

Paul believes that the tiger is cuddly because, presumably, he visually perceives it to be so. This would be a mistake because the tiger does not have the property of being cuddly. Rather, it has the property of being ferocious. Nevertheless, given the rest of Paul's beliefs, it is effective in helping him survive because it causes him to run away. The accuracy of the *contents* of Paul's beliefs does not matter with regard to the effectiveness of his survival behavior. What matters is the behavioral relationship that holds between Paul and tigers—in the presence of tigers, Paul runs.

So, it seems there is reason to believe that evolution does *not* require anything beyond fitness-enhancing behaviors to hone our perceptions of the external world. Our perceptual organs don't have to engender beliefs within us that accurately describe the world. Just because we perceive a flower to be red, it doesn't follow that the flower must be red. In fact, all of our perceptual beliefs may, strictly speaking, be false. Nevertheless, if these perceptual beliefs effectively enhance our ability to survive, then the perceptual organs that give rise to them will be selected. This makes legitimate space for external world skepticism to take root. But is there any reason to think that evolution actively selects perceptual organs that generate false beliefs?

Here, I defer to Hoffman:

> According to standard accounts of evolution, payoffs can vary wildly while the true state of the world remains fixed. It follows that seeing truth and seeing fitness are two distinct strategies of perception, not one strategy seen in different lights. The two strategies can compete. One may dominate and the other go extinct. So it is a central question, not a conceptual mistake, to ask: Does natural selection favor perceptions tuned to truth or to fitness? This can be studied with [evolutionary game theory]. It is a powerful theory. It has the right tools to study our question: Does natural selection favor veridical perceptions? It gives a clear answer: no. This is spelled out in the Fitness-Beats-Truth (FBT) Theorem, which I conjectured and Chetan Prakash proved.

(Hoffman, 2019)

Hoffman's point is that in a competition between perceptual organs that track the truth versus perceptual organs that track fitness, fitness wins every time. Moreover, his theoretical models suggest that this is so. Consequently, we have every reason not to take our perceptual beliefs too seriously. What matters is that they work in keeping us alive, not that they accurately describe the external world.

Returning to our discussion of digital image manipulation may offer us another angle on this claim. Consider again one of the gray images that were introduced at the beginning of this chapter. What is this image in 'reality'? What we are seeing on screen is just a representation of an image file containing RGB values. Basically, the file is a bunch of numbers. Given that the image displayed on the screen is gray, does it follow that the file itself (not the visual representation of the file) is also colored gray? Clearly not. The color of the image on the screen is not the color of the file. So, the visual representation and the file do not participate in a relationship of exact similarity. Beliefs about the visual representation should not, without careful consideration, be transferred over to beliefs about the file itself. In fact, the purpose of the visual representation is not to reveal the 'truth' about the file. The truth about the file is buried in a massive series of numbers (or more accurately electrical signals in intricately organized circuits). Can you imagine trying to figure out what those thousands of numbers represent? It would take you (at least) several hours just to acquaint yourself with all the numbers!

With this in mind, we might argue that evolution selected for the kind of perception we now have because it simplifies the external world and makes operating in it extremely efficient. After all, the world is chock full of information. Consider, for example, the billions (or trillions) of molecules in the air all around us. Would it be evolutionarily efficient to develop perceptual organs that kept track of the trajectories of all these molecules? It would be better to develop perceptual organs that heuristically package all of that information into easily accessible sensations that help with survival behavior. In short, there is reason to believe that evolution selects for *useful* perceptual abstractions and not detailed truth-preserving accounts of the external world.

Key Points

- Conceptual analysis of knowledge yields three components: justification, truth, and belief.
- Skepticism is the claim that we do not have knowledge.
- Dream perception and real perception may be indistinguishable.
- Perception is a causal process from external world objects to visual experience.
- Perception is not passive, but an active construction undertaken by the brain.
- Evolution provides reason to think perception deliberately hides the truth about the external world.

Notes

1 Though this is a popular analysis, it faces a number of well-known counter-examples. Priests and popes, for example, are unmarried males, but they are distinct from bachelors because they can never get married. So the analysis does not provide sufficient conditions for being a bachelor.
2 For a nice discussion of this analysis of knowledge along with its purported shortcomings, see Gettier (1963) and Rosen, Byrne, Cohen, Harman, and Shiffrin (2018).
3 See Marr (2010) for example.

References

Descartes, R. (2003). *Discourse on Method and Meditations*. New York: Dover Publications.

Gettier, E. (1963). Is Justified True Belief Knowledge? *Analysis, 23*(6), 121–123.

Hoffman, D. (2019). *The Case Against Reality: Why Evolution Hid the Truth from Our Eyes*. New York: W.W. Norton & Company.

Marr, D. (2010). *Vision: A Computational Investigation into the Human Representation and Processing of Visual Information*. Cambridge: MIT Press.

Plantinga, A. (1993). *Warrant and Proper Function*. Oxford: Oxford University Press.

Rosen, G., Byrne, A., Cohen, J., Harman, E., & Shiffrin, S. (2018). *The Norton Introduction to Philosophy*. New York: W.W. Norton & Company.

Trivers, R. (2011). *The Folly of Fools: The Logic of Deceit and Self-Deception in Human Life*. New York: Basic Books.

Chapter 8

Functions

In previous chapters, we were introduced to several built-in functions. They included `type`, `len`, `print`, `int`, and `str`, among others. Let's remind ourselves how to use these functions. You first type the name of the function and then follow this with parentheses. What you put in the parentheses are the inputs to the function. Depending on the function, you might supply it without any inputs, with a specific number of inputs, or an indefinite number of inputs. Here are some examples:

```
>>> int()
0
>>> len('hello world')
11
>>> print(1,'hi',True,None)
1 hi True None
```

Defining Functions

While there are plenty of useful built-in functions, Python provides us with the ability to define our own functions. Writing good functions is a skill, and as we will see, both **decomposition** and **pattern recognition** (two pillars of computational thinking) play important roles in developing this skill.

Functions can be created by using the `def` statement. A function definition has a few simple parts: a name, an arbitrary number of comma-separated input variables, and a block of code. Here is the general form of a function definition:

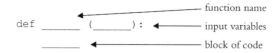

Figure 8.1 The basic structure of a function definition.

DOI: 10.4324/9781003271284-8

Let's start with a simple example:

```
def greet(n):
    print('Hi ' + n + ', how are you?')
```

The name of this function is greet. It takes a single input that will be assigned to the variable n. The body of the function is a single print statement. The name greet acts like any other created variable (e.g., x = 10), but instead of having a number or string assigned to it, it has a function assigned to it. You can verify that this has successfully occurred by typing greet into the interpreter. This should return something like the following:

```
>>> greet
<function greet at 0x03E09C40>
```

This demonstrates that the function was successfully created and assigned to the variable greet. The strange string of characters at the end (0x03E09C40) is a hexadecimal representation of the location in your computer's memory where the function definition is stored (and not something we need to worry about at this point).

You can use the type function on greet to see that it is tied to an object that is of the function type.

```
>>> type(greet)
<class 'function'>
```

To *execute* (or *call* or *run*) the function, we do what we've done before. The name of the function must be followed by parentheses. The parentheses are critical—they signal that the function should be executed. Since greet was defined with a single input variable, a single input must be given. Here is an example of how to use the greet function:

```
>>> greet('Andre')
```

The input value, 'Andre,' is assigned to the input variable n. So, the function should display the following.

```
Hi Andre, how are you?
```

Once the block of code in greet is executed, the function terminates.

This function can be used with a variety of different input strings. It is a completely general way of greeting anyone you'd like:

```
>>> greet('Joshua')
Hi Joshua, how are you?
>>> greet('Elaine')
Hi Elaine, how are you?
```

Local versus Global Variables

More needs to be said about what happens during the execution of a function. When a function is executed, the first thing that happens is the inputs to the function are evaluated.

```
>>> greet('I' + 'saac')
```

In this example, the input is an expression that combines two strings. Evaluating this expression results in the string 'Isaac.' This is then assigned to the newly created variable n. This variable, however, is only accessible to the statements in the block of code within the function definition. Once the execution of greet terminates, n will no longer exist. You can verify this by trying to access n outside of greet. It should return the following error.

```
>>> n
NameError: name 'n' is not defined
```

This is why the input variables in a function definition are often referred to as 'local' variables. They are only available locally to the block of code within the function definition.

By contrast, variables defined outside of a function are often referred to as 'global' variables because they can be accessed anywhere. Consider the following variation on the greet function:

```
def greet2():
    print('Hi ' + n + ', how are you?')
```

It is the same as greet except that it doesn't have any input variables. This function also refers to variable n, but because there is no local variable n in greet2, the global variable n (assuming it already exists) is used.

```
>>> n = 'David'
>>> greet2()
Hi David, how are you?
```

But what happens if there is a variable naming conflict? That is, what if there is a local variable and a global variable that have the same name? In this case, any reference to the variable within a function definition will refer to the local variable. If a local variable of that name does not exist, then the variable will refer to the global variable. If a global variable of that name does not exist, then Python will return an error. The following code should help you see how this works.

```
>>> n = 'David'
>>> greet('Andre')
Hi Andre, how are you?
```

The global variable n is assigned the string 'David,' and the local variable n (which is only accessible within the greet function and exists only during the execution of greet) is assigned the string 'Andre.' This is why the resulting sentence is displayed with 'Andre' instead of 'David.'

Often the best way to learn how these concepts work is to experiment. Try different combinations of local and global variables in the definitions of various functions. See for yourself what happens in a variety of situations and get comfortable with the local versus global distinction.

Exercise 8.1: Write a function called respond that takes a single input n and displays a response like the following: 'Hi _____, doing well, thanks!' where the blank is replaced with n.

Return Values

Though it may not be obvious, all of the functions we've defined so far have *no* output value. Consider the greet function. Although it takes input values, it doesn't have any output values. While the greet function does display something on the screen, the act of displaying something is *not* the output value of the function itself. To get a better handle on this important point, let's first get comfortable with the idea of a function that doesn't take any input values.

```
def f1():
    print('this function has no input or output')
```

Notice that there is nothing in the parentheses of the function definition. The way to execute this function is as follows.

```
>>> f1()
this function has no input or output
```

Again, the parentheses are critical. They signal that the function, f1, should be executed. This is different from simply typing the name of the function.

```
>>> f1
<function f1 at 0x01D93A74>
```

This returns information about the function but does not *execute* it.

Now, consider the following function, called circumference, which takes one input, radius, and (assuming radius represents the radius of a circle) calculates the circumference.

```
def circumference(radius):
    2 * radius * 3.1416
```

We might execute this function as follows:

```
>>> circumference(100)
```

What happens when you execute this function? It looks like it doesn't do anything. In fact, it *is* doing something. It creates a local variable radius, assigns 100 to it, and carries out two multiplication operations. The problem is that the *result* of these operations is not set as the *output* value of the function. Output values must be explicitly specified by using the **return** keyword. Just as you have to specify what inputs (if any) are given to a function, you also have to specify what outputs (if any) a function returns. Here is a function that specifies the output value:

```
def circumference_2(radius):
    return 2 * radius * 3.1416
```

When a function has a return value, it can be used in more complex expressions. Compare the following two addition operations:

```
>>> circumference(100) + 100
>>> circumference_2(100) + 100
```

The first expression will result in an error because circumference has no return value. Although it carries out the multiplication operations, its resulting value is None (signifying that the evaluation of the function has no value). Consequently, the first expression generates an error because it is an attempt to add 100 to None (remember, None and 0 are not the same). The second expression has no problems because circumference_2 has a return value—it evaluates to 628. This results in a simple arithmetic operation that yields 728.

Having to explicitly specify what the output value of a function is makes sense. After all, in functions of increasing complexity, the code in the function definition will be full of statements, resulting in a variety of values. Without specifying which of these values is to count as the output value, it would be completely arbitrary, from Python's perspective, what the output value of a function should be.

It is also important to note that the return statement immediately stops the execution of the function and exits. Any code left in the function that might be present after the return statement is skipped.

Going back to the greet function, now we have an explanation for why it takes inputs but generates no outputs. No return statement was issued in that function, so it carried out the print operation and displayed something on the screen, but no output value was specified. Thus, the resulting value of executing greet is None.

Exercise 8.2: Write a function called volume that takes a number, called r, as input (that represents the radius of a sphere) and returns the volume of the sphere.

To get a bit more practice under our belts, let's revisit the program we wrote in Chapter 5, which counted the number of times 'o' occurs in a given string. Let's write a function that calculates this for us. Let's call it count_os. This function should take a string, S, as input and return the number of times 'o' occurs in S. Since you already have access to the program, it shouldn't be too difficult to translate it into a function.

```
def count_os(S):
    x = 0
    number_of_os = 0
    while x < len(S):
        if S[x] == 'o':
            number_of_os += 1
        x += 1
    return number_of_os
```

Now I can use this function to count the number of times 'o' occurs in *any* string.

```
>>> count_os('Jeff is looking for food!')
5
```

The count_os function, however, is limited in an important way—it can only count the number of times 'o' occurs in S. What if we wanted to count the number of times 'e' occurs in s? We could redefine the function and simply change the 'o' to an 'e.' But what if we wanted to go back and count the number of 'o's again? We'd have to redefine the function again—how frustrating!

Reflecting on these two tasks (counting 'o's and 'e's) gives us another opportunity to work on our pattern recognition skills. By noticing the pattern in these tasks, we can generalize the algorithm and make it work on a variety of different (but structurally similar) tasks.

To exploit the pattern in the task of counting characters, we simply add another input variable to the count_os function. This way, instead of 'hardcoding' an arbitrary character into the function (like 'o'), we can let the input variable dictate which character is to be counted. Let's call this more general function count.

```
def count(S, c):
    x = 0
    num_cs = 0
    while x < len(S):
        if S[x] == c:
            num_cs +=1
        x += 1
    return num_cs
```

Now we can, for example, easily count the number of times 'a' occurs in a string, or the number of times 'i' occurs in the same string without having to change any of the code in our function.

```
>>> count('Jeff is looking for food!', 'a')
0
>>> count('Jeff is looking for food!', 'i')
2
```

As a final example, let's try writing a function called sum that takes a list of integers L as input and returns the sum of all the integers in L.

```
def sum(L):
    total = 0
    for num in L:
        total += num
    return total
```

We begin by creating a variable total that will be used to keep track of the sum of the numbers that have been processed so far. In the beginning, since no numbers have been processed, total is initialized to 0. Next, we use a for loop to sequentially process each number in L. We process each number by adding it to total. By the time the loop is completed, all the numbers in L would have been added. Now we simply specify total as the output value of the function using a return statement.

Exercise 8.3: Write a function called average that takes a list of integers, L, as input and returns the average of all the integers.

Exercise 8.4: Write a function called largest that takes a list of integers, L, as input and returns the largest integer in the list.

Decomposition

Now that we have a rudimentary understanding of how to define functions, let's see how functions might be used to solve the Counterfeit Coin Problem. The Counterfeit Coin Problem was introduced in an earlier chapter as the problem of finding a potential counterfeit coin among three coins. We noted that this problem could be *decomposed* into three sub-problems because there are three possible outcomes whenever a balance scale is used: the scale will either balance, tip to the left, or tip to the right.

Perhaps we can write a function to handle each of these three outcomes. Let's begin with the outcome where the scale balances when coin1 is measured against coin2. When this is the case, we know coin1 and coin2 must be genuine, and that coin3 might be counterfeit. We might write the following function to figure out what coin3's status is:

```
def outcome_balance():
    if coin1 == coin3:
        print('there are no counterfeits')
    elif coin1 > coin3:
        print('coin3 is counterfeit and lighter')
    else:
        print('coin3 is counterfeit and heavier')
```

Since we know that coin1 is genuine, we can use it to determine whether coin3 is a counterfeit or not. If the coins balance, then we know there are no counterfeits. If coin1 is heavier, then we know that coin3 is counterfeit and lighter. If the previous two conditions fail, then we know that coin3 is counterfeit and heavier.

Now consider the outcome where the scale tips to the left in favor of coin1. Since the scale didn't balance, we know that coin3 must be genuine and either coin1 or coin2 must be a counterfeit. It is also evident that if coin1 is counterfeit, it will be heavier and if coin2 is counterfeit, it will be lighter. We might write the following function to figure out which of the two coins is counterfeit:

```
def outcome_tipleft():
    if coin1 == coin3:
        print('coin2 is counterfeit and lighter')
    else:
        print('coin1 is counterfeit and heavier')
```

Finally, consider the outcome where the scale tips to the right in favor of coin2. This is almost exactly like the previous outcome except coin2 is heavier and coin1 is lighter. We might write the following function to figure out which of the two coins is counterfeit:

```
def outcome_tipright():
    if coin1 == coin3:
        print('coin2 is counterfeit and heavier')
    else:
        print('coin1 is counterfeit and lighter')
```

Having written functions for each of the three possible outcomes, we can now write a 'master' function that brings all of these 'helper' functions together as follows:

```
def ccp_3():
    if coin1 == coin2:
        outcome_balance()
    elif coin1 > coin2:
        outcome_tipleft()
    else:
        outcome_tipright()
```

Not only did we decompose the Counterfeit Coin Problem into three sub-problems, writing functions for each of these sub-problems made the code for solving the Counterfeit Coin Problem more succinct. What's more, given that the names of the functions for each of the sub-problems are (reasonably) informative, it is easier to see the logic of the overall solution. That is, it is more readable—other human programmers (or you yourself if you come back to this code after a few months) will more easily understand what the code is intended to accomplish.

Pattern Recognition

What if we wanted to solve the Counterfeit Coin Problem for five coins (instead of three)? Assuming we use the names coin1, coin2, coin3, coin4, and coin5 for the five coins, can you think of a way to exploit the fact that we've already solved the Counterfeit Coin Problem for three coins? Take a moment to think of how you would solve this.

If we begin by comparing `coin4` and `coin5` using the balance scale, there will be three possible outcomes. If the scale balances, then we know that any possible counterfeit must exist among the three remaining coins: `coin1`, `coin2`, and `coin3`. In this case, we can simply use the function we already defined above (`ccp_3`) to solve this. So we really only have to handle the two remaining cases: either `coin4` will be heavier than `coin5` or it will be lighter than `coin5`.

These two remaining cases, where `coin4` and `coin5` have different weights, are analogous to the cases in the Counterfeit Coin Problem for three coins, where `coin1` and `coin2` have different weights. The only real difference is that the names of the coins are different. Despite the similarity, however, the previously defined functions cannot be reused for the two remaining cases in the Counterfeit Coin Problem for five coins, because they are tailor-made for `coin1` and `coin2` (note that `coin1` and `coin2` are both global variables). While we've recognized a pattern (of some kind) this pattern can't be exploited with `outcome_tipleft` and `outcome_tipright` as they are currently defined—they do not generalize to *other* possible coins. To see this, let's consider the `outcome_tipleft` function again:

```
def outcome_tipleft():
    if coin1 == coin3:
        print('coin2 is counterfeit and lighter')
    else:
        print('coin1 is counterfeit and heavier')
```

This function can only be used when the first use of the scale compares `coin1` and `coin2` and it tips in favor of `coin1`. But what if we wanted the first use of the scale to compare `coin4` and `coin5` instead?

Discussion: Take a moment to consider how the algorithm for `outcome_tipleft` might be generalized to handle other coins. What is the significance of `coin1` and `coin3` in the function?

Perhaps the best way to start thinking about this is to redefine `outcome_tipleft` so that it works in the case where `coin4` and `coin5` are compared and `coin4` comes out heavier. Here's what the function might look like:

```
def outcome_tipleft():
    if coin4 == coin3:
        print('coin5 is counterfeit and lighter')
    else:
        print('coin4 is counterfeit and heavier')
```

There are only three differences when compared with the original function—they are bolded above. In order to generalize this function, what we need is the ability to easily change these values without changing the structure of the overall algorithm. This can be done by providing the function with input variables.

In this case, we can try using three input variables (let's call them v1, v2, and v3) that will allow us to control the values that are used in the highlighted locations. The first variable should refer to a number (probably a float) and the two other variables should refer to strings.

```
def outcome_tipleft(v1, v2, v3):
    if v1 == coin3:
        print(v2 + ' is counterfeit and lighter')
    else:
        print(v3 + ' is counterfeit and heavier')
```

With this function, we could handle the case where coin1 is heavier than coin2, as well as the case where coin4 is heavier than coin5, simply by executing the function with different input values. The following two function calls would do this:

```
outcome_tipleft(coin1, 'coin2', 'coin1')
outcome_tipleft(coin4, 'coin5', 'coin4')
```

Note that coin1 and 'coin1' are given as inputs in the first function call. Do you remember what the difference between these two statements is? The first is a variable that refers to a number (probably a float) that represents how much coin1 weighs. The second is a string that contains the characters 'coin1.' They are completely different objects:

```
>>> print(coin1)
0.2153627
>>> print('coin1')
coin1
```

One problem with outcome_tipleft, as it is defined above, is that its input variables do not have meaningful names. We could rename the input variables to better reflect what the variables represent.

```
def outcome_tipleft(heavy_coin, light_name, heavy_name):
    if heavy_coin == coin3:
        print(light_name + ' is counterfeit and lighter')
    else:
        print(heavy_name + ' is counterfeit and heavier')
```

Before proceeding, make sure you understand how this works.

Having come this far, you should see a further pattern. The functions outcome_tipleft and outcome_tipright are also very similar. The only difference is that the heavier coin is given to outcome_tipleft and the lighter coin is given to outcome_tipright. But now that we can specify the names of the heavier and lighter coins, it seems we can handle the case where coin4 is lighter than coin5 with the following statement.

```
>>> outcome_tipleft(coin5, 'coin4', 'coin5')
```

Again, before proceeding, make sure you understand why this works.

Because this function can now handle *both* cases when the scale does not balance, we should rename this function to reflect its further generalized nature. It might be better named as follows:

```
def outcome_imbalance(heavy_coin, light_name, heavy_
name):
    if heavy == coin3:
        print(light_name + ' is counterfeit and lighter')
    else:
        print(heavy_name + ' is counterfeit and heavier')
```

Now we can rewrite the function for solving the Counterfeit Coin Problem for three coins using this generalized function for handling imbalanced outcomes.

```
def ccp_3():
    if coin1 == coin2:
        outcome_balance()
    elif coin1 > coin2:
        outcome_imbalance(coin1, 'coin2', 'coin1')
    else:
        outcome_imbalance(coin2, 'coin1', 'coin2')
```

Finally, we can write a solution for the Counterfeit Coin Problem for five coins by using the existing functions that have now been generalized.

```
def ccp_5():
    if coin4 == coin5:
        ccp_3()
    elif coin4 > coin5:
        outcome_imbalance(coin4, 'coin5', 'coin4')
    else:
        outcome_imbalance(coin5, 'coin4', 'coin5')
```

Exercise 8.5: Given all the functions we've defined, can you write a function to solve the Counterfeit Coin Problem for seven coins? How about for nine coins?

Some Benefits

There are many benefits to writing functions. First, good functions make blocks of code **reusable**. Instead of having to write and rewrite the same blocks of code every time a given task needs to be carried out, the appropriate definition and use of functions minimize what the programmer needs to type. We saw a good example of this in the count function above. By generalizing the block of code used for counting the number of times 'o' occurs in a string, we were able to use (more or less) the same block of code to count the number of times any given character occurs in any given string.

Second, defining and using functions makes code more readable (i.e., easier to understand for human programmers), because they act as an **abstraction** (the relevant features of a task are preserved and the irrelevant features are ignored). When a programmer uses a function, all they have to know about is the function's **input-output behavior**. The actual commands and logic that make the function work can be ignored. The count function we defined above serves as a nice example. We don't need to know that extra variables (e.g., x and num_cs) are being created and while loops are being executed. We simply want an answer! All we need to know is that the function count takes two inputs (a string and a character) and returns the number of times that character occurs in the string. We don't want to get distracted by all the implementation details. In this sense, a function can act as a black box and is the key to abstraction. In order to use a function well, all we need to know is what the function *does*, not *how* it actually does it. You can imagine as the programs you write get larger and more complex, it will get harder and harder to keep track of all the implementation details. By abstracting away from the myriad 'irrelevant' details, you will be able to think of the overall structure of the program with greater ease and facility.

To see this, compare the following function definition for calculating the circumference of a circle with the one above:

```
def circumference_3(radius):
    return (radius + radius) * 3.1416
```

These two functions (circumference_2 and circumference_3) have the exact same input-output behavior. Given the radius of a circle, it will calculate the circumference of that circle. *What* the functions do is clear and is the same. *How* the functions carry out the necessary calculations differ. The original function, `circumference_2`, only uses multiplication operations. The second function, `circumference_3`, uses an addition operation and a multiplication operation. The point is, as a user of these functions, I don't need to know (and perhaps shouldn't know) about these implementation details.

To bring this closer to home, consider what it takes to drive a car. All cars come with a massively useful abstraction built into them. What we are given as a driver are a steering wheel and two pedals. Pressing one of the pedals makes the car move and pressing the other pedal makes the car stop. We have a very simple way of sending information to the car through its input variables, if you will. They are the steering wheel and two pedals. What actually happens when you turn the steering wheel and press or release the pedals is a marvel of science and engineering. All sorts of mechanical devices are set in motion and a variety of chemical reactions are triggered. If we had to keep track of and manage all of these minute details, we'd never be able to drive the car! Thankfully car manufacturers have hidden all these details (the block of code) from us. This allows us to operate at a higher level of organization and focus on the big picture of driving the car. Instead of trying, for example, to precisely regulate the amount of fuel that is combusted, we can simply focus on pressing the accelerator with a certain amount of force.

Key Points

- Functions can be defined in Python.
- Functions can have input and output values.
- Functions can be used to exploit the decomposability of large problems.
- Functions can be used to exploit patterns found across multiple tasks.
- Functions are useful for code reusability and abstraction.

Chapter 9

Mind

Theories of Mind

The branch of philosophy that deals with **reality** (what things exist and what the natures of these things are) is called **metaphysics**. There are a variety of topics that fall under this category, including time, space, and causation. In this chapter, we will focus on the nature of mind (and its relationship to the physical body). We will utilize what we learned in the previous chapter regarding functions to explore the functionalist theory of mind. But before we get to that, we need to start with a little philosophical history to better situate the functionalist theory of mind.

While discourse over the nature of mind goes back thousands of years, the framing of the contemporary debate can arguably be traced back to Descartes. In an earlier chapter, we were introduced to Descartes while exploring external world skepticism—a topic within epistemology. Descartes' philosophical exploration, however, didn't stop there. He leveraged the epistemological issues raised by external world skepticism to argue for metaphysical claims concerning the nature of mind.

He eventually arrived at a view that neatly separates the mind and body into two different categories of things: mental things and physical things. According to Descartes, the concept of mind is a concept about a non-physical thing (or more technically, substance). Consequently, for something to be a mind, it must not have any spatial characteristics. Most obviously, it must not take up any space and, therefore, must not have size or weight. Moreover, the mind, according to Descartes, is grounded in the capacity to doubt, believe, hope, and think. The concept of body, however, is a concept about a physical thing. It takes up space and can be measured. A person's brain, for example, is a physical thing. It might have a circumference of 57 cm and weigh 5.5 kg. The same cannot be said about the mind. Based on this conceptual analysis of mind and body, it would be a category mistake to attribute physical characteristics (like 5.5 kg) to the mind. It might usefully be compared to attributing physical characteristics to the number one. The concept of the number one is a

DOI: 10.4324/9781003271284-9

concept about a non-physical thing, so it doesn't make sense to say that the number one weighs 5.5 kg.

Discussion: Do you agree with Descartes' conceptual analysis of mind?

But Descartes' claim is not simply that the mind and the body are two distinct kinds of things. He also believed that the mind was separable from the body. That is, the mind can continue to exist and function even without a body. Despite this radical difference, the mind and the body are, nevertheless, able to causally interact with each other. This is what makes it possible for our minds to make causal differences to our bodies (mental-to-physical causation) and vice versa (physical-to-mental causation). Mental-to-physical causation occurs, for example, when I decide to pick up the cup in front of me and take a drink. The mental act of deciding causes my physical arm to move. In the other direction, physical-to-mental causation occurs when a raindrop lands somewhere on my body, which triggers a reaction that eventually alerts my mind and I experience a wet sensation. The physical raindrop causes a wet sensation to be experienced in my mind. This position is aptly named **dualism**—a position that espouses some form of duality. Its central claim is that the human person is composed of two things: a non-physical mind and a physical body that causally interact with each other.

Some have argued that dualism is a preposterous idea because it posits a mysterious causal relationship between physical and non-physical entities. How can something non-physical (that doesn't take up any space) cause anything to happen in the physical world? But take a moment to check its plausibility. Consider movies that deal with ghosts or spirits (exemplars of minds that exist without bodies). Do you find the scenarios depicted in such movies difficult to understand or imagine? Chances are you can easily track with and imagine such scenarios. Moreover, movies like *Freaky Friday*, where a mother and daughter swap bodies, exploit most people's natural tendency to understand mind-body dualism. This, of course, is not to suggest that dualism is true—only that it is a position that most people seem to have no trouble imagining. Understanding ourselves in dualistic terms is surprisingly easy.

Discussion: Can you think of other examples of dualistic thinking in your culture?

Discussion: Are the ghosts or spirits depicted in most movies good examples of minds that exist without bodies? If they were completely non-physical, would you be able to see them?

There has always been opposition to dualist theories of mind. Some argue that, contra dualism, the mind and body are really one and the same thing. While they acknowledge that there may be different ways of referring to or thinking about the mind as opposed to the body, it doesn't follow that the mind and body are two different things. This position is aptly named **monism**—a position that espouses some form of singularity. Given Descartes' two categories, the mental and the physical, monism can be fleshed out in one of two ways. One might argue that everything is mental—a *mental* monism (Berkeley, 1982). One might also argue, as many contemporary philosophers do, that everything is physical—a *physical* monism (Melnyk, 2003). This view has come to be known as **physicalism**. The most straightforward way of fleshing this idea out is to say that the mind is just another physical entity and that this physical entity is what we call the 'brain.' This claim is called the **identity theory**—the idea that the mind is identical to the brain (Smart, 1959). It is one of several ways of developing a theory of mind that remains within the boundaries of physicalism.

An Argument for Dualism

Before moving on, however, it will be instructive to consider philosophical arguments in favor of each of these two positions.

Here is a passage from Descartes:

> Examining attentively that which I was, I saw that I could conceive that I had no body, and that there was no world nor place where I might be; but yet that I could not for all that conceive that I was not. On the contrary, I saw from the very fact that I thought of doubting the truth of other things, it very evidently and certainly followed that I was; on the other hand if I had only ceased from thinking, even if all the rest of what I had ever imagined had really existed, I should have no reason for thinking that I had existed... From that I knew that... this 'me,' that is to say, the soul by which I am what I am, is entirely distinct from body. (Descartes, 2003, p. 23)

Discussion: Can you reconstruct Descartes' argument and put it into premise-conclusion form?

Here is one way this might be done.

Descartes' Argument

1. I am such that my non-existence can*not* be conceived.
2. My body is such that its non-existence *can* be conceived.
3. If I am such that my non-existence cannot be conceived, and my body is such that its non-existence can be conceived, then I have a property that my body does not have.
4. Therefore, I have a property that my body does not have.
5. If I have a property that my body does not have, then I am not identical to my body.
6. Therefore, I am not identical to my body.

One thing to note about this argument is that Descartes does not explicitly refer to the mind. Instead, he focuses on the self (what the term 'I' refers to). This essentially amounts to an argument for the non-physicality of the mind because he understands the self as a thinking thing, and thinking is the essence of the mind.

What should we make of this argument? The way I've reconstructed it above, the argument surely seems valid. Premises 1, 2, and 3 entail *sub*-conclusion 4. This, in conjunction with premise 5, entails the conclusion. The conclusion, however, does not ground all the claims embedded in Descartes' dualism (i.e., it does not give us reason to think that minds and bodies causally interact with each other). It does enough, however, to establish a foundation on which a dualist theory of mind can be built—a demonstration of the distinction between mind and body.[1]

What about the truth of the premises? Premise 2 seems to be true. After all, the claim is weak in an important sense. It is focused solely on *conceivability*. The claim is *not* that my body does not exist. Rather, it is the weaker claim that it is conceivable that my body does not exist. It is a claim about what can be imagined.

You may, however, harbor a worry about premise 1. Why, after all, can't we imagine that we don't exist? Don't we sometimes wonder what the world might be like if we had never existed? The catch is that *we* are still doing the imagining and we must exist if we're doing the imagining. That is, conceiving is a function of the mind, so the very act of conceiving of a universe where I don't exist *requires* that I exist and am conceiving this very universe. Though implicit, it seems like solid evidence that I must exist while conceiving of my non-existence.

What about premise 5? This seems to be uncontroversial. It's grounded in the idea that x and y can only be identical with each other if x and y share all the same properties. After all, how can x and y be identical with each other if x has a property, say, the property of being blue, that y doesn't have? The fact that there is a property that x and y do not share is conclusive evidence that x and y must not be identical. This almost amounts to a self-evident truth. So, at least on an initial reading, this seems to be a compelling argument.

Discussion: Do you think the argument accurately captures Descartes' reasoning in the quoted passage? What do you think of Descartes' argument for dualism?

Things, however, are never this tidy in philosophy. One way of responding to this argument is, perhaps surprisingly, to argue that there is a faulty inference that connects premises 1 and 2 to premise 4—namely the conditional in premise 3. Its truth hinges on the question of whether the feature of being conceivable should count as being a 'real' property of an entity. This might be questioned because conceivability is about a certain way that we *think* about an entity (not necessarily something true about the entity itself). It might be argued that my body's being such that its non-existence can be conceived is merely a reflection of the way *we* think about my body, and that this does not necessarily tell us anything about my body itself.

Take Donald Trump, for example. He is, in fact, an American. I may mistakenly think, however, that Donald Trump is Korean. It follows that Donald Trump is such that his *not* being American can be conceived. But, is being such that his not being American can be conceived really be a feature of Donald Trump? Perhaps it's nothing more than a feature of the way that we think about Donald Trump. The latter may seem the more reasonable position.[2] If so, given the fact that Donald Trump is indeed American, there is no guaranteed connection between the way that we think about Donald Trump and the way that Donald Trump actually is.

This gives us a way of constructing a counterexample to Descartes' argument. Consider Superman. As an outside observer privy to his identity, we know that Superman is identical with Clark Kent. Excluding Lois Lane, Lex Luther, and a few others, however, this identity is unknown. Jimmy Olsen, for example, is oblivious to Superman's true identity. Jimmy thinks that Superman has the ability to fly, but simultaneously thinks that Clark Kent does not. So, it seems that Superman has a property that Clark Kent doesn't have—namely the property of being such that Jimmy Olsen thinks he can fly. Does this difference show that Superman and Clark Kent are not identical with each other? Clearly not, because we know that Superman and Clark Kent are identical.

To turn this into a counterexample, we might take the formal structure of Descartes' argument and replace the key bits with Clark Kent, Superman, and Jimmy.

Superman Counterexample

1. Clark Kent is such that Jimmy thinks Clark Kent can*not* fly.
2. Superman is such that Jimmy thinks Superman *can* fly.
3. If Clark Kent is such that Jimmy thinks Clark Kent cannot fly, and Superman is such that Jimmy thinks Superman can fly, then Clark Kent has a property that Superman does not have.
4. Therefore, Clark Kent has a property that Superman does not have.
5. If Clark Kent has a property that Superman does not have, then Clark Kent is not identical to Superman.
6. Therefore, Clark Kent is not identical to Superman.

Because we know that the conclusion is false, it shows that something must have gone wrong in the argument. Because the argument is valid, there must be a false premise. The most likely culprit, according to our brief discussion, seems to be premise 3. We cannot ground a difference between x and y based merely on a difference in ways that someone *conceives* x and y to be. By relying on this premise, it seems we were led to infer a false conclusion.

Discussion: What do you think about this response to Descartes' argument? Does Superman really count as a counterexample to Descartes' argument?

An Argument for the Identity Theory

Over the years growing discontent with dualist theories of mind eventually led to physical monist theories of mind. Let's now look at an argument for the identity theory—the claim that the mind is identical to the brain. Here is a passage from one of the early defenders of the identity theory, J.J.C. Smart:

> Why do I wish to resist [dualism]? Mainly because of Occam's razor. It seems to me that science is increasingly giving us a viewpoint whereby organisms are able to be seen as physicochemical mechanisms: it seems that even the behavior of man himself will one day be explicable in mechanistic terms. There does seem to be, so far as science is concerned, nothing in the world but increasingly complex arrangements of physical constituents. All except for one place: in consciousness... so sensations, states of consciousness, do seem to be the one sort of thing left outside the physicalist picture, and for various reasons I just cannot believe that this can be so. That everything should be explicable in terms of physics (together of course with descriptions of the ways in which the parts are put together-roughly, biology is to physics as radio-engineering is to electromagnetism) except the occurrence of sensations seems to me to be frankly unbelievable.
>
> (Smart, 1959, p. 142)

Smart refers to **Occam's Razor** in this passage. This is also known as the law of parsimony (or simplicity) and is credited to William of Occam, who used this concept to argue for his preferred philosophical views. Occam's Razor is the claim that the simplest explanation is (usually) the best explanation, all else being equal.

Consider a particular phenomenon, say, the movement of the sun and planets across the sky. One theory used to explain the movement is the geocentric theory. It posits the earth as the center of our solar system and the other planets and sun orbiting earth. A competing theory is the heliocentric theory. It posits the sun as the center of our solar system and the planets (including earth) orbiting the sun. Let's assume that both theories are observationally equivalent. In other words, both theories are equally capable of making accurate predictions about the positions of the sun and planets in the sky. So, we can't distinguish these theories in terms of their observational merits.

How then are we to decide which theory is better? According to Occam's Razor, we ought to choose the theory that is simpler. One way Occam's Razor might be used in favor of the heliocentric theory concerns the retrograde motion of the planets. As observers on earth, the movements of the planets appear, at key points, to change direction and move backward. In order to account for this within the geocentric theory, planets not only have to revolve around the earth in a single large orbit, but they also have to revolve around an invisible point within this larger orbit. These smaller orbits within the larger orbit are known as epicycles.

How does the heliocentric theory handle retrograde motion? Since all planets (including the earth) orbit the sun, retrograde motion simply follows as a consequence of the single large orbits each planet takes around the sun. There is no need for any additional smaller orbits to account for the phenomena. In this sense, then, the heliocentric theory is simpler than the geocentric theory because it can account for all the observational data we have regarding the movements of the planets and sun across the sky without needing to postulate epicycles. Given this, we could use Occam's Razor as a rationale for preferring the heliocentric theory over the geocentric theory—because it's simpler, it's probably closer to the truth.

Returning to Smart's argument, we might regiment it as follows:

Smart's Argument

1. The identity theory is simpler than dualism.
2. If the identity theory is simpler than dualism, then the identity theory should be preferred.
3. Therefore, the identity theory should be preferred.

It is clear that premises 1 and 2 entail the conclusion, so the argument is valid. But what are we to make of the truth of premises 1 and 2? Premise 2 is basically an application of Occam's Razor, so given its broad acceptance in theory adjudication (especially in the sciences), the only way to resist Smart's argument is to reject premise 1. But this is no easy task for the dualist.

Smart focuses on the success of the sciences to make his case. Because scientific theories have slowly and successfully brought many existing phenomena under their various physicalist frameworks (e.g., biology, chemistry, and physics), it would not be parsimonious to keep a single phenomenon beyond its reach. Adopting the identity theory would be 'simpler' than adopting dualism because it would make the trajectory of science uniform. However, adopting dualism would mean making an exception.

The thought is that science would eventually explain everything through a physicalist framework, but the mind would, in principle, resist scientific explanation.

More obviously, perhaps, the identity theory is simpler because it doesn't have to posit extra entities to make sense of mental phenomena. Instead of claiming that there are physical states and distinct mental states that are needed to account for mental and physical phenomena, the identity theory, by claiming mental states are identical to physical brain states, only has to account for physical phenomena. So it seems rather obvious if we were to follow Occam's Razor, the identity theory is to be preferred over dualism.

Discussion: Do you think the argument accurately captures Smart's reasoning in the quoted passage? What do you think of Smart's argument for the identity theory?

One natural response to Smart's argument is to question the observational equivalence of the two positions. Occam's Razor, after all, should only be used to decide between theories that are observationally equivalent. Returning to the debates over the solar system, if the geocentric theory had been more accurate in predicting the positions of the sun and planets than the heliocentric theory, then it would have been a mistake to use Occam's Razor to reject it. So, one might question whether the identity theory and dualism are observationally equivalent. Do they each provide an adequate account of all the observations we make concerning minds?

Here, convinced dualists might disagree. They might argue that mental states must be non-physical in order to account for the variety of features that mental states have. These features, they might suggest, are inexplicable as merely physical phenomena. How, for example, are we to account for the way we have feelings and experiences? Can our best scientific theories involving only molecules and electrical signals make sense of our feelings of worry, or our experiences of pain? Why do mental phenomena like these occur in a purely physical universe at all? A dualist might, therefore, argue that mental states cannot be reduced to mere physical processes and that something more is needed to give a full account of the mind.

A dualist might want to revise Smart's argument and make the observational equivalence claim (implicitly found in Occam's Razor) explicit.

Smart's Revised Argument

1. The identity theory is simpler than dualism.
2. The identity theory and dualism are observationally equivalent.
3. If the identity theory is simpler than dualism, *and* the identity theory and dualism are observationally equivalent, then the identity theory should be preferred.
4. Therefore, the identity theory should be preferred.

Stated in this way, the dualist has a ready response. She can argue that premise 2 of the revised argument is false.

Functionalism

Despite its popularity, the identity theory eventually came under fire. Surprisingly, the attack did not come from dualism, but from a new kind of physicalism. Some argued that one of the undesirable consequences of the identity theory is that identifying mental states with *human* brain states would lead to a privileging of human neurobiology in studying the mind. For example, if the mental state of being in pain is identified with the brain state of, say, having C-fibers electrically stimulated, then this seems to preclude other lifeforms (with different physical constitutions) from being in pain. What about other animals that don't have the same kind of nerve fibers that humans have? Should we say that they don't experience pain? If being in pain is *identical* to having one's C-fibers electrically stimulated, and other non-human animals don't have C-fibers, it surely seems that these other non-human animals can't be in pain. But non-human animals do experience pain! Or consider a more far-fetched example involving life in other parts of the universe. Can we be certain that only lifeforms with C-fibers are capable of being in pain? What about an extraterrestrial being that is composed of completely different materials (say, silicon)? The identity theory, by identifying the mind with the brain, is committed to a *very* strong claim. According to the theory, such extraterrestrials, by definition, could not experience pain.

Some have thought that this claim is *too* strong. Hilary Putnam, a very influential 20th-century philosopher, argued that mental states like being in pain can*not* be identified with any particular physical state. The mental state of being in pain is not so limited in its manifestations. Humans with C-fibers can be in pain, animals without C-fibers can be in pain, and extraterrestrial beings (in theory) composed of completely different non-organic matter can also be in pain. In short, Putnam argued that mental states like pain are **multiply realizable**. That is, they can be realized in many different ways. Here's a quote from Putnam:

> Consider what the [identity] theorist has to do to make good his claims. He has to specify a physical-chemical state such that any organism... is in pain if and only if (a) it possesses a brain of a suitable physical-chemical structure; and (b) its brain is in that physical-chemical state. This means that the physical-chemical state in question must be a possible state of a mammalian brain, a reptilian brain, a mollusc's brain... etc. At the same time, it must not be a possible... state of the brain of any physically possible creature that cannot feel pain... [I]t is not altogether impossible that such a state will be found... [I]t is at least

possible that parallel evolution, all over the universe, might always lead to one and the same physical "correlate" of pain. But this is certainly an ambitious hypothesis.

(Putnam, 1967, p. 436)

The concept of multiple realizability does not merely apply to mental states. Consider, for example, the concept of a wine bottle opener. What is its essence? Is it having a corkscrew? If so, what are we to make of the twin-prong cork puller? Should we say that it is not really a wine bottle opener? It seems to me that we should say that the twin-prong cork puller is indeed a wine bottle opener (albeit one without a corkscrew). This is because the essence of a wine bottle opener does not reside in its having a corkscrew. Its essence is grounded in the role it plays. Anything that is capable of removing the cork from a wine bottle is a wine bottle opener. Having a corkscrew is not essential to its being a wine bottle opener. In this sense, we can say that wine bottle openers are essentially characterized by the role they play, and because there are different mechanisms that can perform this role, they are multiply realizable.

Putnam's argument might be regimented in premise-conclusion form as follows:

Putnam's Argument

1. At least some mental states are multiply realizable by distinct physical states.
2. If at least some mental states are multiply realizable by distinct physical states, then at least some mental states cannot be identical to any one specific physical state.
3. At least some mental states cannot be identical to any one specific physical state.

To the extent that you also agree that mental states like being in pain are essentially characterized by the roles they play, you will find it natural to believe that mental states like being in pain are multiply realizable. Consequently, you may find it increasingly difficult to maintain the identity theory. The natural response, then, would be to develop a theory of mind that respects the multiple realizability of mental states. This is where **functionalism** enters the picture. According to functionalism, the essence of mental states is not what they are composed of, but what roles they play within a given mind. The idea then is to treat mental states, not as physical states, but as *functional* states. Consequently, the functionalist theory of mind may be seen as the best of both worlds by straddling the fence between dualism on the one hand and the identity theory on the other. Like dualism, it resists the *identification* of mind with anything physical (since the mind is multiply realizable), but like the identity theory, it endorses physical monism by asserting that the states that realize mental states are physical.

To get a better handle on this, let's return to the function definitions we covered in the previous chapter. What are the key components of a function definition?

The basic structure of a function definition is given in Figure 9.1.

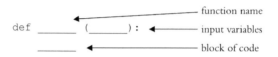

```
def _____ (_____) : ◄——— function name
                     ◄——— input variables
    _____  ◄——————————— block of code
```

Figure 9.1 **The basic structure of a function definition.**

Function definitions are composed of the function name, a set of input variables, and a block of code. A critical part of the block of code is the return statement (or its lack thereof)—which specifies what will or will not be the output value of the function.

As we saw in the previous chapter, one of the benefits of creating and using functions is that they can act as abstractions. An abstraction allows the user of a function to focus only on what is relevant and ignore what is irrelevant. In the case of a good function, all that matters to the user is the function's input-output behavior. The user could care less about what goes on in the block of code. Being able to forget about the implementation details of a function allows the programmer to operate at a higher, more conceptual, level. Remember the example of the car?

What's more, functions, given their role of abstracting away from the implementation details, naturally allow for multiple realizability. Consider the following function:

```
def multiply_1(x,y):
    return x * y
```

Yes, multiply_1 is not a very useful function given the existence of the * operator. Nevertheless, it carries out the relevant input-output behavior. We could write another version of this same function as follows:

```
def multiply_2(x,y):
    result = 0
    for i in range(y):
        result += x
    return result
```

Exercise 9.1: Can you write this function in yet another way? How about using a `while` loop?

Notice that `multiply_2` carries out the exact same function (in terms of input-output behavior) as `multiply_1`. They both take in two numerical inputs, x and y, and they both return a single numerical output that is the product of x and y. As far as input-output behavior goes, the two functions are identical. Given a certain set of input values, the two functions will return the same set of output values. We might say that they are functionally equivalent. Nevertheless, they are *realized* in two different ways. One uses a `for` loop and the other doesn't. One uses a multiplication operator and the other doesn't.

The thought, then, is that we ought to conceive of mental states in terms of their input and output behavior. When the mind of an organism is given a certain set of inputs and those inputs result in a certain set of outputs, we can think of the relevant mental states as the functions that are actively processing these input-output pairings. What kind of input-output pairings might exist for being in the mental state of pain? That is, what kinds of inputs and outputs would the pain function be operating on?

We can think of a variety of inputs both external and internal to the organism's body. Any external event that causes physical damage to an organism's body can serve as an input (e.g., a rock hitting a person's head). Any internal event that causes damage to an organism's organs may also serve as an input (e.g., a virus attacking a person's liver). If these inputs are given to the pain function, the pain function will return certain outputs. These outputs will also include external and internal manifestations. It may cause the organism to emit a scream—'ouch!' It may cause the organism to enter into other mental states, perhaps a desire to bring the mental state of being in pain to an end.

Notice that the actual *implementation* of the pain function was never discussed. We have been silent about the way the function is realized. We never said that C-fiber nerve cells must be used to realize the mental state of being in pain. Of course, as it turns out, C-fibers are what realize the pain function in human beings, but some other kinds of nerve cells might realize the same function in a different organism. And perhaps more exotic, alien beings might realize this function in altogether non-organic matter.

The Turing Test

In the more ambitious areas of AI (artificial intelligence) research, the functionalist theory of mind can naturally be adapted to provide a rationale for the claim that computers can have (or be) minds. If functionalism is true, there is no reason why a computer (of the right sophistication and power) cannot also have mental states. That is, there is no reason why a computer can't itself have (or be) a mind. There is no principled reason (as far as we know now) that precludes silicon-based materials from carrying out the same functions that organic materials (like brains) do. So, assuming intelligence is a feature of a mind, AI is squarely within the realm of possibility. Perhaps, it would be more accurate, given our discussion thus far, to say that artificial *minds* are possible (not just intelligence). Why can't we have computers that have the full range of mental states that we enjoy—including mental states like being in pain?

In 1950, Alan Turing, a British mathematician and pioneer in computing theory, published an influential paper titled "Computing Machinery and Intelligence." In it, he asked the question: "can computers think?" He noted, however, that the word 'think' needed a clear definition if the question was to have any meaningful content. But is there any agreed-upon definition, or a set of necessary and sufficient conditions, for attributing thought to an entity?

Discussion: Take a moment to provide a conceptual analysis yourself. What are the necessary and sufficient conditions for someone or something to 'think'?

Chances are you found it difficult to conceptually analyze 'think.' Moreover, if you asked a random friend to provide an analysis, I wouldn't be surprised if he/she came up with a different analysis from yours.

Turing then did something interesting. He decided to replace this question with one that is "closely related' because he thought the original question was 'too meaningless to deserve discussion." The replacement question, he thought, could be stated in a way that avoids the ambiguity surrounding the word 'think.' We might say that Turing was *operationalizing* the concept of thinking by introducing a variation on the so-called 'imitation game.' Here's how he describes the imitation game:

> It is played with three people, a man (A), a woman (B), and an interrogator (C) who may be of either sex. The interrogator stays in a room apart from the other two. The object of the game for the interrogator is to determine which of the other two is the man and which is the woman. He knows them by labels X and Y, and at the end of the game he says either 'X is A and Y is B' or 'X is B and Y is A.' The interrogator is allowed to put questions to A and B thus: C: Will X please tell me the length of his or her hair? Now suppose X is actually A, then A must answer. It is A's object in the game to try and cause C to make the wrong identification. His answer might therefore be 'My hair is shingled, and the longest strands are about nine inches long.' In order that tones of voice may not help the interrogator the answers should be written, or better still, typewritten. The ideal arrangement is to have a teleprinter communicating between the two rooms. Alternatively the question and answers can be repeated by an intermediary.

The object of the game for the third player (B) is to help the interrogator. The best strategy for her is probably to give truthful answers.

(Turing, 1950, p. 433)

This sounds like an entertaining game that might be played at a party. Turing adapted this game and wondered what would happen if a computer took on A's role in the game and a human (of any gender) took on B's role. This variation on the imitation game has become known as the **Turing Test**. If the computer plays A's role so effectively that C is unable to determine whether X is A (and Y is B) or X is B (and Y is A), then Turing contends that the computer can think. Of course, we can't expect a computer to successfully fool a human interrogator 100% of the time. Even if a computer perfectly mimicked a human, random guessing on the part of the human interrogator will result in 50% accuracy. So, we might say that a computer passes[3] the Turing Test if the human evaluator cannot *reliably* distinguish the machine from the human with more than 50% accuracy. That is, if C is left simply to guess, then Turing would be satisfied that the computer actually thinks!

Discussion: What do you think about the Turing Test? Is it a good gauge for a computer's ability to think?

The claim that a computer can actually think may sound like a preposterous claim. But consider what it would be like to live in a world where computers are conversationally indistinguishable from normal human beings. You might be on the phone talking with an automated voice or purchasing products through automated text messages or having a casual conversation with an automated chatbot. In all these instances, you might very well be convinced that you are interacting with a human being. When you later discover that these interactions were with AI-enabled computers, how would you react? Remember, when you imagine these interactions, you must not make the mistake of thinking that you can subtly detect any abnormalities.[4] Regardless of your initial reactions, over time and with enough exposure, you might start to wonder what the difference (at least conversationally) is between a human and a computer. If computers ever reach this level of sophistication, we might be inclined to agree with Turing that "the use of words and general educated opinion will have altered so much that one will be able to speak of machines thinking without expecting to be contradicted."

The Chinese Room

It's an open question whether computers will ever reach this level of sophistication. If they did, they may very well alter the way we use the word 'think.' Nevertheless, you might feel there's something missing! One version of the idea that something *is* missing was more formally articulated by John Searle, an American philosopher.

He begins by making a distinction between two conceptions of AI: weak and strong. Weak AI is the claim that computers can be used to help us study the mind. Strong AI is the claim that computers not only help us study the mind, but that computers can actually *be* minds. Though Searle is a proponent of weak AI he is, to this day, an adamant opponent of strong AI.[5]

He has a principled reason why strong AI is impossible, a reason that is not contingent on the state of computer technology. The fundamental issue, for Searle, is that 'syntax is not sufficient for semantics.' To put this another way, there is a distinction between what is purely formal (or syntactic) and what has content (or semantics). His main point is that what is purely syntactic is never (on its own) going to be enough for semantics.

Recall our discussion of validity from the chapter on logic. Consider again the way we extracted the formal structure from the different arguments in the chapter on logic. Do you remember how the formal structure was important for assessing the validity of an argument? This formal structure could be shared by a variety (in fact an infinite number) of arguments with different content. In this domain, the claim that syntax is not sufficient for semantics might be interpreted as follows: the formal structure of an argument is not sufficient for determining the actual content of the argument. Consider the following representation of the *modus ponens* argument structure:

Argument$_{FS}$

1. If p then q.
2. p.
3. Therefore, q.

The formal structure explicitly captured in Argument$_{FS}$ is the same formal structure found in the following two arguments.

Argument$_1$

1. If Alan Turing is British, then Alan Turing is human.
2. Alan Turing is British.
3. Therefore, Alan Turing is human.

Argument$_2$

1. If Hilary Putnam is a businessman, then Hilary Putnam is Chinese.
2. Hilary Putnam is a businessman.

3.   Therefore, Hilary Putnam is Chinese.

The point here is that the purely formal (or syntactic) structure of Argument$_{FS}$ is not sufficient for determining the actual content of the argument. It is compatible after all with both Argument$_1$ and Argument$_2$.

Now if you add Searle's claim that computer programs are entirely defined by their formal or syntactic structure, then we have a recipe for arguing that computer programs can never have content or semantics. More colloquially, computer programs can never have *meaning*. Here's Searle:

> But this feature of programs, that they are defined purely formally or syntactically, is fatal to the view that mental processes and program processes are identical. And the reason can be stated quite simply. There is more to having a mind than having formal or syntactical processes. Our internal mental states, by definition, have certain sorts of contents. If I am thinking about Kansas City or wishing that I had a cold beer to drink or wondering if there will be a fall in interest rates, in each case my mental state has a certain mental content in addition to whatever formal features it might have. That is, even if my thoughts occur to me in strings of symbols, there must be more to the thought than the abstract strings, because strings by themselves can't have any meaning. If my thoughts are to be about anything, then the strings must have a meaning which makes the thoughts about those things. In a word, the mind has more than a syntax, it has a semantics. The reason that no computer program can ever be a mind is simply that a computer program is only syntactical, and minds are more than syntactical. Minds are semantical, in the sense that they have more than a formal structure, they have a content.
>
> (Searle, 1984, p. 29)

Question: Can you logically analyze Searle's argument into premise-conclusion form?

Here's one way of putting Searle's argument into premise-conclusion form.

Searle's Argument

1.   Computer programs are entirely defined by their syntactic structure.
2.   If computer programs are entirely defined by their syntactic structure, then computer programs cannot have semantic content.
3.   Computer programs cannot have semantic content.
4.   Minds can have semantic content.

5. If computer programs cannot have semantic content, and minds can have semantic content, then computer programs cannot be minds.
6. Therefore, computer programs cannot be minds.

Stated in this way, the argument is valid. But what reason do we have to believe that premise 1 is true? Moreover, why think the inference embedded in premise 2 is valid? To provide intuitive support for these premises, Searle developed his so-called Chinese Room Argument. Here it is in his own words:

> Imagine that you are locked in a room, and in this room are several baskets full of Chinese symbols. Imagine that you (like me) do not understand a word of Chinese, but that you are given a rule book in English for manipulating these Chinese symbols. The rules specify the manipulations of the symbols purely formally, in terms of their syntax, not their semantics. So the rule might say: 'Take a squiggle-squiggle sign out of basket number one and put it next to a squiggle-squoggle sign from basket number two.' Now suppose that some other Chinese symbols are passed into the room, and that you are given further rules for passing back Chinese symbols out of the room. Suppose that unknown to you the symbols passed into the room are called 'questions' by the people outside the room, and the symbols you pass back out of the room are called 'answers to the questions.' Suppose, furthermore, that the programmers are so good at designing the programs and that you are so good at manipulating the symbols, that very soon your answers are indistinguishable from those of a native Chinese speaker. There you are locked in your room shuffling your Chinese symbols and passing out Chinese symbols in response to incoming Chinese symbols. On the basis of the situation as I have described it, there is no way you could learn any Chinese simply by manipulating these formal symbols. Now the point of the story is simply this: by virtue of implementing a formal computer program from the point of view of an outside observer, you behave exactly as if you understood Chinese, but all the same you don't understand a word of Chinese.
>
> (Searle, 1984, p. 32)

Of course, this thought experiment will *not* work very well for you if you already speak Chinese. But there's an easy fix. Simply replace Chinese with another language that you are completely unfamiliar with. Perhaps, Swahili, Vietnamese, or Hindi? For you, then, the thought experiment might be more aptly named the Swahili Room.

The key to the Chinese Room is that the person inside is doing everything that a computer does when executing a program. The computer doesn't really understand what it's doing—it simply translates the symbols into the appropriate electrical signals, according to established rules, and then outputs symbols. What is plainly obvious, however, is that the person inside the Chinese Room, despite perfectly mimicking the linguistic behavior of a native Chinese speaker, doesn't understand Chinese. No matter how good this person might get at shuffling the symbols, the person will not make the slightest progress toward understanding Chinese. Here's how Searle sums up these ideas:

> If the [person inside doesn't] understand Chinese, then no other computer could understand Chinese because no computer... has anything that you don't have. All that the computer has, as you have, is a formal program for manipulating uninterpreted Chinese symbols. To repeat, a computer has a syntax, but no semantics.
>
> (Searle, 1984, p. 33)

If Searle is right about all this, then it seems we have a reason to believe that functionalist theories of mind cannot be correct. Because the possibility of strong AI seems to follow from functionalism, if Searle's argument shows that strong AI is impossible, then it seems functionalism must be false.

Discussion: What do you think about this reconstruction of Searle's argument? Do you think it's a charitable reconstruction of Searle's reasoning? Are there any weaknesses in the argument?

One popular response to Searle's argument is the so-called 'Systems Response.' The proponent of this response agrees that the person inside the Chinese Room does not understand Chinese, but disagrees with Searle about the right question to ask. We shouldn't ask if the *person* inside the room understands Chinese. We should ask whether *the entire room* understands Chinese. Otherwise, it would be like asking if a certain part of the computer, like the CPU (central processing unit), understands Chinese. But we wouldn't want to say that—we would want to refer to something more holistic about the computer. Similarly, we wouldn't say that just a part of me, say my temporal cortex understands, Chinese. Rather, it's me (the whole person) who understands Chinese. Perhaps, the CPU plus the memory, plus the circuitry on the motherboard, plus the program, etc. working in conjunction with each other is what understands Chinese. Similarly, we wouldn't say the *person* inside the room understands Chinese, but it might make more sense to say that the entire complex, including the person plus the baskets full of Chinese symbols, plus the instructions for manipulating these symbols, etc. understands Chinese.

The verdict is still out and the debates over the Chinese Room are still alive and well. Will computers ever be able to think or become minds? It's very difficult to predict the future, but with the remarkable changes in computing power along with the rapid evolution of machine learning techniques over the past several years, it's not difficult to imagine computers becoming verbally (and perhaps behaviorally) equivalent to human beings. Nevertheless, Searle may be right that syntax will never be sufficient for semantics and so no matter how good technology gets, computers will never truly think or have minds. On the other hand, Turing may also be right that enough experience with verbally equivalent computers may change the way we conceptually analyze the term 'think' (and other allied mental terms).

Key Points

- Dualism is the claim that humans are composed of two distinct things: a mind and a body.
- Identity Theory is a version of Monism that claims minds are identical to brains.
- Functionalism is a physicalist theory of mind that respects the multiple realizability of the mind.
- The Turing Test was an attempt to operationalize the question: can machines think?
- The Chinese Room Argument was developed to show that Strong AI is impossible.

Notes

1 This alone is not enough to count as a dualist theory of mind because there are so-called non-reductive physicalist theories of mind that also affirm the distinction between mind and body. These physicalist theories of mind retain their physicalism by maintaining that the mental supervenes on the physical. That is, that the mental is, in some way, constrained by the physical. A proper definition of supervenience and the varieties of supervenience, however, will take us too far afield.

2 This claim can easily lead to a discussion about essential (versus contingent) properties. Some philosophers have argued that being human is a part of our essence. For example, supposing Barack Obama is a human, it seems we cannot imagine Obama as an inanimate object. That is, being human is an essential property of Obama. On the other hand, Obama may have lost the 2008 U.S. presidential election. His being the 44th president of the U.S. is a contingent property of Obama.

3 Some have claimed that computers have already passed the Turing Test. Look up, for example, Eugene Goostman's computer program that simulates a 13-year-old Ukrainian boy. Nevertheless, it's safe to say that this is still a highly contentious claim, and most believe that computers have yet to successfully pass the Turing Test.

4   At the time of my writing this, OpenAI recently released GPT-3 (Generative Pre-trained Transformer), a language model that uses deep learning to produce human-like text. As amazing as this technology is, there are many shortcomings. The point is, it does not pass the Turing Test and is still a far cry from being indistinguishable from a human. We must not smuggle such limitations into this imaginative exercise!

5   Listen, for example, to my interview with Searle here: https://danielflim.org/2021/01/17/interview-john-searle-artificial-intelligence/.

References

Berkeley, G. (1982). *A Treatise Concerning the Principles of Human Knowledge*. Cambridge, MA: Hackett Publishing Company.

Descartes, R. (2003). *Discourse on Method and Meditations*. New York: Dover Publications.

Melnyk, A. (2003). *A Physicalist Manifesto: Thoroughly Modern Materialism*. Cambridge: Cambridge University Press.

Putnam, H. (1967). Psychological Predicates. In W. Capitan, & D. Merrill, *Art, Mind, and Religion* (pp. 37–48). Pittsburgh, PA: University of Pittsburgh Press.

Searle, J. (1984). *Minds, Brains, and Science*. Cambridge, MA: Harvard University Press.

Smart, J. (1959). Sensations and Brain Processes. *The Philosophical Review, 68*(2), 141–156.

Turing, A. (1950). Computing Machinery and Intelligence. *Mind, 59*(236), 433–460.

Chapter 10

Game of Life

In this chapter, we will work on an ambitious program—one that simulates the evolution of life! In order to do this, we will have to deploy all the tools we've acquired so far regarding Python and computational thinking. This will give us a working platform to help us think about philosophical issues regarding determinism and free will in the following chapter.

Cellular Automata

Stanislaw Ulam, a Polish mathematician and physicist, is credited with discovering the concept of a cellular automaton (CA) (Bialynicki-Birula & Bialynicki-Birula, 2004). John Conway, a British mathematician, devised a particular CA that made the concept famous (Gardner, 1970). Conway's so-called 'Game of Life' is a CA that operates within a two-dimensional grid of square cells. Each cell is in one of two possible states (alive or dead) and has up to eight possible neighbors that are horizontally, vertically, and diagonally adjacent. Cells that populate the edges of the grid do not have eight neighbors. For example, corner cells only have three neighbors.

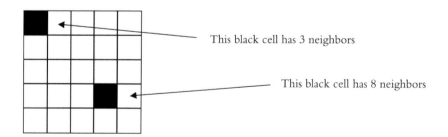

This black cell has 3 neighbors

This black cell has 8 neighbors

Figure 10.1 5x5 two-dimensional cellular automaton.

DOI: 10.4324/9781003271284-10

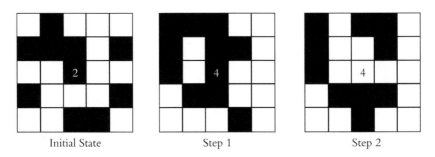

| Initial State | Step 1 | Step 2 |

Figure 10.2 Evolving a 5x5 two-dimensional cellular automaton given an initial state.

Conway's CA evolves according to four simple rules that anyone can easily understand—no high-level mathematics here!

1. Any live cell with less than two live neighbors will be dead in the next step.
2. Any live cell with two or three live neighbors will remain alive in the next step.
3. Any live cell with more than three live neighbors will be dead in the next step.
4. Any dead cell with exactly three live neighbors will be alive in the next step.

Using these rules, make sure you can confirm the next two steps of evolution in the 5×5 grid given the initial state shown in Figure 10.2.

Calculating whether a given cell will be alive or dead in the *next* evolutionary step depends only on the *current* state of the cell's neighbors. Consider the cell at the center of the grid in the initial state (labeled with a 2). It is currently alive and because it has two live neighbors, it will remain alive in the next step. Consider the same center cell in Step 1. How many live neighbors does it have? It now has four live neighbors. Because of this, it will become dead in the next step, as seen in Step 2.

Computational Thinking

Let's think through a way of implementing this in Python. This is the first large program we are attempting to write. Because of its size, the creation and use of functions will help us break down this daunting task into smaller, more manageable parts. This is the **decomposition** component of computational thinking.

Before we get to writing any code, however, we must decide how to represent Conway's CA in Python. This is the component of computational thinking known as **data representation**. I hope, given our discussion in Chapter 6, that you would've naturally turned to two-dimensional lists when considering how to represent the Game of Life grid. But what objects should we store in the two-dimensional list? It really doesn't matter what we store as long as we consistently store one of two different objects in each location of the two-dimensional list. This is because, from a formal standpoint, all that matters for the Game of Life is that each cell be in one of two different states. We might call these states 'alive' or 'dead.' All that matters is that there are two distinct states. Our two-dimensional list can be populated with 0s and 1s, where the 0s are treated as dead cells and the 1s are treated as live cells (or vice versa). We might also populate our two-dimensional list with ' 's (spaces) and '*'s (asterisks) and treat the ' 's as dead cells and the '*'s as live cells. It's completely arbitrary what two objects we end up settling on to represent the two possible states of a cell.

Let's represent the 5×5 grid in the initial state above with the following two-dimensional list using ' 's and '*'s.

```
grid = [[' ','*',' ',' ',' '],
        ['*','*','*',' ','*'],
        [' ',' ','*',' ',' '],
        ['*',' ',' ',' ','*'],
        [' ',' ','*','*',' ']]
```

Exercise 10.1: How should the 5×5 grid at Step 1 in Figure 10.2 be represented?

Explicitly writing out the value of every element in the 5×5 grid would be extremely tedious. What if we wanted to work with a 50×50 grid? This would require writing out 2,500 values—no easy task! It would be helpful to have a function that creates this two-dimensional list for us. More generally, it would be helpful to have a function that creates a two-dimensional list of *any* given dimension.

Exercise 10.2: Write a function called create_row that takes an integer, n, as input and returns a list of n space characters.

Exercise 10.3: Write a function called create_grid that takes two integers, rows and cols, as inputs and returns a two-dimensional list of space characters with rows and cols as its dimensions (where rows represents the number of rows and cols represents the number of columns). You should use the create_row function defined in the previous exercise.

As an initial state for your Game of Life grid, however, a grid full of dead cells would be rather boring. Nothing will ever happen in this world. What we would want is a grid of cells that had a reasonable distribution of live and dead cells. One way of creating such a grid would be to manually code in the values. With a 5×5 grid, manually coding in the values of every cell is manageable (barely). But what if we wanted to work with a 50×50 grid? This will require up to 2,500 manually coded cells! One alternative, if we are not interested in a particular starting state, would be to *randomly* populate the cells in a grid with live and dead cells.

The Random Library

An important set of functions is available through the random library. As the name suggests, it not only provides functions that generate a variety of random numbers, but it also provides functions that will randomly extract elements out of a list. In this section, we'll just stick with random number generation.

To access the library, we first need to import it.

```
>>> import random
```

Once imported, we can use any of the functions within this library by prefixing the function with the name of the library. To access the random function[1] in the random library, we can type the following:

```
>>> random.random()
0.5717435612218142
```

Don't worry if the number you see differs from the number written here. This is as it should be since the random function returns a random number between 0 and 1. The chance that our numbers match is statistically impossible.

Using this function, we can model probabilities to a very high level of accuracy. Say, for example, that you wanted to model an event that happens exactly 34.125% of the time. We can use the random function to help us accomplish this. Consider the following Boolean expression.

```
>>> random.random() <= 0.34125
```

Will this expression evaluate to True or False? Well, it depends on what number the random function generates. If the number is less than or equal to 0.34125, then the expression will evaluate to True. If the number is greater than 0.34125, then the expression will evaluate to False. Can we say anything about the probability that the expression will evaluate to True? Yes! Given that the random function generates an even distribution of random numbers between 0 and 1, we can see that this expression will evaluate to True exactly 34.125% of the time. We can get a rough approximation that this is indeed the case by running the following code:

```
num_true = 0
num_total = 1000
probability = 0.34125

for i in range(num_total):
    if random.random() <= probability:
        num_true += 1

print(num_true / num_total)
```

What does this code do? It executes the random function 1,000 times and counts the number of times the randomly generated number is less than or equal to 0.34125. My first three times executing this resulted in the following values:

```
0.36, 0.326, 0.34
```

Pretty close to the 0.34125 probability we were aiming to model. Of course, if the number of times the random function is used is increased, the more closely the desired probability will be approximated. When I run it 1,000,000 times, I get the following results:

```
0.341162, 0.341386, 0.340946
```

Notice that the percentages are even closer to 0.34125.

Exercise 10.4: Write a function called flip that has no input or output values. When it is executed, it will simply print 'heads' or 'tails' where each string is displayed with 50% probability.

Exercise 10.5: Write a function called roll that has no input value. This function will model what it's like to roll a six-sided die. The percentage of times it will land on any given number between 1 and 6 is 16.66%. This function should return a number between 1 and 6.

Returning to the Game of Life grid, what if we wanted to randomly populate the grid with live cells? Perhaps I want each individual cell to have a 50% chance of being alive. This would be like flipping a coin to decide for each cell whether it's going to be alive. We might manage this by iterating over every cell in the grid using a nested loop and then using the random function to simulate a coin flip.

```
>>> random.random() <= 0.50:
```

This expression will evaluate to True about 50% of the time. We can populate the grid with any probability of live cells we desire by changing the 0.50 to a number in the range from 0 to 1.

Exercise 10.6: Write a function called populate that takes a two-dimensional list, grid, and a number, prob (signifying the probability a given cell will be alive), and updates grid so that the relevant cells are made alive. Note that the values in grid are being modified so there is no need for a return value. Hint: it may be helpful to find out the dimensions of grid before doing anything else using the len function.

Before going on, it would be nice to test your two functions and make sure they are working properly. The following code should create a 5×5 two-dimensional list of spaces and assign it to the variable grid.

```
>>> grid = create_grid(5,5)
>>> grid
[[' ',' ',' ',' ',' '],
 [' ',' ',' ',' ',' '],
 [' ',' ',' ',' ',' '],
 [' ',' ',' ',' ',' '],
 [' ',' ',' ',' ',' ']]
>>> len(grid)
5
>>> len(grid[0])
5
```

Make sure this works with differing input values so that you are confident that you can create a two-dimensional list of spaces with an arbitrary number of rows and columns.

Now let's make sure the populate function works. The following code should populate the existing grid so that roughly 50% of its cells are alive.

```
>>> populate(grid,0.5)
>>> grid
[['*',' ','*',' ',' '],
 [' ','*',' ','*','*'],
 [' ','*','*',' ',' '],
 [' ',' ','*','*',' '],
 ['*','*',' ',' ','*']]
```

If you run these two statements over again, your grid should have a different distribution of ' 's and '*'s with each covering roughly 50% of the total spaces in grid.

Evolving the Grid

Now that we have a representation of the Game of Life grid and the ability to create and randomly populate it, we need to figure out how we can process the information in this grid so that we can evolve the states of the cells one step at a time. Since we know that the evolution of the grid requires, among other things, the calculation of the number of live neighbors each cell has, creating a function to handle this logic seems to be a good idea. This can be seen as a possible step in **decomposing** the problem of modeling the Game of Life into smaller sub-problems.

In writing a function that calculates the number of neighbors a given cell has, let's first decide what the inputs and outputs of this function will be. Take a moment to think through this yourself.

One of the inputs to this function should be the location of the cell under consideration in terms of its row and column indices. Another important input is the grid itself. Given this, we might write a function that takes three objects as inputs: a two-dimensional list that represents the grid, the row index of the cell, and the column index of the cell. What should this function output? It should output an integer between 0 and 8 (inclusive) that represents the number of live neighbors this cell has.

With a clear set of inputs and output in mind, we have, in essence, created an abstraction to think about the computational process of counting a cell's live neighbors. Let's say, as inputs, we gave our function the grid shown in Figure 10.2 in its initial state, along with the row and column indices 1 and 2.

Now that we've specified the cell we're interested in (colored in gray), we'll have to check its eight adjacent cells for live neighbors. This can be seen in Figure 10.3. Notice that the gray box enclosing the eight adjacent cells is a 3×3 two-dimensional list. The rows for just these neighbors are

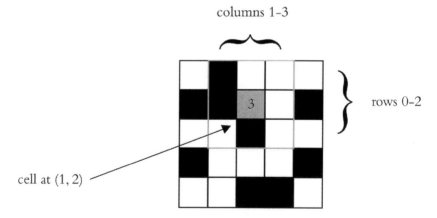

Figure 10.3 The cell at row 1 and column 2 has three live neighbors.

between indices 0 and 2 (inclusive) and the columns are between indices 1 and 3 (inclusive). These indices can be calculated based on the row and column indices of the specified cell. So, one way of solving this problem would be to iterate over every cell in this 3×3 two-dimensional list (except the cell at row 1 and column 2) and count up all the live cells. This should then output 3 since there are three live neighbors. Note, however, that cells along the edge of the grid do not have a full set of neighbors. The cell at row 0 and column 1, for example, only has five neighbors.

Exercise 10.7: Write a function called `neighbors` that takes three inputs: a two-dimensional list called `grid`, an integer, `row`, which stands for the row index, and an integer, `column`, which stands for the column index. This function should return the number of live neighbors that the cell located at `row` and `column` in `grid` has.

Make sure that your function works correctly! Test it on various cells within `grid` and make sure it yields the right number of live neighbors. Don't forget to test your function on edge cells and corner cells.

Before going on, it would be nice to have a rudimentary way of visualizing the Game of Life grid. Since we haven't learned how to use Zelle's `graphics` library for drawing polygons yet, we can visualize grid using text and `print` statements. One way of doing this is as follows.

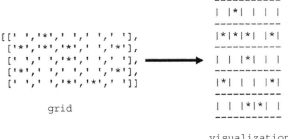

grid

visualization

Exercise 10.8: Write a function called `visualize` that takes a two-dimensional list, `grid`, as input and visualizes `grid` by displaying formatted text.

If you've successfully coded the `neighbors` and `visualize` functions, then you've finally reached the core of the Game of Life logic. Now we need to figure out how to evolve the information stored in a grid one step at a time. This will be a matter of applying the four rules listed above to every cell in this grid. Implementing the relevant rules, given the `neighbors` function, should be a fairly straightforward task. It is important to remember, however, that applying the rules to a given cell must be done based on the current, *unaltered* state of the grid. The rules must be applied to the cells in the grid 'all at once.'

To see why this is important, consider the 3×3 grid in Figure 10.4.

If we apply the rules to the cell at row 0 and column 0 (colored gray), which is currently dead, the cell should be made alive since it has exactly three live neighbors.

Now if we update the grid and try to apply the rules to the cell (highlighted with a gray border) at row 0 and column 1, the cell should be made dead since it has more than three live neighbors. You can see this in Figure 10.5. The cell at row 0 and column 1 has 4 live neighbors. But notice, if we tried to apply the rules to the same cell in the original, unaltered grid, we would get a different result. You can see this in Figure 10.6. The cell at row 0 and column 1 has three live neighbors.

In this case, the cell should remain alive since it has exactly three neighbors. This would lead to two very different results. This is why it is critical that the rules be applied to the cells 'all at once.'

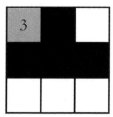

Figure 10.4 The dead cell in the top-left corner of the grid has three live neighbors.

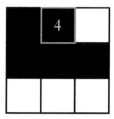

Figure 10.5 The live cell in the middle of the top row of the grid has four live neighbors.

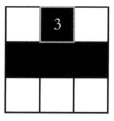

Figure 10.6 The live cell in the middle of the top row of the grid has three live neighbors.

In order to apply the rules simultaneously to all cells, the changes to the cells must be made to a separate, *temporary* grid with the exact same dimensions as grid.[2] This way, changes to the state of a given cell will not be reflected in the existing grid while the rules are still being applied. Once the new states of *all* the cells are recorded in the temporary grid, this temporary grid can be assigned to grid.

Exercise 10.9: Write a function called evolve that takes a two-dimensional list, grid, as input and returns a new two-dimensional list (with the same dimensions) with cells that reflect the next step in the evolution based on the four rules of the Game of Life.

Testing your code will now become more difficult. My suggestion is to create a small 5×5 grid and populate it with 50% live cells. You can see what the grid looks like using the visualize function. Then run the evolve function on the grid and use the visualize function again. Now you must carefully inspect whether the Game of Life rules were properly applied. This may be a painstaking process if you find that your grid is not evolving correctly. You'll have to carefully look through your code to make sure there are no mistakes in your logic. Is your neighbors function working correctly? Are you applying the Game of Life rules correctly?

Since we've decomposed the original problem into several sub-problems, we now need to put the solutions to these sub-problems back together. If all the functions are working properly then the following code should provide text-based visualizations that mirror the first two steps in the evolution of the 5×5 grid depicted above.

```
grid = [[' ','*',' ',' ',' '],
        ['*','*','*',' ','*'],
        [' ',' ','*',' ',' '],
        ['*',' ',' ',' ','*'],
        [' ',' ','*','*',' ']]
visualize(grid)       # initial state[3]
evolve(grid)
visualize(grid)       # step 1
evolve(grid)
visualize(grid)       # step 2
```

Do your text-based visualizations of the first two steps of evolution accurately match the grids displayed at the beginning of this chapter? Make sure that everything is working properly before proceeding.

Given the repetitive nature of this code, it would be nice to put this into a loop. In fact, we could put this into an *infinite* loop since the Game of Life really has no end. We might simply use the following code to do this.

```
while True:

    visualize(grid)
    evolve(grid)
```

Notice how simple the code is for running the Game of Life (given you've already decomposed the problem into smaller parts)! It's just a matter of visualizing grid, evolving grid, and doing these two things over and over again. Because all the implementation details are abstracted away, it should be obvious to someone trying to understand your code what you're trying to accomplish.

To run a Game of Life CA, we can put everything together as follows.

```
grid = create_grid(50,50)
populate(grid,0.5)

while True:

    visualize(grid)
    evolve(grid)
```

If you've successfully reached this point, then you've accomplished a great task! You've written your first large program that simulates Conway's Game of Life.

Graphics

Sadly, this is a very clunky implementation of the Game of Life since we are using text to visualize the evolution of the grid. In this section, we will use Zelle's graphics library (introduced in an earlier chapter) to develop a graphics-based visualization of the Game of Life using the code that you've already written.

Assuming you already have the graphics.py file placed in the right location, here is some code to get started.

```
from graphics import *
window = GraphWin('Game of Life',500,500,autoflush=False)
```

This much, hopefully, is already familiar. The GraphWin statement should generate a new 500×500 pixel window with the title: 'Game of Life.' The one new detail is the autoflush input. By setting this attribute to False, we are actively suppressing the tkinter GUI from continually updating the image. This is important because continually updating the window can be time-consuming and may affect the smoothness of the animation we hope to achieve (more on this later).

What is critical for our purposes is the ability to draw rectangles in this window. This is easy to achieve with the Rectangle function.

```
rect = Rectangle(Point(0,0),Point(100,25))
rect.draw(window)
```

The Rectangle function takes two inputs that are Point objects. The Point function in turn takes two integer inputs that specify the x–y coordinates in the window. The coordinate system, if you recall, works the way you'd expect for the x-axis (numbers increase moving to the right) but works the opposite way for the y-axis (numbers increase moving down). Moreover, the origin (0,0) is located at the top-left of window (not at the center).

The two Point objects, which are given as input, represent the top-left and bottom-right corners of the Rectangle object. So, the statement above creates a Rectangle object with a top-left corner aligned with the top-left corner of window and a bottom-right corner located at (100,25). The draw function must be executed in order for the Rectangle to be displayed (or drawn) in window.

Note that once the draw function is executed for an object, it should never be called again for that object. Calling this function more than once for an object will generate an error because the object has already been displayed. Any visual changes in the objects in window will be handled with the update function (not the draw function).

You can manipulate the color of the Rectangle object using two functions. The setFill function takes a single input, an RGB color value, and sets the internal color of the rectangle. The setOutline function takes a single input, an RGB color value, and sets the outline color of the rectangle. Try experimenting with this yourself.

```
rect.setFill(color_rgb(255,0,255))
rect.setOutline(color_rgb(0,255,0))
```

Exercise 10.10: Write code that creates a 500×500 GraphWin object titled: 'Face.' Then create four Rectangle objects of different colors that represent the eyes, nose, and mouth of a person's face. Finally, display the Rectangle objects in the GraphWin object using the draw function.

Now we have the tools to visualize a two-dimensional grid of cells. Let's try this with the 5×5 grid in the initial state described earlier in this chapter. The first thing we need to do is to create a two-dimensional list of Rectangle objects that are located at the proper locations in window. Let's begin by assigned an empty list to the variable grid_visual.

```
grid_visual = []
```

Since we need five `Rectangle` objects to stretch across window's width, each `Rectangle` object should be 100 pixels wide. Since we also need five `Rectangle` objects to stretch down window's height, each Rectangle object should be 100 pixels tall. To create the first sub-list in `grid_visual` (which represents the first row of the grid), we might do the following.

```
row1 = [Rectangle(Point(0,0),Point(100,100)), Rectangle
(Point(100,0),Point(200,100)), Rectangle(Point(200,0),P
oint(300,100)), Rectangle(Point(300,0),Point(400,100)),
Rectangle(Point(400,0),Point(500,100))]
grid_visual.append(row1)
```

We can repeat this process for the remaining four rows with corresponding changes in coordinates for each of the `Rectangle` objects. Successfully completing `grid_visual` will result in a 5×5 two-dimensional list of `Rectangle` objects that is structurally identical to the 5×5 two-dimensional list of strings we will assign to `grid`.

The problem, at this point, is that the `Rectangle` objects are all the same color. To properly represent the information in `grid`, two distinct colors need to be used to mirror the ' 's and '*'s. This way, every `Rectangle` object that is 'alive' will be colored one way and every `Rectangle` object that is 'dead' will be colored the other way.

```
[[' ','*',' ',' ',' '],          [[Rec,Rec,Rec,Rec,Rec],
 [' ','*',' ',' ','*'],           [Rec,Rec,Rec,Rec,Rec],
 [' ',' ','*','*',' '],           [Rec,Rec,Rec,Rec,Rec],
 ['*',' ',' ','*',' '],           [Rec,Rec,Rec,Rec,Rec],
 ['*','*',' ',' ','*']]           [Rec,Rec,Rec,Rec,Rec]]

        grid                           grid_visual
```

The process of assigning appropriate colors for each `Rectangle` object in this two-dimensional list can be done elegantly with a nested loop.

Finally, note that without explicitly executing the `draw` function for each of the Rectangle objects that were created above, none of the objects will be displayed in window.

Exercise 10.11: Write a function called `create_grid_visual` that takes two integers, rows and cols, and a `GraphWin` object, window, as inputs. rows and cols specify the number of `Rectangle` objects that should exist in any given row or column (respectively). This function should return a two-dimensional list of Rectangle objects. Don't forget to use the draw function to display each of the Rectangle objects in window. It may be helpful to use the create_grid function since it can create a two-dimensional list of arbitrary dimensions. Hint: the dimensions of window can be accessed through the getWidth and getHeight functions.

We are now extremely close to a complete computer program! Now that we have two structurally identical two-dimensional lists (one from our text-based representation of the Game of Life grid and the other from our graphics-based representation of the Game of Life grid), we only need one final function. We need a way to use the information in grid (the text-based representation) to inform the way our graphical visualization, grid_visual, will be displayed. Perhaps we want every '*' in grid to be mirrored by a black Rectangle in grid_visual and we want every ' ' in grid to be mirrored by a white Rectangle in grid_visual.

Recall that we can access the cell in grid at row 0 and column 1 with the following statement:

grid[0][1]

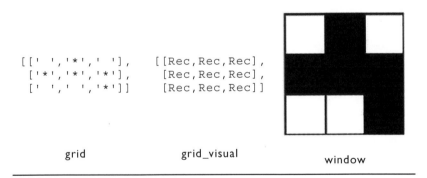

| grid | grid_visual | window |

The corresponding Rectangle object in grid_visual can be accessed with the same indices. Once accessed, the color of the Rectangle object can be changed to black since the corresponding cell in grid is a '*.' Since the cell at row 0 and column 2 in grid is a ' ', we can set the corresponding Rectangle to white.

```
grid_visual[0][1].setFill(color_rgb(0,0,0))
grid_visual[0][2].setFill(color_rgb(255,255,255))
```

In this way, we can ensure that the Rectangle objects in grid_visual mirror the live and dead cells in grid.

Exercise 10.12: Write a function called `mirror` that takes two structurally identical two-dimensional lists, `grid` and `grid_visual`, as inputs and ensures that every `'*'` in `grid` is mirrored by a black `Rectangle` in `grid_visual` and every `' '` in `grid` is mirrored by a green `Rectangle` in `grid_visual`.

If you've managed to get this far then your implementation of the Game of Life should be finished. I can now write the code needed for running the Game of Life as follows.

```
window = GraphWin('Game of Life',500,500,autoflush=False)
grid = create_grid(50,50)
grid_visual = create_grid_visual(50,50,window)
populate(grid,0.5)

while True:
    mirror(grid,grid_visual)
    window.update()
    grid = evolve(grid)
```

The only new function in this final bit of code is `update`. When this is called from `window`, it forces `window` to update the GUI with all the changes that have been made to the colors of the `Rectangle` objects. This is needed because when `window` was first created, it was created with the `autoflush` input set to `False`. Setting `autoflush` to `False` ensures that `window` does not automatically update its visual appearance—it will only do so upon command. Consequently, though the `mirror` function changes the colors of the `Rectangle` objects in `grid_visual`, these changes are not visually reflected in `window`. It's only after the `update` function is executed that `window` visually reflects the changes that have occurred to the `Rectangle` objects in it.

Let's review what we've accomplished in developing a program to run the Game of Life in Python. First, we made a decision regarding the representation of the structures we would use in the Game of Life. We used a two-dimensional list of two possible strings: `' '`s (spaces) and `'*'`s to represent the grid of live and dead cells.

Then we decomposed the task of running the Game of Life into smaller sub-problems. We designed the `neighbors` function to handle the task of counting the number of live cells surrounding a given cell. We then used this function to write the `evolve` function that applied the rules of the Game of Life to the cells. In order to visualize this without graphics, we wrote the `visualize` function, which displayed representative text on the screen. The final piece was to add graphics. This was done by creating a two-dimensional list of `Rectangle` objects from Zelle's graphics library that corresponds to each of the cells in the two-dimensional list of strings. Then the `mirror` function was developed so that the `Rectangle` objects' colors would mirror the live and dead cells in the two-dimensional list of strings.

Key Points

- The `random` library can be imported and used to generate random numbers.
- The Game of Life is a CA that can be represented as a two-dimensional list.
- The Game of Life can be decomposed into manageable parts through the defining of functions.

Notes

1 See the Appendix for a different way of generating random numbers using the `randint` function.
2 Remember, it should be easy to create a temporary grid since you've already written the `create_grid` function! Don't reinvent the wheel every time you need to solve something you've already solved.
3 The # `character` is used in Python to tell the interpreter not to do anything with it and the characters that follow it. Python will simply ignore these characters. These, therefore, act as ways programmers can add comments to their code. Usually they are descriptive phrases that explain what the code is doing at a more conceptual level.

References

Bialynicki-Birula, I., & Bialynicki-Birula, I. (2004). *Modeling Reality: How Computers Mirror Reality.* Oxford: Oxford University Press.
Gardner, M. (1970). *Mathematical Games: The Fantastic Combinationvs of John Conway's New Solitaire Game "Life".* Scientific American, 233, 120–123.

Chapter 11

Free Will

In this chapter, we will consider a classic topic in western philosophy: free will. To do this, we will begin with conceptual analyses of the terms 'free will' and 'determinism.' Then we will consider some reasons for and against the claim that free will and determinism are compatible with each other. Finally, we will use Conway's Game of Life (which we implemented in the previous chapter) to consider Daniel Dennett's approach to thinking about the relationship between free will and determinism.

Free Will

We believe that we are agents—beings with the ability to act intentionally. Moreover, we believe that we are agents who can be held morally accountable (both positively and negatively) for our intentional actions. When Moses helps an elderly woman with her groceries, most people would consider this a praiseworthy action. When Moses instead steals groceries from an elderly woman, most people would consider this a blameworthy action. Holding one another (and ourselves) morally responsible for our actions is a foundational feature of our social practices.

But what makes our being morally responsible agents possible? It seems we have a certain control over our actions that makes us morally responsible. One common view is that this control comes from our having **free will**. Free will is often characterized as the control an agent has such that an agent could have done otherwise than what she actually does. So, for example, Moses might have helped an elderly woman with her groceries, but he could easily have done otherwise. Instead of helping her, he could have simply walked past her and attended to his own shopping priorities. He was presented with at least two **alternate possibilities**. Because Moses could have legitimately chosen either possibility, he is morally responsible for the possibility he actually chooses. He, being an agent, is the difference with respect to whether or not the elderly woman receives help with her groceries.

DOI: 10.4324/9781003271284-11

We might summarize this with the following requirement on free will.

AP (alternate possibilities): the universe is such that, at least sometimes, there are at least two possible futures.
   FW → AP

Assuming 'FW' stands for the claim that free will exists and 'AP' stands for the claim that there are alternate possibilities, the conditional FW → AP expresses the claim that alternate possibilities are a necessary condition for free will.

Discussion: Do you agree with this condition? Are alternate possibilities necessary for free will? Are alternate possibilities sufficient for free will?

A bit of reflection on this concept of free will, however, yields a puzzle given our growing scientific understanding of who and what we are. Here is how this puzzle is described in a popular article from *The Atlantic*:

> The challenge posed by neuroscience is more radical: It describes the brain as a physical system like any other, and suggests that we no more will it to operate in a particular way than we will our heart to beat. The contemporary scientific image of human behavior is one of neurons firing, causing other neurons to fire, causing our thoughts and deeds, in an unbroken chain that stretches back to our birth and beyond. In principle, we are therefore completely predictable. If we could understand any individual's brain architecture and chemistry well enough, we could, in theory, predict that individual's response to any given stimulus with 100 percent accuracy.
>
> (Cave, 2016)

If all our behavior can be traced back to the firing of the neurons in our brains, and our brains are physical systems, how can free will exist? After all, if the complexes of neurons in our brains are no different from the complexes of muscle cells in our hearts, why think that one physical system generates free will while the other doesn't? It's not as though our hearts have a choice about whether they beat or not. They cannot do other than what they actually do. How can brains be any different? But if this is the case, then the AP requirement is not met, and free will cannot exist.

At the heart of this intuition is an underlying claim that is explicitly made in the quote above: "in principle, we are therefore completely predictable." Why would an unbroken chain of causes from the firing of neurons in our brains to our behaviors make everything we do 'completely predictable'? It must be that each causal link is completely fixed by the previous causal link in this unbroken chain. So long as the causes remain the same, the effects *must* remain the same. There is no room for things to have happened differently than they actually do. We might say that the scientific image of the world gives us a *deterministic* understanding of how events unfold. But if **determinism** is true, how is free will possible? How can anything in a deterministic world be such that it could have done otherwise than what it actually does? According to this line of thought, if determinism is true, there is only one way events can unfold, and no other alternatives are possible.

Determinism

The inspiration for Cave's quote can be traced back to the 18th-century French mathematician Pierre-Simon Laplace. He is credited with offering one of the more popular and enduring descriptions of determinism.

> We ought then to consider the present state of the universe as the effect of its previous state and as the cause of that which is to follow. An intelligence that, at a given instant, could comprehend all the forces by which nature is animated and the respective situation of the beings that make it up, if moreover it were vast enough to submit these data to analysis, would encompass in the same formula the movements of the greatest bodies of the universe and those of the lightest atoms. For such an intelligence nothing would be uncertain, and the future, like the past, would be open to its eyes.
>
> (Laplace, 1995, p. 2)

Others have referred to the 'intelligence' in this passage as **Laplace's demon** to honor the super-human abilities this intelligence would have. Given exhaustive information about the present state of the universe, Laplace's demon, using its knowledge of the laws of nature, could extrapolate all future states of the universe with perfect accuracy. These future states would, of course, include the behaviors of every human being on earth. We can try to imagine what Laplace's demon might need to carry out these calculations. Perhaps something like super-human memory and super-human processing speed are minimal requirements. Put in these terms, Laplace's demon might be considered a future descendant of the modern-day supercomputer.

The Game of Life cellular automaton discussed in the previous chapter provides a useful illustration of Laplacean determinism. We can consider the two-dimensional grid of cells within the Game of Life as the 'entire universe.' The configuration of live and dead cells constitutes exhaustive information about the exact state of the universe at a given point in time. This universe obeys a set of simple rules that dictates whether any given cell lives or dies as the universe evolves—what we might call the 'laws of nature' in that universe. The important point is that these laws operate deterministically. Given this, we can confidently say that there is only a *single*

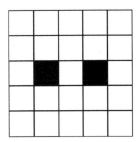

Figure 11.1 State 0.

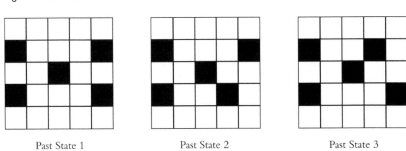

Past State 1   Past State 2   Past State 3

Figure 11.2 Three possible past states that are compatible with State 0.

possible future for the way the two-dimensional grid of cells will evolve given any particular initial configuration.

Care is required. Though determinism entails a *single* possible future, it does not entail a single possible past. In fact, a given state of a deterministic system may have multiple possible past histories. Consider the following state in the Game of Life, let's call it State 0:

This is compatible with at least the following three past states:

In fact, if we assume an infinite two-dimensional grid of cells, there would be an infinite number of distinct past states that are compatible with State 0. We could, for example, make an infinite number of variations on Past State 1 by adding a single live cell to any location in the infinite grid that is sufficiently far from the five live cells in Past State 1 such that it cannot interact with any of them. That is, this single live cell must not affect and must not be affected by the five live cells in Past State 1. So, we can confidently claim that there are an infinite number of past states that are compatible with State 0, but there is only a *single* possible future that is compatible with State 0. We might rightly say that a deterministic system has an 'open' past but a 'closed' future.[1]

What this means is that, given enough memory and processing speed, a computer would be able to calculate every future state of the Game of Life universe. There would be nothing uncertain about what the future of this universe will be like. Moreover, if you rewind the history of this universe and play it back again, the history will unfold in exactly the same way every time. It is in this sense that we can say that the Game of Life represents a deterministic universe.

If the universe we live in were deterministic in this way, many might be persuaded (in agreement with the AP requirement) that free will could not exist. After all, given the previous state of the universe, how could Moses have done other than what he actually did? If Moses helps an elderly woman with her groceries, it seems the previous state of the universe (plus the laws of nature) determined that Moses would help. Indeed, the previous state of the universe made it impossible for Moses to have done otherwise. Rewinding this universe and playing it back will result in Moses' helping the elderly woman every time. Put another way, the only thing Moses *could* do given the prior state of the universe is to help the elderly woman. He had no choice in the matter, no matter how much he thought that he did!

Given this, the following conditional must be true:

D → ~AP

Here, 'D' stands for the claim that determinism is true, and the conditional D → ~AP expresses the claim that the absence of alternate possibilities is a necessary condition for determinism. Juxtaposing this with the requirement on free will we are faced with a tension:

FW → AP
D → ~AP

Free will entails alternate possibilities, but determinism entails the impossibility of alternate possibilities. So, it seems, in a rather straightforward way, that free will and determinism are not compatible with each other.

Does this mean that free will doesn't exist? That depends on whether or not determinism is true of our universe. The question of whether or not our universe is deterministic, however, is (at least at the moment) an open question. Given the recent progress in quantum physics, we might be convinced that our universe could not be deterministic. Some philosophers think, however, that this makes no difference regarding free will. Even if the universe were *in*deterministic, the existence of free will would still be threatened since it's unclear how randomness (at the quantum level, or anywhere else) can give rise to the relevant kind of control at the human level needed for free will. Be that as it may, we will limit our discussion to the *relationship* between free will and determinism (and set aside the question of whether determinism is true). We will limit our reflection to the following conditional: *if* our universe were deterministic then what would this mean about the existence of free will?

There are two main positions in this debate. One is the claim that free will and determinism are not compatible with each other. This position is aptly called **incompatibilism**, which we just discussed. The other is the claim that free will and determinism are compatible with each other. This position is aptly called **compatibilism**.

Incompatibilism and Compatibilism

Carl Ginet, a contemporary philosopher of mind, has offered an argument for incompatibilism. Here is a representative passage:

> The occurrence of free and responsible action is incompatible with determinism because: (a) having alternative possible courses of action (or inaction) open to one at a given time entails indeterminism at that time and place, that is, it entails that the causal laws and the antecedent state of the world do not determine which of those alternative possibilities will then occur; and (b) [free will] entails having alternative possibilities open, that is, an agent is morally responsible for a given action only if she had it open to her to avoid that action.
>
> (Ginet, 2003, p. 588)

Question: Can you logically analyze Ginet's argument and put it in premise-conclusion form?

Given the discussion so far, we might offer a straightforward interpretation of Ginet's argument using the two conditionals provided above.

Incompatibilist Argument

1. D → ~AP
    If determinism is true, then it is false that there are alternate possibilities.
2. ~AP → ~FW (i.e. FW → AP)
    If it is false that there are alternate possibilities, then it is false that free will exists (because if free will exists then there must be alternate possibilities).
3. Therefore, D → ~FW

If determinism is true, then it is false that free will exists.

Discussion: Is this a charitable reconstruction of Ginet's reasoning? Are there any weak premises?

We might classify compatibilist responses to this kind of reasoning into two broad categories. In the first category, attempts are made to show that AP is in fact compatible with determinism. In the second category, attempts are made to show that AP is not a necessary condition for the kind of free will that really matters.

Let's begin with a response that fits into the first category. The so-called **'conditional analysis'** can be seen as an attack on premise 1 of the Incompatibilist Argument. The idea is to argue that determinism does not rule out alternate possibilities. G.E. Moore seemed to have supported this kind of a compatibilist response. Here is a suggestive quote:

> What is the sense of the word 'could', in which it is so certain that we often could have done what we did not do? What, for instance, is the sense in which I could have walked a mile in twenty minutes this morning, though I did not? There is one suggestion, which is very obvious: namely, that what I mean is simply after all that I could, if I had chosen; or (to avoid a possible complication) perhaps we had better say 'that I [would], if I had chosen'. In other words, the suggestion is that we often use the phrase 'I could' simply and solely as a short way of saying 'I [would], if I had chosen'.
>
> (Moore, 2005, p. 110)

So when we say that 'Moses *could have done otherwise* (than help the elderly woman),' what we really mean is '*if* Moses had chosen not to help the elderly woman, then Moses would not have helped the elderly woman'. This interpretation of 'could have done otherwise' is clearly compatible with determinism because it posits an alternate past history. What actually happened was Moses chose to help the elderly woman and this choice led Moses to help the elderly woman. If, contrary to fact, Moses had chosen *not* to help the elderly woman, then this choice would have led Moses to *not* help the elderly woman.

How might the conditional analysis be applied to the Game of Life? Let's assume that State 0 is the *current* state of the Game of Life universe and that it was immediately preceded by Past State 1.

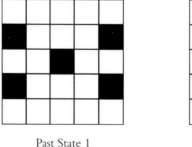 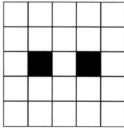

Past State 1   State 0

Figure 11.3 Past State 1 must evolve to State 0 according to the Game of Life rules.

We can ask: what is meant when one says that the current state 'could' have been different from State 0? What this means is if Past State 1 had been appropriately different, then the current state would have been different from State 0. If this analysis is correct, then no deterministic rules within the Game of Life universe would have been violated. Consequently, we could say that the current state of the Game of Life universe could have been different than it actually is in a way that is compatible with the deterministic rules within the Game of Life universe.

Discussion: How satisfying is the conditional analysis to you? Is it really the case that 'I could' can be translated into 'I [would], if I had chosen'?

A natural incompatibilist response might be to wonder how this even helps. If the only way Moses could have refrained from helping the elderly woman was for Moses to have chosen *not* to help the elderly woman (i.e., for a different past to have occurred), then it's unclear how this helps. According to determinism, even the past could not have been different than what it actually was, given the initial state of the universe. So long as the initial state of the universe is kept constant, Moses could not have chosen not to help the elderly woman.

Moreover, perhaps a counterexample can be provided against this analysis. Peter van Inwagen gives us a 'recipe' for constructing such a counterexample. He writes:

> Simply pick one of those logically possible cases in which someone COULD HAVE chosen to do something, but could not have chosen to do it (and, of course, construct the example in such a way that his choice would have been effective). This will be a case in which our imaginary person could not have performed a certain act, though, according to the proposed definition, he could have.
>
> (Van Inwagen, 1983, p. 117)

Suppose Sora is psychologically unable to *want* to taste mustard. I am unaware of this condition and I bring Sora two hot dogs. One has only ketchup and the other has both ketchup and mustard. I ask her to choose which hot dog she wants to eat. Sora happily chooses the hot dog that only has ketchup. The question is: when Sora reached out for the hot dog that only has ketchup, could she have done otherwise and reached out for the hot dog with both ketchup and mustard? Given her unique psychological condition, the answer must obviously be no. She cannot develop a desire to taste mustard. Nevertheless, given the conditional analysis, we have to say yes. For *if* she wanted to reach out for the hot dog with ketchup and mustard then she would have done so. But if she had wanted to reach out for the hot dog with ketchup and mustard, then she would not have had her unique psychological disorder. So, it seems the conditional analysis gives us the wrong result regarding Sora's actual abilities.

Discussion: What do you think about these responses to the conditional analysis? Are they convincing? What might the compatibilist proponent of the conditional analysis say to defend her position?

Now let's consider a response that fits into the second category. The idea here is to show that free will doesn't require alternate possibilities—at least not the kind of free will that really matters to us. The kind of free will that really matters to us is that which makes moral responsibility possible. What the defender of this response attempts to show is that a person can be morally responsible for an action even if this person had no alternate possibilities (i.e., this person could not have done otherwise). This can be seen as an attack on premise 2 of the Incompatibilist Argument. The idea is to argue that free will (that is necessary for moral responsibility) does not require alternate possibilities.

Harry Frankfurt famously developed a response along these lines. He offers a kind of recipe for generating examples that show how people can be morally responsible even if alternate possibilities do not exist. Frankfurt writes:

> Suppose someone—[Bob], let us say—wants Jones to perform a certain action. [Bob] is prepared to go to considerable lengths to get his way, but he prefers to avoid showing his hand unnecessarily. So he waits until Jones is about to make up his mind what to do, and he does nothing unless it is clear to him that Jones is going to do something *other* than what he wants him to do. If it does become clear that Jones is going to decide to do something else, [Bob] takes effective steps to ensure that Jones decides to do, and that he does do, what he wants him to do. Whatever Jones's initial preferences and inclinations, [Bob] will have his way... Now suppose that [Bob] never has to show his hand because Jones, for reasons of his own, decides to perform and does perform the very action [Bob] wants him to perform.
>
> (Frankfurt, 1969, pp. 835–836)

To make this a little more concrete, let's say that Bob was betrayed by Walt and now wants Walt assassinated. To avoid punishment, Bob intends to have Jones assassinate Walt. Bob has the ability to ensure that Jones will assassinate Walt (Frankfurt offers several ways: Bob can pronounce a terrible threat, Bob can put Jones under hypnosis, or Bob can manipulate the minute processes of Jones' brain) should Bob believe that Jones will do something other than what Bob wants him to do. In short, there are no alternate possibilities for Jones regarding his assassinating Walt—one way or another, Jones *will* assassinate Walt. Either Jones will assassinate Walt without Bob's intervention, or Jones will assassinate Walt because of Bob's intervention. As it turns out, Bob never has to intervene. Bob simply observes what happens as a silent bystander. Jones, based on his own deliberation and decision, assassinates Walt. Though Jones could not have done otherwise (because of Bob's presence), it is plain that Jones is morally responsible for the assassination.

It seems we have a straightforward counterexample to premise 2. If we construe free will as the kind of free will necessary for moral responsibility, then Frankfurt's scenario shows that free will doesn't require alternate possibilities.

Discussion: How satisfying is Frankfurt's counterexample?

Frankfurt's counterexample radically changed the way debates over free will developed in the second half of the 20th century and the impacts are still being felt today. Nevertheless, some incompatibilists have been unimpressed. Carl Ginet, for example, thinks that adding sufficient details to Frankfurt's counterexample will reveal that Jones did indeed have alternate possibilities. Let's revisit what Bob wants—he does not simply want Jones to assassinate Walt. Bob wants Jones to assassinate Walt by a certain time, say, t_3 (after all, the assassination cannot happen at *any* time—given enough time Walt might simply die of natural causes). Bob sets things up so that if Jones has not already assassinated Walt by time t_2, then Bob will intervene so that Jones does assassinate Walt by t_3. But Bob never has to intervene because Jones assassinates Walt at time t_1. So it seems that Jones could not have done otherwise than assassinate Walt by t_3. For if Jones refrained from assassinating Walt at t_1, then Bob would have ensured at t_2 that Jones would assassinate Walt by t_3.

It seems we've exposed an alternate possibility that is more fine-grained in terms of time. Jones actually assassinated Walt at t_1 and couldn't have done other than assassinate Walt by t_3. But now it seems clear that Jones could have done otherwise with respect to his assassinating Walt at t_1. After all, isn't this precisely the alternate possibility Bob was so intently studying in order to ensure Walt's guaranteed assassination by t_3? And isn't this what grounds Jones' moral responsibility for Walt's assassination at t_1?

Avoidance Machines

As you can see from the previous brief discussions, the philosophical debates over various incompatibilist and compatibilist arguments have evolved in subtle directions over the years and have shed light on the intricacies of the relationship between free will and determinism (and moral responsibility). While there is merit to delving deeper into these debates, we might opt for a different take on these matters. Following

Daniel Dennett (2003), perhaps a bit of reflection on the Game of Life can help us entertain new possibilities.

Typical executions of the Game of Life that are visually understandable for humans are carried out on grids with relatively small dimensions, say, 100×100 cells. When configured with initial states that are randomly populated with live and dead cells, higher-level patterns emerge. Though these patterns are interesting at first, the patterns can quickly become stale. Yes, it's true that the patterns are almost always different because the initial states are almost always different. But the patterns seem 'messy' and hard to understand. Because it's difficult to predict how the various patterns will behave, it amounts to little more than chaos.

In the midst of this messiness, however, you may have noticed certain stable structures. There are structures that can (if left alone) last forever. Consider the square still life in Figure 11.4.

Given the rules of the Game of Life, you should be able to work out the stability of this 2×2 cell structure. Though boring, it has the virtue of eternal existence.

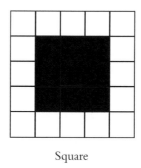

Square

Figure 11.4 **Square.**

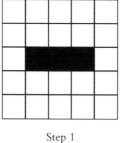 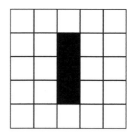

Step 1   Step 2

Figure 11.5 **Flasher.**

Other structures add a bit more variation. They are equally stable and (if left alone) will last forever, but have cyclic variations. Consider the flasher in Figure 11.5.

This structure will alternate between a three-cell horizontal bar (Step 1) and a three-cell vertical bar (Step 2) in an endless two-step cycle.

We can even consider structures that 'move' like the glider in Figure 11.6.

In a four-step cycle, the glider is able to move[2] diagonally toward the bottom right of the grid. You can see this because the same structure is present in Step 1 and Step 5 with the sole difference being its position (it is now one cell to the right and one cell below).

There are all sorts of interesting structures that one can find when carefully exploring the space of possibilities within the Game of Life. Experimenting with these higher-level structures, one can start to make

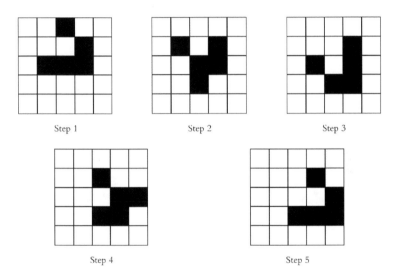

Step 1   Step 2   Step 3

Step 4   Step 5

Figure 11.6 **Glider.**

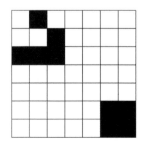

Figure 11.7 **A Glider and a Square.**

predictions and design initial configurations that yield fascinating results. As Dennett suggests, when we move up to this so-called 'design' level, we can introduce a new language that provides useful abbreviations for the painstaking descriptions that occur at the level of individual cells. Consider the initial configuration in Figure 11.7.

We can describe its evolution with the following language. In the top left of the grid is a glider and in the bottom right is a square still life. The glider moves diagonally toward the square still life and when they make contact with each other, they ultimately destroy each other. Dennett writes:

> Notice that something curious happens to our "ontology"—our catalog of what exists—as we move between levels. At the level [of individual cells] there is no motion, only [alive] and [dead], and the only individual things that exist, [cells], are defined by their fixed spatial location, {x, y}. At the design level we suddenly have the motion of persisting objects; it is one and the same glider (though composed each generation of different [cells]) that has moved [diagonally toward the bottom-right].
>
> (Dennett, 2003, p. 40)

The previous example of a glider colliding with a square still life ending in mutual destruction serves as a reminder, however, that the fate of many collisions in the Game of Life end in 'death.' Though structures like squares can live eternally, this is predicated on the condition that they live undisturbed. Is there any way for structures in the Game of Life to persist even in the presence of other objects that pose potential collision threats? Or, even more, can they survive and reproduce?

This brings us to the origins of the Game of Life. The Game of Life was actually a result of discussions that began in the 1950s with John von Neumann, one of the great mathematicians of the 20th century. Being interested in the design of possible machines, von Neumann wondered: could we ever create a machine that could manufacture itself? That is, could we ever create self-replicating machines? Moreover, he wondered: could we ever create a machine that could manufacture machines more complex than itself? These are intriguing questions! Moreover, affirmative answers to these questions might give us hints at what might be possible in a deterministic universe.

Technology during von Neumann's day, however, wasn't sophisticated enough to pursue answers to these questions experimentally. It took inspiration from Stanislaw Ulam, a fellow mathematician on the Manhattan Project, to provide von Neumann with the idea of experimenting via simulations on a computer. Ulam encouraged von Neumann to build imaginary worlds on the computer with rules that mimic a simplified physics. If the worlds were appropriately designed, Ulam opined, von Neumann would be able to construct 'machines' and run virtual experiments on them. Von Neumann eventually created a world with cells consisting of 29 possible states and rules that decided how the cells would evolve. He even went on to prove that there are initial configurations of these worlds that contain self-replicating patterns!

The problem with many amazing discoveries like von Neumann's, however, is that almost no one ever hears about them—at least no one in the general public. Years later, Conway, familiar with Ulam's pattern games, devised what we now know as the Game of Life. Because of its simplicity (a world consisting of cells with two possible states instead of von Neumann's 29) and publicity (through publication in Martin Gardner's extremely popular 'Mathematical Games' column in *Scientific American*), Conway's cellular automaton gained a cult following in the 1970s and has captured the imaginations of countless people ever since.[3]

Consider two notable discoveries in the Game of Life. In 2010, Andrew Wade devised a self-replicating structure dubbed 'Gemini.' Gemini replicates itself in 34 million steps and, among its accolades, has the ability to move in a non-diagonal, non-orthogonal manner. Because of this, it is considered the first *oblique* spaceship. A couple of years later, in 2013, Dave Greene devised the first self-replicating structure that not only replicates a complete copy of itself but also replicates the instructions needed to carry out the replication.

But how is this self-replication possible? To see this, we might benefit from a helpful abstraction. If we construe the presence or absence of gliders as 'bits' of information (akin to the 1s and 0s inside a computer), what kind of structures are possible within the Game of Life? It turns out we can actually construct Universal Turing Machines within the Game of Life. That is, we can construct virtual machines that do what *any* computer can do! And it is through virtual machines like these that the computations necessary for self-replication become possible. While we will not explore Turing Machines in any depth, we will take a peek into some of the structures that make these machines possible in the Game of Life.

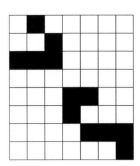

Figure 11.8 A Glider and an Eater.

In order to accomplish this self-replication, a few additional structures are needed: eaters and glider guns. These structures are critical because they enable the detection and control of 'information.' Figure 11.8 is a diagram of a glider in the top-left corner and an eater in the bottom-right corner.

Eaters are remarkable structures. They are aptly named because they are able to destroy (or 'eat') other structures while preserving themselves. In this example, the glider moves toward the eater and when they encounter each other, the glider is destroyed in four steps, and the original structure of the eater is restored. Here is how William Poundstone describes this interaction:

> An eater can eat a glider in four generations. Whatever is being consumed, the basic process is the same. A bridge forms between the eater and its prey. In the next generation, the bridge region dies from overpopulation, taking a bite out of both eater and prey. The eater then repairs itself. The prey usually cannot. If the remainder of the prey dies out as with the glider, the prey is consumed.
>
> (Poundstone, 2013, p. 31)

Exercise: Try running your Game of Life simulation with an initial state that includes a configuration like the one shown above and see for yourself how gliders and eaters interact.

Now let's take a look at a more complex structure, the glider gun. As shown in Figure 11.9, it is composed of several pieces: two shuttles and two still life squares.

When the shuttles collide, the collision generates a glider that shoots off toward the bottom right of the grid. The shuttles then horizontally reverse directions toward the two still life squares. When the shuttles make contact with the squares, the shuttles reverse directions again leaving the squares intact and the entire process repeats itself. This is a complex composite structure that endlessly generates gliders in 30-step cycles! If you

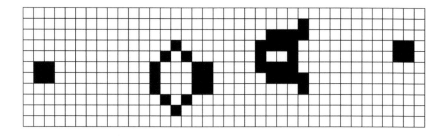

Figure 11.9 Glider Gun.

have a large enough screen, you will see a steady stream of gliders (roughly five diagonal cells apart) shooting out of this structure at regular intervals.

Practice: Try running your Game of Life simulation with an initial state that includes a configuration like the one shown above and see for yourself how glider guns endlessly generate gliders.

With these structures, we can now begin manipulating gliders in a way that allows us to treat them as bits of information. By treating the presence of a glider as a 1 and the absence of a glider as a 0, we can construct the rudimentary building blocks of a computer. Let's see how (in an abstract way with many missing details!) a simple operation might be executed using glider guns, gliders, and eaters.

One of the basic building blocks of a computer is the AND operation. It takes 1s and 0s as inputs and returns a 1 or 0 as an output. This operation returns 1 if and only if both inputs are 1s. If either (or both) of the inputs are 0, then this operation returns 0. If we interpret the 1 as being True and 0 as being False, this is how we would expect the logical and operator to work in Python.

Figure 11.10 depicts how an AND operator might be implemented in the Game of Life. G represents a glider gun and E represents an eater. The arrows represent the paths a glider might take. The arrow going from G to E represents a steady stream of gliders that are generated by G and eaten by E. Inputs A and B, depending on whether they are 1s or 0s, will either have a glider or not have a glider. The 'X's along the arrow going from G to E represent potential fatal collisions between gliders. Should Input A send out a glider (representing a 1), the system is set up so that this glider will collide with one of the gliders in the stream from G to E, and both gliders will be destroyed. The point is that any glider sent out by Input A will be destroyed by one of the gliders in the stream generated from G.

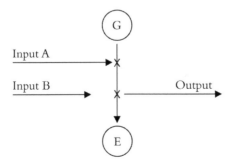

Figure 11.10 A schematic for an implementation of the AND operator in the Game of Life.

Notice that the arrow representing Input A is longer than the arrow representing Input B. This signifies that the glider representing Input B must lag behind Input A by the precise number of steps that it takes for G to generate gliders. That is, the gliders must be staggered. If gliders from Input A and Input B are not staggered and sent out together, then both gliders will be destroyed by gliders in the stream from G to E.

Given this setup, if Inputs A and B are staggered and send out gliders, the glider from Input A will collide with the glider generated by G that would have collided with the glider from Input B. This allows the glider from Input B to proceed unobstructed. If there were no glider from Input A then the glider from Input B would have collided with the glider generated by G. In this way, a glider will only appear in the Output if both Inputs A and B send gliders. That is, this structure will only yield a 1 (i.e., a glider) in the output if both inputs are 1s.

This is a remarkable accomplishment! Using eaters, gliders, and glider guns, we are able to create a mechanism that simulates the AND operation in circuit design. While we are just barely getting a glimpse of how a Universal Turing Machine might be constructed, it is at least a tantalizing glimmer! If you want to explore how to actually implement a Universal Turing Machine in the Game of Life, I invite you to look through the documentation in Rendell (2000).

The upshot of this discussion is that something at least as sophisticated as a computer—like the one on your desk—can exist in the Game of Life! Take a moment to consider all the amazing things that we're doing today with computers. We can type essays on word processors, we can have video conference calls over the internet, we can watch movies, etc. Moreover, consider the many recent breakthroughs in machine learning that are making once-intractable problems tractable. We use computers to recognize faces, synthesize speech, and translate languages. It turns out *all* of the computations necessary for such breakthroughs can be executed within this extremely simple system—a two-dimensional grid of cells with two possible states and a few deterministic rules.[4]

Here's how Dennett summarizes this:

> The information-handling ability of gigantic Life-forms is equivalent to the information-handling ability of our real three-dimensional computers. Any competence you can "put on a chip" and embed in a 3-D contraption can be perfectly mimicked by a similarly embedded Life constellation in a still larger Life-form in two dimensions. We know it exists in principle.
>
> (Dennett, 2003, pp. 45–46)

Bringing matters back to the issues introduced at the beginning of this chapter, how does all this potentiality help us think about free will? What we know is that all the necessary ingredients are available in the Game of Life for the evolution of structures that can carry out complex tasks (including glider discrimination and self-replication).

These structures will have various 'powers.' But which of these structures will be the best at persisting (or surviving)? As we've seen, some have the power to move, while some even have the power to consume. Clearly, structures with additional powers like these will have better ways of surviving. But we can easily dream up fancier structures that have the power to 'observe' their environments. Turing Machines within the Game of Life have just this power. They are able to discriminate between the presence and absence of gliders.

Here is where we get to Dennett's more adventurous ideas. If we assume that observation is the ability to gather information about the environment and further assume that gliders are photons of light in the Game of Life (entities that set the absolute limit on how quickly information can travel), then the ability to detect gliders can be construed as a kind of sight. And with such a power comes the potential for avoiding threats. Dennett writes:

> This is the birth of avoidance; this is the birth of prevention, protection, guidance, enhancement, and all the other fancier, more expensive sorts of action. And right at the moment of birth, we can discern the key distinction we will need later on: Some kinds of harms can, in principle, be avoided, and some kinds of harms are unavoidable.
>
> (Dennett, 2003, p. 43)

> [The existence of avoiders] is what we need to break the back of the cognitive illusion that yokes determinism with inevitability.
>
> (Dennett, 2003, p. 51)

Dennett thinks that many who are worried about the incompatibility of free will and determinism are worried because of the *inevitability* that lurks within determinism. If everything is determined, then everything is inevitable. When everything that happens is inevitable, how can we ever exercise the ability to make choices?

But consider for a moment that 'inevitable' might be translated as 'unavoidable.' If this is right, then there seems to be tension in what is possible within a deterministic world, like the Game of Life. Not everything is unavoidable. With the development of complex structures that can make observations and use this information to react, avoidance becomes a distinct possibility. Dennett writes:

> We have seen that in a deterministic world such as the Life world we can design things that are better at avoiding harms in that world than

other things are, and these things owe their very persistence to this prowess.

(Dennett, 2003, p. 56)

So, it seems not everything is 'inevitable' in a deterministic world.

Question: Can you logically analyze Dennett's argument and put it in premise-conclusion form?

One way to reconstruct his argument is as follows:

Dennett's Argument

1. In some deterministic worlds, there are avoiders avoiding harm.
2. Therefore, in some deterministic worlds some things are avoided.
3. If something is avoided, then something is avoidable (or not inevitable).
4. Therefore, in some deterministic worlds, something is not inevitable.
5. Therefore, determinism does not imply inevitability.

Discussion: Is this a charitable reconstruction of Dennett's reasoning? Are there any weak premises? What do you think of Dennett's use of the Game of Life to introduce structures that have the ability to avoid collisions? Does this help with a defense of compatibilism?

A natural response to Dennett's argument is to complain that the kind of avoidance occurring in the Game of Life is not 'real' avoidance. What real avoidance requires (the kind necessary for free will) is the ability to *change* something that was going to happen into something that doesn't happen.

But what does 'going to happen' mean in this context? There are a variety of avoidance responses we see in the actual world. They lie on a spectrum of simple 'hard-wired' responses to extremely complex responses. On the simple 'hard-wired' end, consider the blink reflex most humans have. Our eyes are so sensitive to swiftly moving objects and small debris that we blink reflexively even when there is nothing present that can harm our eyes. This is a very simple, involuntary avoidance response. But even in this simple case, the blink reflex succeeds in avoiding debris from entering your eye and thereby changes something that was going to happen (i.e., debris entering your eye) into something that doesn't happen (i.e. debris not entering your eye).

You might complain that the blink reflex didn't really change what was going to happen. The blink reflex itself and the debris not entering your eye should have also figured into the prediction of what was going to happen. So, there was no real avoidance of debris in the sense that the blink reflex changed what was going to happen (i.e., debris entering your eye) into something that doesn't happen (i.e., debris not entering your eye). Given the blink reflex, it was never the case that the debris was going to enter your eye. The blink reflex, after all, is another part of the unfolding of the universe that must be accounted for.

But now consider a more complex example. A ball is thrown at you in a game of dodgeball that you deftly avoid. In what sense was the ball's hitting you going to happen? Perhaps the ball was never really going to hit you since your biological avoidance system, acting much like the blink reflex, instinctively reacted to your observation of the incoming ball. Everything is unfolding in a deterministic way so the ball was never going to hit you! Notice, however, that you can respond to *additional* information. Maybe you also know that if you get hit and exit the game at that point in time, your team will have a better chance of winning. So, you ultimately decide to resist your pending avoidance behavior. Of course, you could even resist resisting your initial avoidance behavior if you had a hidden strategy that, contrary to popular wisdom in the sport of dodgeball, staying in the game actually gives your team a better chance for victory. This is a very complex and nuanced form of avoidance!

Should we treat the entire spectrum of avoidance behaviors as being not 'real' avoidance? Perhaps a case can be made that the complex avoidance of avoidance should count as 'real' avoidance. Dennett, of course, considers many more objections in his book. This overview gives a flavor of how the Game of Life opens up conceptual space to think about the latent possibilities in deterministic worlds and even generates novel ways of understanding complex behaviors.

Key Points

- Incompatibilists and compatibilists disagree over the compatibility between free will and determinism.
- Some incompatibilists argue that alternate possibilities are necessary for free will.
- Some have developed the conditional analysis as a way of defending compatibilism.
- Some have developed examples that purport to show that moral responsibility does not require alternate possibilities as a way of defending compatibilism.
- Conway's Game of Life may be used as a practical aid to think about these issues.

Endnotes

1   This is not to say that there are many *actual* past histories. While there is only one actual past history, given information about a given state of the grid, it is impossible to deduce which of a set of possible past histories the actual past history is.

2   Technically speaking, there is nothing that is moving—only stationary cells that live and die. The death of cells on one side and the growth of new cells on the other make it appear as if the glider moving.
3   See, for example, the online community of Game of Life enthusiasts at https://www.conwaylife.com/.
4   Some are convinced that something akin to biological evolution can occur within the simple deterministic world of the Game of Life that might eventually produce self-replicating structures (they don't simply have to be created by programmer-gods like Rendell). To get a feel for how this might be possible, see Mark Niemiec's (2010) paper on the structures that can be created purely through the collisions of gliders. He showed, for example, how a glider gun can be constructed through the collision of seven gliders.

References

Cave, S. (2016, June). There's No Such Thing as Free Will. *Atlantic*. https://www.theatlantic.com/magazine/archive/2016/06/theres-no-such-thing-as-free-will/480750/

Dennett, D. (2003). *Freedom Evolves*. New York: Viking.

Frankfurt, H. (1969). Alternate Possibilities and Moral Responsibility. *Journal of Philosophy, 66*, 829–839.

Ginet, C. (2003). Libertarianism. In M. Loux, & D. Zimmerman, *The Oxford Handbook of Metaphysics* (pp. 587–612). Oxford: Oxford University Press.

Laplace, P.-S. (1995). *Philosophical Essay on Probabilities*. New York: Springer.

Moore, G. (2005). *Ethics*. Oxford: Oxford University Press.

Niemiec, M. (2010). Object Synthesis in Conway's Game of Life and Other Cellular Automata. In A. Adamatzky, *Game of Life Cellular Automata* (pp. 115–134). London: Springer.

Poundstone, W. (2013). *The Recursive Universe: Cosmic Complexity and the Limits of Scientific Knowledge*. New York: Dover.

Rendell, P. (2000, April 2). *Turing Machine Implemented in Conway's Game of Life*. Retrieved from Paul's Home Page on Rendell-Attic: http://rendell-attic.org/gol/tm.htm

Van Inwagen, P. (1983). *An Essay on Free Will*. Oxford: Oxford University Press.

Chapter 12

Recursion

We've learned about and defined our own functions in previous chapters, and we've seen that functions are very useful for a variety of purposes. By writing good functions, we can create abstractions and then use these abstractions to think about problems at higher, more conceptual levels. So far, however, we've only looked at functions that call other functions. What would happen if we created a function that called *itself*?

Well, that's precisely what we do when we use **recursion**. As a programming technique, recursive programming can be thought of as a method for solving a problem by solving a slightly easier version of the same problem. At a more theoretical level, it is an important concept that is found in all sorts of other domains. Recursion, for example, is used in mathematics for generating inductive proofs. Consider the summation formula:

$$1 + 2 + 3 + \ldots + n = \frac{n(n+1)}{2}$$

How can we prove that this formula holds for all values of n? We can do this recursively by making sure this formula works for a trivial case like $n = 1$ since we already know what the answer should be, namely 1.

If we plug $n = 1$ into the formula, we get $1(1 + 1)/2$, which resolves to 1. We know that the formula works in the simplest case. Now we can simply check whether the formula is consistent when applied to adjacent values of n. We know, for example, that the summation of n (the original problem) should be equal to the sum of the summation of $n - 1$ (a slightly simpler version of the original problem) and n. We can represent this as follows.

$$1 + 2 + 3 + \ldots + n = (1 + 2 + 3 + \ldots + n - 1) + n$$

Using the summation formula, we can calculate the summation of $n - 1$:

$$1 + 2 + 3 + \ldots + n - 1 = \frac{(n-1)n}{2}$$

DOI: 10.4324/9781003271284-12

Taking this and adding n eventually yields the original formula:

$$1 + 2 + 3 + \ldots + n = \frac{n^2 - n}{2} + n$$

$$1 + 2 + 3 + \ldots + n = \frac{n^2 - n + 2n}{2}$$

$$1 + 2 + 3 + \ldots + n = \frac{n^2 + n}{2}$$

$$1 + 2 + 3 + \ldots + n = \frac{n(n+1)}{2}$$

This proves that the summation formula works for all positive integers greater than or equal to 1.

Languages can also have a recursive structure. Consider the following sentence:

Computer science is fun.

This sentence has a simple structure: subject-verb-adjective. Now that we have a rule for sentence structure, we can use this in defining another sentence structure: subject-'thinks that'-*sentence*. Notice this second rule for defining sentence structure involves sentences themselves. It allows us to produce a sentence that embeds the previous sentence like this:

Lila thinks that computer science is fun.

This sentence, in turn, can be embedded in a further sentence:

Dana thinks that Lila thinks that computer science is fun.

We could continue constructing sentences like this indefinitely.

Discussion: Where else do you see recursion at work?

Recursive Programming

To get a handle on using recursion, let's think of a simple function that has a recursive structure. Consider the multiplication of two positive integers: x*y. How can this be conceived of in terms of a slightly simpler problem of the exact same structure? We might note the following:

```
x * y = x * (y-1) + x
```

Here, we are trying to answer the original problem, x*y, by using the answer to a slightly simpler problem of the same structure, x* (y-1). If I knew the answer to this slightly simpler problem, all I'd have to do is add x to this in order to solve the original problem. So, I'm solving a multiplication problem by solving a slightly simpler multiplication problem. The hope is that once this simplifying process reaches a point of sufficient simplicity, I will have solved the original problem. As a first pass, we might write a function that recursively solves multiplication as follows.

```
def multiply(x,y):
    return x + multiply(x,y-1)
```

Notice the return value of this function is precisely what I described in the previous paragraph. x is being added to the result of multiplying x and y-1. What do you think will happen when you execute the following statement?

```
multiply(5,4)
```

Unfortunately, this will result in an error.

```
RecursionError: maximum recursion depth exceeded
```

This means that the recursive process of multiply calling itself went into an infinite loop. At some point, the number of recursive calls that can be handled by the computer reaches a limit because the computer simply doesn't have enough memory. Let's take a closer look at why this happens by tracing out the evaluation of the original function call.

```
multiply(5,4)
5 + multiply(5,3)
5 + 5 + multiply(5,2)
...
5 + 5 + 5 + 5 + 5 + multiply(5,-1)
...
```

You can see that the input value for the y variable gets decremented by one at every recursive call. The problem, however, is that there is no instruction within the function to *stop* the recursive calls when y reaches a certain level of simplicity.

Question: At what point should the recursive calls end?

The recursive calls should end when y is equal to 1. It can be considered the 'simplest' case in trying to solve the problem of multiplying two positive integers. We know the answer immediately because the calculation is trivial, it's simply whatever the value of x is. To reflect this insight, we might change the original function as follows.

```
def multiply(x,y):
    if y == 1:
        return x
    return x + multiply(x,y-1)
```

The y == 1 condition specifies what programmers often call the **base case**. It is the case that stops the recursion, and it should include a solution to the most trivial version of the problem you're trying to solve.

We see from this example that there are two parts to writing a good recursive function: (1) a base case and (2) a recursive case. In more complicated recursive functions, however, you might need multiple base cases and multiple recursive cases. But we'll set that worry aside for now.

Let's consider the classic problem (found in many textbooks) for introducing recursive functions: factorial. The factorial of a positive integer n, written as n!, is the product of all the positive integers less than or equal to n. It follows from this definition that 5! is 5*4*3*2*1, which equals 120. It's pretty easy to see the recursive nature of factorial because 5! is really just 5*4!. More generally, n! is really just n*(n-1)!.

So, we can see what the recursive case amounts to. But what about the base case? Another way to ask this question might be: what is the *simplest* case for calculating factorials? The case that requires no thought to compute is when n is equal to 1. 1! is simply 1. We can put these two ideas together and write a recursive function that computes factorials.

```
def factorial(n):
    if n == 1:                # base case
        return 1
    return n * factorial(n-1) # recursive case
```

Notice that this is structurally very similar to the implementation of multiply above.

Exercise 12.1: Write a recursive function called summation that takes a single positive integer n as input and returns the sum of all the positive integers that are less than or equal to n.

Exercise 12.2: Write a recursive function called exponent that takes two non-negative integers, x and y, and returns xy.

So far, we have been writing recursive functions that deal with numbers as inputs, but what about recursive functions that deal with structured objects, like lists or strings, as inputs? Consider the problem of adding up all the numbers in a list like the following.

```
[24, 55, 19, 92, 1, 42]
```

How can I generate a solution to this problem by solving a slightly simpler version of the same problem? Solving the same problem with the *same* list *without* the first number would be slightly simpler.

```
[55, 19, 92, 1, 42]
```

If I could calculate the sum of all the numbers in this slightly simpler list, then all I'd have to do to solve the original problem is add the first number, 24, to this sum. This is the recursive call. But what about the base case? What kind of list would be trivial to solve? The easiest case would be the empty list. We know the answer to this immediately: zero. There are no computations to execute since there are no numbers to add! We can implement this as follows.

```
def sum_list(L):
    if len(L) == 0:              # base case
        return 0
    return L[0] + sum_list(L[1:])  # recursive case
```

One way to check for an empty list is to see if the length of L is equal to 0. Another way would be to check the following equality: L == []. Accessing the first number of the list can be done by indexing the list at 0. Creating a new list that is a copy of L without the first number can be done with a slice L[1:]. Remember this slices the list beginning at index 1 (the second number in L) and ending at the last number in the list. This is useful to remember when trying to recursively work through lists (or strings or any other structured type that can be indexed and sliced).

Exercise 12.3: Revise the sum_list function so that it can take lists with numbers and other types of objects and return the sum of *only* the numbers (e.g., [5, 'Hi', 8, True, 1] should return 14). Hint: use the type function to ensure that you will only add int or float objects. You must solve this recursively!

Now let's consider a recursive function that deals with lists as inputs *and* outputs. What if, given a list of integers, I wanted to filter out all the even numbers so that what's left is a list of only the odd numbers? Given the following list:

```
[1,2,3,4,5]
```

This function should return:

```
[1,3,5]
```

Let's begin thinking about this problem by figuring out what a base case might be. The simplest list to filter would be an empty list. Since there are no numbers in it to begin with, there's nothing to filter—we'd simply return an empty list. So much for the base case.

What about the recursive case? Well, a slightly simpler problem to solve, given the initial input list, would be the same list without the first number.

```
[2,3,4,5]
```

Now, if we had the solution to this problem, which is the list [3,5], what should we do with the first number, 1? It depends on whether that number is even. If it's even, we don't have to do anything—the solution to the slightly simpler problem will literally be the solution to the original problem. If it's odd, however, we should add it to the front of the solution to the slightly simpler problem. Since the first number is 1 and it's odd, it should be added to the front of [3,5]. And that's pretty much it.

We can implement these ideas as follows.

```
def filter_odd(L):
    if len(L) == 0:     # base case
        return []
    if L[0] % 2 == 0:   # first number is even, do nothing
        return filter_odd(L[1:])
    else:               # first number is odd, add it
        return [L[0]] + filter_odd(L[1:])
```

Make sure you understand how each line of code corresponds to the logic laid out in the previous paragraph. It may seem a bit like magic that this works. So long as a proper base case has been given, it can be assumed that *all* recursive calls to the function itself (filter_odd) within the function will produce the correct answer. Given this, we simply have to deal with the first number of L when dealing with the recursive cases.

If you're still having trouble understanding the code for filter_odd, it may be helpful to get clear on the type of object that is returned by filter_odd. The object returned by any successful call of filter_odd is a list. With this in mind, if L is the list [1,2,3,4,5], then the recursive call filter_odd(L[1:]) can simply be seen as the list [3,5]. All that would be needed to generate an answer to the original problem would be to add 1 to the beginning of this list.

Don't worry if you still feel a bit overwhelmed by recursive programming. It can feel unnatural at first, and it takes a bit of practice to get the hang of it. So, the key is to work on a lot of exercises.

Exercise 12.4: Write a recursive function called count that takes a list of numbers L and a number n as input and returns the number of numbers in L that are less than n.

Exercise 12.5: Write a recursive function called palindrome that takes a string S as input and returns True if it is a palindrome and False otherwise. A palindrome is a word that is spelled the same backward. For example, the strings 'pop' and 'racecar' are both palindromes.

Hint: the base case is when S has a length that is less than or equal to 1. All such strings are automatically palindromes. And don't forget that the return value of this function, unlike previous functions, is a Boolean value (not a number, a list, or a string).

Hanoi Tower

Now you might be thinking that recursive programming is actually quite difficult! The problems above could be solved by using for or while loops. That is, we could've solved them *iteratively*. In fact, most of the problems above might have been solved more easily had they been solved iteratively (by the way, rewriting all the functions above iteratively would be great practice!).

But this is not always the case. Consider the so-called **Hanoi Tower** problem. You have a board with three pegs labeled A, B, and C. There are a variable number of disks that are labeled 1, 2, 3, and so on. Disks can be stacked on top of each other as depicted in Figure 12.1. Disk 1 is stacked on top of disk 2 which, in turn, is stacked on top of disk 3. Only the top disk of any stack can be moved to another peg. So, given the state of the board depicted in the figure, only disk 1 can be moved and it can be moved to either peg B or C. Disks 2 and 3, at least in this situation, cannot be moved. The other critical constraint is that bigger disks can never be

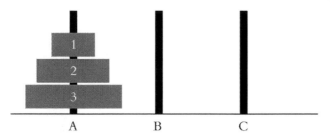

Figure 12.1 Hanoi Tower.

stacked on top of smaller disks. For example, disks 2 and 3 can never be stacked on top of disk 1. And disk 3 can never be stacked on disk 2.

The task is to generate step-by-step instructions that will move a stack of blocks beginning on a certain peg to a destination peg. For example, I may want to move the stack of disks from peg A to peg C. Given only three disks, we can figure this out without the help of a computer. Here are the instructions.

```
Move the disk from peg A to peg C.
Move the disk from peg A to peg B.
Move the disk from peg C to peg B.
Move the disk from peg A to peg C.
Move the disk from peg B to peg A.
Move the disk from peg B to peg C.
Move the disk from peg A to peg C.
```

Can you verify that the steps above correctly solve the problem?

But what if there are five disks in the initial stack? What if there are ten disks?! I would have no idea how to begin, let alone program a computer to solve it for me. This could become a nightmare to figure out. Here, we can think up a rather elegant recursive solution. The key is to figure out the base case and the recursive cases.

Let's start with the base case. What is the easiest case to solve? It would be the case where the initial stack of disks only contains a single disk. The solution, in this case, would be trivial—simply move the disk from the starting peg to the desired destination peg. That was easy!

Now that the base case is taken care of, we just have to figure out the recursive case. Let's assume that we have a stack of n disks on peg A and we want to move this stack to peg C. What slightly easier problem do we need to solve in order to do this? Well, a slightly easier problem would involve moving a stack of n-1 disks. If we could move the first n-1 disks from peg A to peg B (the peg that is neither the starting peg nor the destination peg), then we could easily move the one remaining disk on peg A (the largest disk) to peg C. Then we simply move the stack of n-1 disks from peg B to peg C. And we're finished!

But how would we implement this?

Given that the recursive logic is pretty straightforward, the most important step may be to carefully specify the inputs to the function we want to write. The inputs must include an integer, n, which specifies the number of disks that are in the initial stack and the names of the labels of the pegs that represent the starting peg, s, the destination peg, d, and the leftover peg, l (the peg that is neither the starting peg nor the destination peg).

Here is one way to implement the algorithm:

```
def hanoi(n, s, d, l):
    if n == 1:
        print('Move the disk from peg ' + s + ' to peg ' +
d + '.')
    else:
        hanoi(n-1, s, l, d) # move n-1 disks from s to l
        hanoi(1, s, d, l)   # move 1 disk from s to d
        hanoi(n-1, l, d, s) # move n-1 disks from l to d
```

Note how succinct the code is! Try executing this with a stack of 3 disks to verify that it works correctly. Does it generate the same set of instructions as above?

```
>>> hanoi(3,'A','C','B')
```

Try executing this with a stack of 5 disks (or 10). Does it generate the right instructions? It never ceases to amaze me how elegant the *recursive* solution to the Hanoi Tower problem is. By conceptualizing the problem in terms of simpler versions of the same problem, the solution was relatively easy to implement.

Recursive versus Iterative Programming

Recursive programming can be very useful. In many cases, the code needed to solve a problem is just plain beautiful. More importantly, recursive programs can be very easy to understand and explain to another person. The conceptual logic can often be directly translated into code. Should you go on to do more programming, you may also find that recursive programming lends itself to elegant code for processing grammars, trees, and graphs among other things (not to mention my favorite sorting algorithm: merge sort!). But this goes beyond the scope of this book. The take-home message is that there are certain problems that are more intuitively solvable when using recursion.

One of the major drawbacks of recursive programming is that it may require a lot more memory than iterative programming. If you go back to the recursive implementation of multiplication, you'll notice that multiply(5,4) would end up executing 5 + multiply(5,3). But notice that the + operator cannot be executed because we still don't know what multiply(5,3) evaluates to. Evaluating multiply(5,3), in turn, ends up executing 5 + multiply(5,2). But the + operator in this case also cannot be executed because we still don't know what multiply(5,2) evaluates to. This goes on, of course, until the base case is reached and the pending + operations will complete executing in reverse order.

Why does this require the use of more memory? If you recall, every time a function is called, it must keep track of its own set of local variables. Among other things, this helps us avoid potentially confusing naming conflicts. So if I have a variable called x outside of a function definition, and I also have a variable called x inside a function definition (either as an input variable or as a variable within the block of code comprising the function body), these two xs must carefully be distinguished. Storing and distinguishing the values of these two variables requires memory. Python has to remember the x that exists outside the function and the x that exists inside the function (which is distinct from the previous x).

In a recursive function, with each recursive call to the same function, a new set of local variables must be tracked that are distinct from all previous recursive calls and all future recursive calls. As the number of recursive calls grows, the amount of memory required to remember all the variables in each recursive call grows. This is why, when we initially defined a recursive function without a base case, it led to an infinite loop that quickly exhausted the amount of memory available for performing recursion.

The upshot is that recursive programming often produces elegant and easily understandable code, but at the cost of potentially overusing available memory. Nevertheless, it is a powerful programming tool that has a number of interesting applications and, some may argue, lies at the heart of computer science itself.

Key Points

- Recursion is found in other domains like math and linguistics.
- Recursion in computer science requires base cases and recursive cases.
- Recursion can be elegant and easy to understand.
- Recursion is different from iteration in important ways.

Chapter 13

God

The **philosophy of religion** is a branch of philosophy that deals with concepts and issues pertaining to religious traditions. Among the central issues in this branch of philosophy is the existence of God.[1] A variety of arguments for the existence of God have been developed over the centuries. The most enduring might be categorized into three broad groups: ontological arguments, teleological arguments, and cosmological arguments.

Discussion: What is your concept of God? Do you think there are good reasons to think that God does or does not exist?

Arguably, the most famous ontological (meaning 'being') argument can be traced back to the work of St. Anselm, an 11th-century Benedictine monk.[2] He argued that reflection on the very concept of God shows that God must exist. God, for Anselm, could be understood as a being than which no greater can be conceived.[3] Such a being *must* exist. For suppose that we believed, as atheists do, that such a being failed to exist. If this were the case, we would only be able to conceive of God (a being than which no greater can be conceived), but God would not exist. That is, God would only exist as an idea in one's mind, not in reality. But now it seems we would be able to conceive of a greater being. We could conceive of God as actually existing in reality! Surely the concept of an actually existing God is greater than the concept of God that does not exist. But this is a logical contradiction. How could we conceive of a being that is greater than a being than which no greater can be conceived? So, Anselm argued, the only way to avoid this contradiction is to reject the initial supposition—that God does not exist in reality, but only in one's mind. Therefore, God must exist in reality.

Teleological (meaning 'end' or 'purpose') arguments focus on features of things that exist within the universe (and even the universe itself) that suggest they are the result of design. A well-known version of the teleological argument can be traced back to William Paley, an 18th-century philosopher.[4] He argued that finding a watch on the ground would cause us to infer design—that the watch was a product of a designer, and not merely the result of chance. Paley went on to claim that plants, animals,

DOI: 10.4324/9781003271284-13

and particularly the biological eye naturally lead to the same design inference—that these entities must be the products of a designer. This designer, according to Paley, is God.[5]

Finally, cosmological (meaning 'order' or 'world') arguments focus on the claim that certain entities or events within the universe are dependent on something else for their existence. We know, for example, that our existence depends on our biological parents. The same can be said for our parents—their existence depends on their parents. The same can be said for our parents' parents, and so on. This observation might then be used to infer a *first* set of parents that makes the existence of all other parents in the human lineage possible. If we suppose a first set of parents did not exist, we would be left with an *infinite* regress of parents. This would be problematic (for reasons that aren't always so obvious).

Here is how Thomas Aquinas explains the problem:

> If we remove a cause the effect is removed; therefore, if there is no first among efficient causes, neither will there be a last or an intermediate. But if we proceed to infinity in efficient causes there will be no first efficient cause, and thus there will be no ultimate effect, nor any intermediate efficient causes, which is clearly false. Therefore it is necessary to suppose the existence of some first efficient cause, and this men call God.
>
> (Aquinas, 2006, p. 2)

Let's consider a concrete example. George Walker Bush (B_{10}), the 43rd president of the U.S., is someone who (at the time of my writing this) exists. A partial cause of George Walker Bush's existence was George Herbert Walker Bush (B_9), the 41st president of the U.S. A partial cause of George Herbert Walker Bush's existence was Prescott Bush (B_8). If we go back far enough we might eventually reach a *first* cause (B_1)—perhaps the first homo sapien. We might capture this causal series as follows:

$$B_1 \rightarrow \dots \rightarrow B_8 \rightarrow B_9 \rightarrow B_{10}$$

But let's assume that the causal series were infinite. This would mean, as Aquinas rightly observes, that there would be no first cause, B_1. Coupled with Aquinas' claim that if we remove a cause the effect is removed, it seems we are faced with a tension. If B_1 were to be removed, then its effect, B_2, would not occur. This, in turn, would result in the removal of B_2's effect and so on until we eventually reach the removal of B_8. The removal of B_8 would result in the removal of B_9 and ultimately the removal of B_{10}. But we all know that B_{10}, George W. Bush, exists (at the time of my writing this). The best way to resolve this tension, it seems, would be to reject the initial assumption that the causal series is infinite. So, we see that there must be a first cause in this causal series.

Discussion: Can you reconstruct Aquinas' argument in premise-conclusion form?

Here's how his argument might be reconstructed in premise-conclusion form:

Aquinas' Argument

1. Assume: causal series H has an infinite number of members.
2. If H has an infinite number of members, then H has no first cause.
3. If H has no first cause, then the present moment (i.e., the newest member of H) does not exist.
4. It is false that the present moment does not exist.
5. Therefore, it is false that H has no first cause.
6. Therefore, it is false that H has an infinite number of members.

This style of argument is sometimes called a *reductio ad absurdum*. Translated from Latin, this literally means "reduction to absurdity." It is an attempt to argue for a claim by showing that the falsity of that claim will lead to an absurdity. In Aquinas' case, he wanted to argue for the claim that the number of members in causal series H must be finite. So, he began with the negation of this claim: it is false that the number of members in causal series H must be finite (i.e., the number of members in H is infinite).

Discussion: What do you think of Aquinas' reasoning? Now that it has been explicitly reconstructed in premise-conclusion form, which premise do you think is the weakest? Why?

Paul Edwards (2006) has a succinct response to this argument. Returning to George W. Bush's causal history, if B_1 did not exist, one could reasonably argue that B_2 could not have existed. And if B_2 did not exist, one could reasonably argue that B_3 could not have existed, and so on. Indeed if B_1 did not exist, none of the subsequent members in this causal series would have come into existence.

But it seems that Aquinas fails to make a distinction between B_1's not existing and B_1's being caused. To say that this series is infinite is not to claim that B_1 does not exist. Rather, it is to claim that B_1 (like all the other members of this series) is caused. What follows is that B_1 *must* have a cause, B_0. B_0 must also have a cause, B_{-1}, and so on *ad infinitum*. Edwards offers the following example to develop this point:

> Suppose Captain Spaulding had said, "I am the greatest explorer who ever lived," and somebody replied, "No, you are not." This answer

would be denying that the Captain possessed the exalted attribute he had claimed for himself, but it would not be denying his existence. It would not be "taking him away." Similarly, the believer in the infinite series is not "taking [B_1] away." He is taking away the privileged status of [B_1]; he is taking away its "first causiness." He does not deny the *existence* of [B_1] or of any particular member of the series. He denies that [B_1] or anything else is *the first member* of the series.

(Edwards, 2006, p. 74)

Edwards, it seems, has provided an interesting response to Aquinas' argument. More specifically, we might say that Edwards attacks premise 3 of Aquinas' argument. Just because H has no first cause, it doesn't follow that a certain member in H stops existing. The only thing that follows is that there is no member of H that has the designation of being the first cause.

To look at this from a computational perspective, consider the following recursive implementation of factorial:

```
def factorial_r(n):
    if n == 1:
        return 1
    return n * factorial_r(n-1)
```

Using this definition, we can try executing the statement: `factorial_r(99)`. Since n is initially equal to 99 this will result in the following return value:

```
99 * factorial_r(98)
```

Notice that this product cannot be calculated until `factorial_r(98)` is executed. Since n is now equal to 98, this will result in the following return value:

```
98 * factorial_r(97)
```

If we plug this back into the original return value by substituting `factorial_r(98)` with `98 * factorial_r(97)`, we get the following:

```
99 * 98 * factorial_r(97)
```

As we continue to work out the calculation of recursive calls, we will drive the value of n down toward 1. In the meantime, the original return value, which involves a growing list of multiplication operators, will continue to expand.

```
99 * 98 * 97 * ... * 32 * 31 * factorial_r(30)
```

Notice that *not a single* multiplication operation has been calculated yet. Only when the recursive calls reach the base case, where n equals 1, will the recursion cease, and the multiplication operations actually get executed.

So how is this relevant to Edwards' response? Consider the slightly modified version of the factorial_r function:

```
def factorial_r(n):
    return n * factorial_r(n-1)
```

It no longer has a base case. Perhaps we should rename the 'base' case to be the 'first' case. So, assuming our computer has an infinite amount of memory, executing factorial_r(99) will result in a never-ending expansion of multiplication operations.

```
99 * 98 * 97 * ... * 2 * 1 * 0 * -1 * -2 * ...
```

By removing the 'first' case, the ever-expanding series of multiplication operations did not get eliminated. Notice that the 1 still exists as part of the multiplication expression. What has changed, however, is that the 1 no longer has the privileged status of being the 'first' number in the multiplication expression. So, it seems, we have a way of corroborating Edwards' insight by reflecting on the way a recursive function like factorial_r gets evaluated.

The Kalam Cosmological Argument

Rather than take a historical look at the different versions of cosmological arguments that have been developed since Aquinas, let's consider a recent version of the cosmological argument developed by William Lane Craig (1979) that may bypass Edwards' response to Aquinas' argument. Here is how Craig regiments his argument:

Kalam Argument

1. Everything that begins to exist has a cause of its existence.
2. The universe began to exist.
3. Therefore, the universe has a cause of its existence.

The upshot of the argument is to provide evidence for a first cause of the universe that transcends time and space. The reason it is called the 'Kalam' cosmological argument is because it was inspired by ideas that arose through medieval Islamic scholasticism referred to as the *kalam*, which is short for *Ilm al-Kalam* (Arabic for "science of discourse").

Because premise 1 is 'so intuitively obvious,'[6] the critical premise in this argument, according to Craig, is premise 2. In defense of premise 2, Craig offers two philosophical arguments and two scientific arguments. The scientific arguments are based on the empirical merits of big bang cosmology and the second law of thermodynamics. Big bang cosmology is the (currently) most well-attested cosmological theory of the universe's origin, and it strongly suggests that there was a beginning to the universe. The second law of thermodynamics can be stated as follows: all systems have the tendency to pass from a more ordered to a less ordered state. What this suggests about our universe is that all the energy within it will eventually become evenly distributed—the so-called 'heat death' of the universe. If this is so and the universe had existed for an infinite amount of time, then it would be puzzling that the universe had not already reached heat death. The fact that the energy in the universe is *not* yet evenly distributed suggests that the universe could not have existed for an infinite amount of time.

Craig's first philosophical argument in defense of premise 2 is based on the claim that an *actual* infinite cannot exist. Borrowing from Zermelo-Fraenkel's axiomatic set theory, he defines an actual infinite set as:

> ... any set R that has a proper subset that is equivalent to R. A proper subset is a subset that does not exhaust all the members of the original set, that is to say, at least one member of the original set is not also a member of the subset. Two sets are said to be equivalent if the members of one set can be related to the members of the other set in a one-to-one correspondence, that is, so that a single member of the one set corresponds to a member of the other set and vice versa.
>
> (Craig, 1979, p. 68)

Why think actual infinites cannot exist? Craig offers a memorable example developed by mathematician David Hilbert, affectionately called "Hilbert's Hotel." Imagine an ordinary hotel with a finite number of rooms that is fully occupied—there are no empty rooms. If a new guest arrives, the manager will reluctantly be forced to turn the guest away. Now imagine Hilbert's Hotel. It's an extraordinary hotel with an actual infinite number of rooms that is also fully occupied—there are no empty rooms. If a new guest arrives, the manager will happily accept the guest. The manager simply shifts the guests over one room. The guest in room 1 is moved to room 2, the guest in room 2 is moved to room 3, and so on *ad infinitum*. This leaves room 1 open for the new guest. But this is absurd! How can a fully occupied hotel have room for a new guest? It seems that countenancing actual infinites entails the absurd possibility of Hilbert's Hotel.

The situation, however, may be worse than it first appears. Imagine Hilbert's Hotel again, fully occupied. This time, not one, but an actual infinite number of new guests arrive. The manager happily accepts them all. The manager simply shifts all the current guests to rooms with numbers that are twice as large as the numbers of their original rooms. So the guest in room 1 is moved to room 2, the guest in room 2 is moved to room 4, the guest in room 3 is moved to room 6, and so on *ad infinitum*. The result of these room changes results in all the even-numbered rooms being occupied and all the odd-numbered rooms being available. Since the set of odd numbers is a set with an actual infinite number of members, Hilbert's Hotel is now ready to welcome an actual infinite number of new guests despite being fully occupied! These absurd results stem from the nature of actual infinites—that the number of elements in a proper subset of a set with an actual infinite number of elements can be equivalent to the number of elements in the set itself.[7]

Discussion: What do you think about Craig's first philosophical defense of premise 2? Is it convincing? Can you think of counterexamples?

There is much more to be said about Craig's first philosophical defense of premise 2, but let's now focus our attention on his second philosophical defense. It's based on the claim that it is impossible to form an actual infinite by successive addition. Craig regiments this in premise-conclusion form as follows:

Defense-of-P2 Argument

4. The temporal series of events is a collection formed by successive addition.
5. A collection formed by successive addition cannot be an actual infinite.
6. Therefore, the temporal series of events cannot be an actual infinite.

Craig uses the term 'the temporal series of events' to refer to the events that comprise the past history of our universe. If the universe does not have a beginning then the temporal series of events *must* have an actual infinite number of members. This is how one might describe the universe as having an infinite or beginning-less past. The term 'successive addition' can be thought of simply as counting in increments of one. Experience seems to verify the truth of premise 5. If you start counting from one in increments of one, you will never reach infinity. At any point in your counting, you would only have reached a finite number. Although you will be able to increment this number by one and generate another finite number, this process will never generate infinity.

Unlike the first philosophical defense of premise 2, this defense does not require the rejection of actual infinites. The point here is that, even if actual infinites exist, they could not have been constructed by successive addition. In a sense, they would have to exist all at once. The incremental creation of an actual infinite seems hopeless. Here is Craig in his own words:

> Sometimes this is described as the impossibility of counting to infinity for each new element added to the collection can be counted as it is added. It is important to understand exactly why it is impossible to form an actual infinite by successive addition. The reason is that for every element one adds, one can always add one more. Therefore, one can never arrive at infinity.
>
> (Craig, 1979, pp. 103–104)

If the temporal series of past events were a set with an actual infinite number of members, then it would be impossible to count through every member of this series. It would be like trying to count from zero to negative infinity. This might be illustrated with the following series:

```
Present → Past
0, -1, -2, -3, ...
```

We would have to count through all the past events in the universe's infinite history starting from the present moment. But this surely seems like an impossible task since we would have to count through an actual infinite number of past events. Consider the following function that simulates this counting:

```
from math import inf as infinity

def count(n):
    while n != -infinity:
        n = n - 1
        print('event',n)
```

The first line of code here simply imports the `inf` object (which represents infinity) from Python's `math` library and gives it the name `infinity`. Executing `count(1)` will print the following in an infinite loop:

```
event 0
event -1
event -2
...
event -10000
event -10001
event -10002
...
```

Now consider what would happen if we wanted to execute the following two statements:

```
count(1)
print('reached -infinity!')
```

Because `count(1)` would run forever, the subsequent `print` statement would never be reached.

Similarly (but in the reverse direction), if an infinite number of past events had to be counted in order for the present moment to be reached, then the present moment could never be reached. The critical observation, however, is that the present *has* been reached! This strongly suggests that there cannot be an actual infinite number of past events.

To hammer this point home, Craig goes on to use a vivid image:

> Before the present event could occur the event immediately prior to it would have to occur; and before that event could occur, the event immediately prior to it would have to occur; and so on ad infinitum. One gets driven back and back into the infinite past, making it impossible for any event to occur.
>
> (Craig & Sinclair, 2009, p. 118)

Here, I emphasize an important corollary from Craig's exposition. If the temporal series of events were an actual infinite, this would make "it impossible for *any event* to occur." Now, this sounds a lot like the reasoning Aquinas used in his argument. So it seems this image may have led Craig astray.

To illustrate Craig's corollary, consider again the recursive version of the factorial function defined above with a modification to the base case:

```
from math import inf as infinity

def factorial_r(n):
    if n == -infinity:
        return 1
    return n * factorial_r(n-1)
```

What happens when we execute `factorial_r(99)`? We saw that this generates a series of multiplication expressions like this:

```
99 * 98 * 97 * ... * 2 * factorial_r(1)
```

Because the base case is different, the recursive calls will not stop when n is 1. The recursive calls will only stop when n is -infinity. So, the number of multiplication expressions that get chained together continues to grow. The interesting observation here is that not a single multiplication expression will ever get evaluated because the base case will never be reached. If we treat the evaluation of a multiplication expression as an event then we could see, following Craig, that it would be 'impossible for *any event* to occur.'

Now let's compare the recursive version of the factorial function with an iterative version:

```
from math import inf as infinity

def factorial(n):
    total = 1
    while n > -infinity:
        total = total * n
        n = n - 1
    return total
```

Like the recursive version, `factorial` will enter an infinite loop. The critical difference, however, is that despite entering an infinite loop, the iterative version manages to evaluate multiplication expressions along the way. Every iteration of the `while` loop will handle the evaluation of a multiplication expression. The first iteration of the `while` loop when executing `factorial(99)` will result in the successful evaluation of `99 * 1`.

It seems, therefore, that Craig's corollary, when applied to the calculation of factorials, depends on certain features of how the relevant functions are defined. When factorial is computed recursively (according to `factorial_r`), we have a nice illustration in support of Craig's corollary. However, when computed iteratively, we seem to have a counterexample. Absent a reason to believe that the temporal series of events in the history of the universe unfolds recursively (and not iteratively), we might have a rationale for safely sidestepping Craig's corollary.

Key Points

- There are a variety of arguments for the existence of God.
- The cosmological argument for the existence of God depends on the nature of infinite series.
- Craig offers at least two reasons for thinking that the universe must begin to exist.
- Recursion and iteration may provide insights into the traversing of infinite series.

Notes

1 The philosophers' conception of God is not the Christian conception, the Jewish conception, nor any other conception from a particular religious tradition. It usually includes certain features like being omnipotent and omniscient.
2 See his book *Proslogion* (Anselm, 1965).
3 Note that this way of conceptually analyzing God does not necessarily coincide with the conceptual analysis of God consistent across the monotheistic religions like Judaism, Islam, and Christianity (i.e., an omnipotent, omniscient, and omnibenevolent being).
4 See his book *Natural Theology* (Paley, 1963).
5 Note that this way of conceptually analyzing God is limited to God's being a designer (an agent with intentions). This doesn't necessarily coincide with a being than which no greater can be conceived nor does it necessarily coincide with an omnipotent, omniscient, and omnibenevolent being.
6 You may disagree with this claim, but it seems to me that it's not completely obvious there are examples of things that *begin* to exist that have no cause.
7 Although this is not absurd when it comes to sets, it *is* absurd if we take Hilbert's Hotel to be an actual, physical hotel.

References

Anselm, S. (1965). *Proslogion*. (M. Charlesworth, Trans.) Oxford: Oxford University Press.

Aquinas, T. (2006). The Five Ways. In L. Pojman, *Philosophy: The Quest for Truth*. Oxford: Oxford University Press.

Craig, W. L. (1979). *The Kalam Cosmological Argument*. London: Macmillan Press.

Craig, W. L., & Sinclair, J. D. (2009). The Kalam Cosmological Argument. In W. L. Craig, & J. Moreland, *The Blackwell Companion to Natural Theology* (pp. 101–201). London: Blackwell.

Edwards, P. (2006). A Critique of the Cosmological Argument. In L. Pojman, *Philosophy: The Quest for Truth* (pp. 72–81). Oxford: Oxford University Press.

Paley, W. (1963). *Natural Theology*. Indianapolis, IN: Bobbs-Merrill.

Chapter 14

Data

Files

Python allows programmers to remember information in at least two different ways. One is through variables, as we discussed early on in this book, the other is through **files**. The key difference between these two ways of remembering is that the former only lasts as long as the session of Python you're running. The latter, however, is persistent—it not only lasts beyond any given Python session, but it persists even after the computer is turned off. You can think of the two ways of keeping track of things as short-term and long-term memory.

Files are also important because they serve as a way of sharing information between different programs and computers (and hence people). Very large amounts of data are stored and shared through files. Often the amount of data is so vast that only computers can process them in a manageable way.

Consider the file `info.txt`. Its contents, when opened in a text editor, might look like this:

```
This is a test.
Line 2.

Line 4.
```

Note that the third line is blank.

We can access files like `info.txt` by using the `open` function. This function usually takes two strings as inputs. The first specifies the name (and location) of the file, and the second specifies the mode with which the file should be opened (the second input is optional and will default to `'r'`).

```
>>> f = open('info.txt','r')
```

DOI: 10.4324/9781003271284-14

The name of the file is `'info.txt'` and the mode is `'r,'` which means that the file will only be available for reading—it can't be written to or revised. While there are a few different possible modes, the only other mode we will be considering is `'w,'` which means that the file will be created and ready to be written to. If a file with the specified name already exists, the file will be erased and a new file (with the same name) will be created.

Don't forget that file names are case sensitive. If you spelled the name wrong or the capitalizations are not exactly right, this function will generate a `FileNotFoundError`. Moreover, for convenience, the file should be in the *same* directory (or folder) as the Python files you are running. Otherwise, the file may not be opened successfully. You can add path information to the filename to specify where in your file system the file is located. For more on this, see the Appendix.

If everything goes right, then a file handle will be returned by the `open` function. This file handle is then assigned to the variable `f`. You can check to see what type of object this file handle is.

```
>>> type(f)
<class 'io.TextIOWrapper'>
```

Basically, a file handle is a way of dealing with input and output (or 'io') behavior regarding the file. Moreover, it's important to note that the input and output are treated as text. That is, the information in the file is treated as the characters found in a human-readable language.

Now that we've opened a file, we want to be able to access its contents. We can do this in a couple of different ways. The `read` function will return the entirety of the file as a single string.

```
>>> f.read()
'This is a test.\nLine 2.\n\nLine 4.'
```

Though the contents of `info.txt` were spread across four separate lines, the reason this was compressed into a string that fits in a single line is that the carriage returns (what happens when you press <Enter> or <Return> on your keyboard) are actually represented as a single character in Python. In a text editor, this character is visually displayed by moving to the next line. As information in a file, however, this is simply another character—the newline character. It is represented by the following string:

```
'\n'
```

Notice that this character is actually shown to us as *two* characters: a backslash and the letter `'n.'` The backslash signals to Python that whatever character immediately follows, that character should be treated in a special way. Instead of treating 'n' as the letter 'n, ' it is treated as a newline character. Given this, you can see why the string above contains an empty line. This is because there are two newline characters (back-to-back) following the second line—'\n\n. '

Extracting the contents of a file in its entirety, however, is a bit cumbersome to manipulate. You will have to do various things to split the text into manageable parts. To handle the contents of a file in a more manageable way, one might use the readline function. This extracts a single line of information from the file.

```
>>> f.readline()
''
```

You'll notice, however, that when you execute this function, it returns an empty string. Not quite what we expected.

It didn't return the first line of the file (as we might have expected) because when a file is opened to be read, there is a pointer that moves through the file keeping track of where we are in the process of reading the file. Since the read function extracted *all* the information in the file, the reading pointer was moved to the end of the file. All subsequent attempts to read anything from the file will result in an empty string since there's literally nothing left to read.

In order to try the readline function, we can either use the seek function or *re*-open the file so that we get a new file handle with a pointer that starts at the beginning of the file. By giving 0 as an input to the seek function, the reading pointer for f is relocated to the beginning.

```
>>> f.seek(0)
>>> f.readline()
'This is a test.\n'

>>> f = open('info.txt','r')
>>> f.readline()
'This is a test.\n'
```

This retrieves the first line of the file. Notice that the first line includes the newline character. Since the first line has been read, the pointer is now moved to the beginning of the second line. The next use of the readline function will retrieve the second line of the file. This can be repeated until an empty string is returned. Once we retrieve an empty string, we know that we've reached the end of the file. So we might iterate over all the content in a file, one line at a time, by using the following while loop.

```
line = f.readline()
```

```
while line != '':
    print(line)
    line = f.readline()
```

Notice that this prints out an extra empty line after each line. This is because the `print` function automatically adds a newline character to whatever is being displayed. Since each line being extracted from the file ends with a newline character, this amounts to having two newline characters at the end of each line.

The same functionality can be achieved using a `for` loop without the use of the `readline` function.

```
for line in f:
    print(line)
```

This works because `f` is considered a sequence of strings that each end with a newline character. So each iteration of this loop assigns the next line of text to the variable `line`.

Finally, you can extract every line as separate elements in a list by using the `readlines` function (don't confuse this with the `readline` function—the only difference is the 's' at the end of `readlines`). When applied to the file handle for info.txt, a list containing four strings is returned.

```
>>> lines = f.readlines()
>>> lines
['This is a test.\n', 'Line 2.\n', '\n', 'Line 4.\n']
>>> lines[1]
'Line 2.\n'
```

Whenever we finish using a file handle, it is important that we properly end the session of file manipulation. This can be done with the `close` function. This should be executed whenever your file manipulation tasks are complete. In certain cases, without explicitly closing the file handle, changes made through the file handle may not properly be reflected in the file itself.

```
>>> f.close()
```

Exercise 14.1: Create a text file (using your favorite text editor) and use Python to open the file and print out all of its lines. Make sure you can do this with the different methods discussed above. It's very important that you create a *text* file (with a `.txt` suffix) and not, say, a Microsoft Word file (with a `.doc` or `.docx` suffix). This is because you want a file that deals only with human-readable characters (many word processor files contain information about formatting, for example, that are not human-readable; however, most word processors can save a file, or export a file, *as* a text file).

So much for reading information out of a file. If we want to create a new file and record information in it, we must open the file in 'w' mode. This allows us to *write* characters to the file. Once open, we can use the file handle to call the write function. This function does exactly what you think it does. It takes a string as input and writes it to the file.

```
f = open('new.txt','w')
f.write('Hello World')
f.write('Does this work?')
f.close()
```

Here, we created a file named 'new.txt,' wrote two strings to the file, and then closed the file. If you inspect the file using a text editor, you may be surprised to see that it has the following single line of information:

```
Hello WorldDoes this work?
```

The reason the two sentences appear on the same line is because the write function does not add anything to the string you provide. Because there are no newline characters explicitly included in the input strings, there are no new lines that are written to the file—the two pieces of text are joined together. In order to add new lines, we have to explicitly include the newline characters at the end of every string.

```
f.write('Hello World\n')
f.write('Does this work?\n')
```

This should have fixed the problem. Make sure it works for yourself.

But be careful, because when you open an *existing* file in 'w' mode, then the contents of the file will effectively be deleted.

Exercise 14.2: Create a text file called 'test.txt' that, starting from 1, has all the numbers from 1 to 1000 written on separate lines.

Exercise 14.3: Open the file you just created, 'test.txt,' and print out every fifth line.

Data Processing

Now that we have the basic ability to handle files, we can start working with data. I downloaded some files from the FiveThirtyEight website using the following URL https://data.fivethirtyeight.com/. One interesting file contains data on the U.S. National Basketball Association's (NBA)

ELO ratings. An ELO rating is a way of quantifying the strength of a team based on game-by-game results. For an explanation of how ELO ratings are calculated, see https://fivethirtyeight.com/features/how-we-calculate-nba-elo-ratings/.

The name of the file we'll be working with is 'nbaallelo.csv.' This file can be found on my website (https://danielflim.org/phil-through-cs/resources/). The suffix of this file, .csv, signals that the file is a comma-separated-values (CSV) file. You will see that many datasets are made available online as CSV files. This means that the data in these files are organized by rows, and every row is populated with data items that are separated by commas. If you open this file in a text editor, you'll see something like this:

```
gameorder,game_id,lg_id,_iscopy,year_id,date_game,    …
1,194611010TRH,NBA,0,1947,11/1/1946,1,0,TRH,           ...
1,194611010TRH,NBA,1,1947,11/1/1946,1,0,NYK,           ...
...
```

It contains information about every game played in the NBA and the ABA (American Basketball Association) from 1946 to 2015. The file is over 17 megabytes in size and includes 126,314 total records.

You can think of the data in this file as a two-dimensional list of strings with rows and columns. The first row (or line) in a CSV file sometimes contains names that describe the contents of each column. So, we can see that the sixth column (named date_game) of each row will be the date of the game that was played. The ninth column of each row will be the three-letter code for team names, and so on. Strictly speaking, this first row of information is not necessary. It is *meta*-data—data that describe the data in the file. So long as we know, in some way (perhaps through a companion document), what the contents of each column are supposed to represent, the first row can be omitted.

The second row is where the data begin in earnest. The sixth column of data in this row is the date 11/1/1946. The ninth column of data is the code for the team: TRH (Toronto Huskies). The 12th and 13th columns of data are the ELO ratings for the team before and after the game: 1300 and 1293.277.

Now that we have a basic understanding of the structure of this CSV file, let's iterate over the rows and simply print out all the information in this file.

```
f = open('nbaallelo.csv','r')
for line in f:
    print(line[:-1])
```

This will dump all the information in the file to the screen. Notice, when printing, that line is sliced with [:-1]. This will return everything in line except the last character. This is useful for display purposes because

the last character is a newline and the print function already adds a newline to the string being displayed. So, this slice will remove the redundant
newline.

What if I wanted to focus on certain columns of data? It would be nice
if I could access, by index, particular data in a given row. This should be
manageable since there is a structure to each row created by the commas.
The commas delimit each piece of data. In order to separate these pieces
of data, we can use the split function. This function takes a single string
as input that acts as a delimiter for separating the pieces of data within a
string. Because we're dealing with comma separated values, we should set
the delimiter to ', .' Here is an example where we take a string ('hel-
lo,12345,world,!') and split it into comma-separated parts.

```
>>> 'hello,12345,world,!'.split(',')
['hello', '12345', 'world', '!']
```

The split function returns a list of four strings. This makes it easy to
access any of these four strings through indexing.

```
>>> parts = 'hello,12345,world,!'.split(',')
>>> parts[1]
'12345'
>>> parts[3]
'!'
```

Exercise 14.4: Write a function called word that takes a string, sentence,
and integer, n, as inputs and returns the nth word in sentence.

We can go back to our ELO rating file and extract, using split, only the
name and postgame ELO rating of each team for every game.

```
f = open('nbaallelo.csv','r')
lines = f.readlines()
for line in lines[1:]:
    data = line.split(',')
    print(data[8],data[12])
```

Several things are worth noting here. I used the readlines function so
that all the lines of data in the file are separated into distinct elements and
placed sequentially into a list that is assigned to the variable lines. I then
iterate over every line in that list except the first line by using a for loop
and using the [1:] slice to exclude the first line of data (the metadata).
Within the loop, I split each line into comma-separated parts and then
print out the ninth (name of the team) and 13th (the postgame ELO rating) elements of the resulting list.

Exercise 14.5: Write a function called `team_ELO` that takes a string, code, and a string, year, as inputs and returns a list of all the ELO ratings (i.e., `elo_n`) for the team with code (e.g., `LAL` for Los Angeles Lakers) as their `team_id` (ninth column) and year as the `year_id` (fifth column).

Make sure you spend some time experimenting with the functions you've learned so far. They should provide you with enough functionality to do a variety of things with the data stored in CSV files.

Visualization

When there is a lot of data to analyze, it is often useful for humans to visualize the data through graphs. Python has a very nice graphing library called `matplotlib`. Within this library, we will use the `pyplot` object. The standard way of importing this object is as follows:

```
import matplotlib.pyplot as plt
```

It has become standard practice to rename the `pyplot` object as `plt`. Make sure that you can execute this `import` statement without generating any errors before proceeding.

Let's assume that I have five data points:

(1,2), (2,5), (3,4), (4,7), (5,9)

In order to generate a basic line plot based on these data points (as shown in Figure 14.1), we can use the `plot` function.

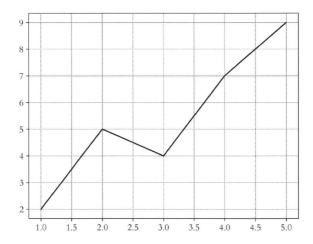

Figure 14.1 A line plot of the five data points.

This function takes two lists as inputs. The first list is a list of all the x values and the second list is a list of all the corresponding y values. It is critical that the order of these values is properly coordinated and that both lists have exactly the same number of elements. Given this, the following code will generate our desired graph.

```
X = [1,2,3,4,5]
Y = [2,5,4,7,9]
plt.plot(X,Y)
plt.grid()
plt.show()
```

The five data points are reconfigured into two lists (called X and Y) so that the x and y values are separated (but correspond to each other based on their locations in their respective lists). The plot function, using these two lists, will generate the line graph. The two additional functions are self-explanatory. The grid function generates the grid of vertical and horizontal lines that can make reading the graph easier. The show function ensures that the graph is made visible on your computer screen.

The key to visualizing data through a line graph is really quite simple: it's just a matter of creating two lists of x and y values. Returning to our ELO ratings for NBA teams, let's try to visualize the ELO ratings over the course of the season for a team as a line graph.

Since I'm originally from Los Angeles, I'm interested in getting all the available ELO ratings for the LA Lakers during their 2008–2009 season *before the playoffs*. To do this, we need to iterate over the nbaallelo.csv file and make sure to record the relevant ELO ratings for LAL during the 2009 year.

There is one very important detail that we must not forget. When opening the CSV file, we are treating all data within the file as *strings*. That's why we're able to use the split function and carve up each line of data into substrings that are separated by commas. The problem is that each of these smaller strings are, well, strings! ELO ratings, however, are meant to be treated as numbers. So, after extracting the relevant data from the lines involving the Lakers, we must convert the corresponding ELO rating into an object of type float.

Let's take another look at the code we wrote above for printing out the name and ELO rating for a given team. I want to draw your attention to the print statement.

```
print(data[9],data[12])
```

For the first row of data in the file, it should display the following.

```
Huskies 1293.277
```

But note that 1293.277 is a string. It is important, therefore, to explicitly convert data that you intend to use numerically with the appropriate type. So when using data in the 13th column, be sure to convert it into a float.

```
print(data[9],float(data[12]))
```

This is important for visualization purposes because the lists that are given to the plot function must be lists of numbers.

Exercise 14.6: Write code that will put all the ELO ratings for the Los Angeles Lakers (LAL) during the 2009 season into a list called LAL_ELOS. In order to extract only the regular season games, you must also use the eighth column of data is_playoffs. When this column has a value of '0,' it is a regular season game, and when it has a value of '1,' it is a playoff game.

The ELO ratings (as numerical values) for LAL are the y values that will be used in our graph. But, we still haven't generated the corresponding x values. Don't forget that we must have the same number of x and y values. We can use the length of the list LAL_ELOS to ensure that this is the case.

```
LAL_X = []
for i in range(len(LAL_ELOS)):
    LAL_X.append(i)
```

This will create a list of numbers from 0 to n-1 for a total of n numbers "where n is the length of LAL_ELOS". A shortcut for doing this is by using list comprehensions. More on list comprehensions can be found in the Appendix, but the code is relatively clear.

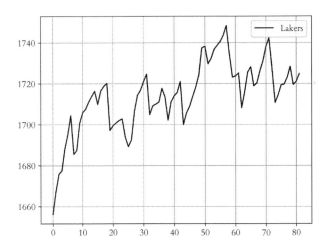

Figure 14.2 Los Angeles Lakers' ELO ratings in 2009.

```
LAL_X = [i for i in range(len(LAL_ELOS))]
```

Now that we have the x and y values in lists, it's easy to generate a graph of the Lakers' ELO ratings over the course of the season. You should have generated a graph that looks something like Figure 14.2.

We can immediately see the upward trajectory of the Lakers' strength. After beginning the season around 1,650, we can see that the Lakers steadily improved and headed into the playoffs with an ELO rating clearly above 1,720. That puts the Lakers squarely in the category of being a 'title contender.'

If you look carefully, you'll notice that there is a legend at the top right of the graph. Generating this requires you to add a couple of bits of information. First, you need to add a label when using the plot function. This label will be associated with the line being plotted.

```
plt.plot(LAL_X, LAL_ELOS, label='Lakers')
```

Second, you to need to call the legend function.

```
plt.legend()
```

This will automatically display a legend with the labels corresponding to the different lines in a graph. The location of the legend will automatically be placed in a region of the graph that leaves the actual data visible.

Exercise 14.7: Write code that will generate a line graph of the ELO ratings for the Golden State Warriors (GSW) over the course of the 2009 season. Can you generate a line graph of the ELO ratings for the LA Lakers (LAL) in the same visualization?

Another useful tool is the scatter function. Instead of adding lines between every data point, this function simply plots all the data as points in the graph. Its usage is exactly the same as plot, so its application is straightforward.

```
plt.scatter(LAL_X, LAL_ELOS, label='Lakers',
color='gray')
```

A color input value can be given so that you can control the color of your data points. This is useful when trying to visualize multiple sets of data points in the same graph. For a list of valid color names, search the documentation at the official website: https://matplotlib.org/.

You now have the tools to visualize some interesting things. There is, of course, a lot more to learn about using matplotlib.pyplot. With an

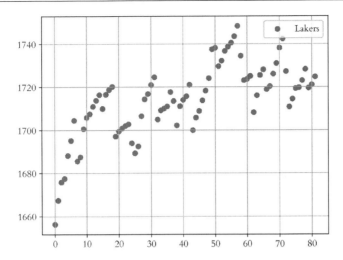

Figure 14.3 A scatter plot of the Los Angeles Lakers' ELO ratings in 2009.

understanding of the `pyplot` object, the best way to learn more is to explore. There is a lot of good documentation online and plenty of examples. Practice, practice, practice!

Key Points

- Files can persistently store data (even when the computer is turned off).
- A common way of representing data in a file is through the CSV format.
- A common way of visualizing data in Python is through the `matplotlib` library.

Chapter 15

Machine Learning

Artificial Intelligence

The 1956 Dartmouth Conference is often cited as the event that kick-started the field of Artificial Intelligence (AI). Among the luminaries in attendance were Marvin Minsky, Claude Shannon, Herbert Simon, and Allen Newell—all important figures in the development of computer science. John McCarthy, one of the organizers of the conference, boldly proposed that:

> significant advances can be made [so that machines can use language, form abstractions and concepts, solve kinds of problems now reserved for humans, and improve themselves] if a carefully selected group of scientists work on [these] together for a summer.

Quite a prediction—he thought it would only take a mere summer to solve problems like natural language processing!

Although a number of groundbreaking ideas emerged out of the conference, it's safe to say that McCarthy's prediction failed to materialize. Problems like natural language processing proved far more difficult than many had imagined, and for decades little progress was made in these domains. The initial excitement surrounding AI was followed by periods of protracted disappointment. It's no wonder some have called the intervening years the 'AI Winter.'

Work being done at the turn of the 21st century, however, has pumped new life into AI research in the form of machine learning. Instead of trying to imbue machines with all the logic to solve problems at the outset, the idea was to let machines learn the logic for themselves. It would be a mistake, however, to think this was a *new* way of approaching AI.

DOI: 10.4324/9781003271284-15

Alan Turing suggested early on that there are at least two different ways of approaching AI:

> Instead of trying to produce a program to simulate the adult mind, why not rather try to produce one which simulates the child's? If this were then subjected to an appropriate course of education one would obtain the adult brain.
>
> (1950, p. 456)

One way is to program a computer to directly simulate an adult mind. The other way is to program a computer to simulate a child's mind and then educate it so that, through a process of learning, it would eventually simulate an adult mind. Turing was prophetic because two camps naturally formed in the years following the Dartmouth Conference that mirrored these two approaches. One camp pushed what might be called Symbolic AI. This camp represented the approach of directly simulating an adult mind. The other camp pushed brain-based connectionist models. This camp represented the learning-based approach of simulating a child's mind. Perhaps it's surprising today, given all the excitement over machine learning, that the Symbolic AI camp 'won' the early contest over which approach would be adopted by the majority of AI researchers. Consequently, much of the energy and resources within the AI research community were dedicated to the Symbolic AI approach, leaving the learning-based approach to flounder.

Two remarkable changes at the turn of the 21st century helped pave the way for the resurrection of the learning-based approach. First, there was a dramatic increase in computing power. What modern-day computers can do in a mere second of processing would've taken years (literally) to process with the computers available to McCarthy in the 1950s. Second, there was a dramatic increase in machine-readable data. The advent of the Internet and social media radically transformed (and continue to transform) the way we communicate with each other and handle tasks. Among other things, we communicate through electronic (not physical) mail on platforms like Google, and exchange digital (not physical) photos on platforms like Facebook. The critical point is that an ever-growing proportion of our communications are being mediated by computers (Varian, 2010). Every time you send an email, receive a text message, post on Facebook, play a video game, etc., you are sending information through a computer over the Internet. Because everything is being processed by computers, it's a trivial task to also record everything that's being processed. There is so much digital information in the world now that we no longer simply call it data—we have to call it 'big data.' And big data, coupled with advances in computing power, is making it possible for machines to efficiently process gargantuan amounts of data and, by learning the patterns that exist in the data, turn the data into action-guiding information.

Discussion: How many emails are processed by Google every day? How many images are processed by Facebook every day? What other companies are processing large amounts of our data?

Machine Learning Taxonomy

Machine learning is not a single monolithic technique. Rather, it is a variety of different techniques used to solve a variety of different problems. Some techniques are excellent at solving some problems, while other techniques are excellent at solving other problems. For conceptual simplicity, these techniques can be divided into two broad categories: **supervised** and **unsupervised** techniques.

Supervised machine learning algorithms are ones that learn through the help of a 'supervisor.' The basic idea is that many examples of inputs and outputs are given to a machine so that the machine can find a pattern for matching these inputs to their corresponding outputs. If the learned pattern is robust enough, the machine will then be able to use this pattern to suggest outputs for new inputs (that the machine may not have encountered before).

So, as a classic example, if I want to help a machine learn how to classify digital images as containing either dogs or cats, what I need to do is provide the machine with lots of inputs (i.e., digital images of dogs and cats). And with each of these inputs, as its supervisor, I also need to tell the machine what each of its corresponding outputs is (i.e., whether the digital image contains a dog or a cat). That is, I have to tell the machine what the right output is. So, the key to *supervised* machine learning is that each input is paired with an output (provided by the supervisor) that the machine can analyze in order to discern some pattern that reliably correlates the inputs and outputs.

Look at the following digital images. As inputs to a machine learning algorithm, they are simply collections of color pixels. How does a computer know whether a given collection of color pixels is a dog or a cat? This is where the human supervisor comes in. As shown in Figure 15.1, each digital image must be labeled by a human who can reliably discern whether a given image contains a dog or a cat. So, the corresponding outputs ('dog' or 'cat') are generated by human supervisors.

And lest you think there is some magical process by which digital images are labeled, I'm here to tell you there is *no* magic process. The labeling of these digital images is a painstaking *human* process. Consider the ImageNet project (Li, 2021). It contains over 14 million images labeled based on a taxonomy of 20,000 different categories! It took over two and a half

Figure 15.1 Labeled images of dogs and cats.

years to compile using a vast array of human workers assembled through the Amazon Mechanical Turk platform.

Unsupervised machine learning algorithms also seek to discern patterns in data, but there is no 'supervisor' to provide the right outputs. That is, unsupervised machine learning algorithms work with *un*labeled data. Consequently, the data contain inputs but no corresponding outputs.

For example, I might have a lot of data about the viewing patterns of Netflix users. What I would like to know is how best to categorize each user. Perhaps I want to split these users into three broad groups according to viewing preference similarities. For any given user, I have input data (i.e., what each user watched on Netflix) but I have no output data (i.e., what group each user should be a part of).

Matthew's Netflix viewing history reveals a lot of science-fiction films. Ray also has a lot of science-fiction films in his Netflix viewing history. So it might be helpful to put the two of them into the same group. As it turns out, unlike Ray, there are also a lot of comedy films that show up in Matthew's history. Abraham, unlike Ray, also has a lot of comedies in his history, but no science-fiction films. Should Matthew then be put into the same group as Abraham? These kinds of questions might be repeated for the millions of users on Netflix—a daunting task! How can the 'best' groupings of Netflix users be discerned? The purpose of an unsupervised learning algorithm is to *discover* the structure latent in the data and produce meaningful groupings.

So much for a conceptual introduction to supervised and unsupervised machine learning algorithms. Let's now jump into concrete examples of each.

Supervised Machine Learning: Regression

Regression is a supervised machine learning algorithm that can be used to predict *continuous* value outputs. A continuous value output between 0 and 1, for example, would include any decimal value in this range (e.g., 0.0215). You can think of the output of a regression model as a number.

Consider a small dataset composed of the heights (in centimeters) and weights (in kilograms) of five different people.

1: 164 cm, 61 kg
2: 171 cm, 74 kg
3: 180 cm, 75 kg
4: 187 cm, 77 kg
5: 192 cm, 94 kg

This might be visualized as points plotted on a graph (Figure 15.2).

Given this data, we want to figure out a model that best captures the pattern that exists between the heights and weights of people. We might want, for example, to use a person's height to predict this person's weight. It's easy to see that there is a clear upward trend in weight that is correlated with an upward trend in height. One way to capture such a trend is with a straight line. The mathematical formula for a straight line is:

$$y = a_1 x^1 + a_0 x^0$$

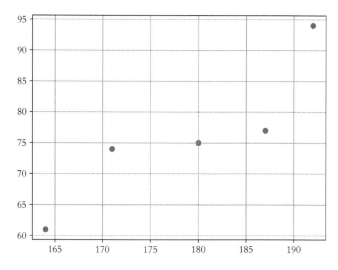

Figure 15.2 Five people's heights and weights.

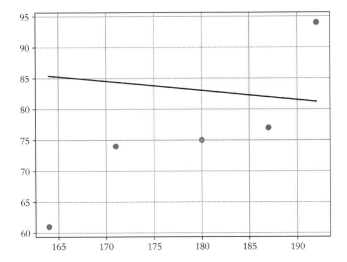

Figure 15.3 y = -0.15x + 110

In Figure 15.3, a straight line is plotted along with the data points. The formula for this line is:

$$y = -0.15x^1 + 110x^0$$

Or more simply:

$$y = -0.15x + 110$$

How well do think this line approximates the relationship that holds between the heights and weights of the five people depicted? We can simply see with our eyes that the line is headed in the wrong direction—it has a downward slope, but the data clearly suggest an upward slope.

The problem is computers can't 'see' the data the way we do. We need to come up with a way of quantifying how well this line **fits** the data. One way of doing this is to calculate the distances between each data point and the corresponding point on the line. So, as shown in Figure 15.4, the distance between the line and the second data point is 10.35. If we calculate the distances between all of the data points and their corresponding points on the line, then we get a total distance of 60.5.

Now compare this with the line in Figure 15.5. We can see that this line does a better job of fitting the data. We can also see that the total of the distances between the data points and their corresponding points on the line is much smaller: 24.4. If we then assume that the line that minimizes the total distance with the data points is the line that best fits the data, then we can say that the second line is a better fit than the first.

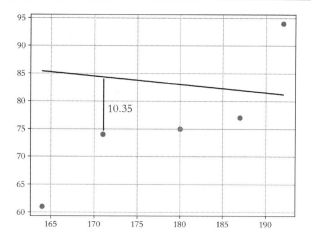

Figure 15.4 The distance between the line and (171, 74) is 10.35.

Cast in this light, the problem of finding the line that best fits the data becomes a mathematical problem with a very precise solution. Problems in real life can have thousands, if not millions, of data points. Processing these many data points is impossible for a human, but with the kind of computing power that is at our disposal, the task of finding the line that best fits the data becomes trivial.

So far, we've focused on **linear** regression. That is, straight–line models for capturing the relationship between inputs and outputs. But straight lines don't always do the best job of capturing trends in data. Sometimes we want lines that can bend. To allow for this kind of flexibility, we can use higher-order polynomials. Here is a second-order polynomial that describes a line with one possible bend.

$$y = a_2 x^2 + a_1 x^1 + a_0 x^0$$

The key point is that the higher the order polynomial, the more bends that can be described in the line that models the data. A fifth-order polynomial, for example, can describe a line with four bends. Given that we only have five data points, a fifth-order polynomial line can be used to fit the data perfectly.

In Figure 15.6, we see the fifth-order polynomial that best fits the five data points. As you can see, the line goes through every single data point. The calculated distance between these points and the line is zero. The lesson here is that higher-order polynomials will always fit the data as well as or better than lower-order polynomials.

Now compare the linear model with the fifth-order polynomial model. Which model is 'better'? Regarding only the five given data points, there is no question. The fifth-order polynomial does much better than the linear model at fitting the *existing* data.

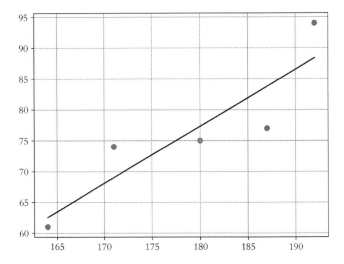

Figure 15.5 Linear Regression.

But what about when using the model to make predictions? That is, which model does a better job of fitting *new* data—which model generalizes better? Here, the linear model does better. Consider, for example, using these models to predict how much an average person who is 200 cm tall weighs. The linear model predicts such a person would weigh about 95 kg—not an unreasonable guess. The fifth-order polynomial model, however, predicts such a person would weigh about 189 kg! So there is a trade-off. Even though models based on higher-order polynomials will always fit the existing data better than models based on lower-order polynomials, that does not necessarily mean models based on higher-order polynomials will do a better job of generalizing to new data (i.e., making accurate predictions).

Discussion: A variety of models can be used to fit a given dataset (linear, second-order polynomial, third-order polynomial, etc.). How can we decide which model fits the existing data best while also generalizing well to new data?

Finally, regression can work with correlating an entire set of variables (not just one) with an answer. We might call this **multivariate** regression. Instead of trying to predict the weight of an average person solely based on a person's height, we might also include a person's age. We'd be trying to model the relationship between *two* variables (height and age) with one other variable (weight). So, in this case, we'd be searching for the plane (and not the line) that best fits the data points. As shown in Figure 15.7, multivariate regression on two variables can be displayed as a two-dimensional plane that models the data points plotted in three-dimensional space. Unfortunately, anything above three-dimensional space is difficult to visualize.

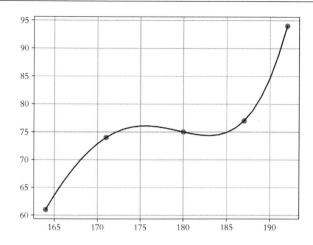

Figure 15.6 Polynomial Regression.

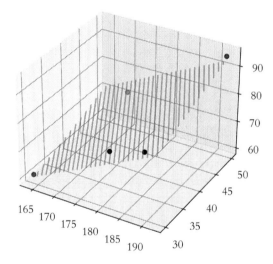

Figure 15.7 Multivariate regression.

Regression can be used to handle complicated datasets by deploying higher-order polynomials or by using multiple variables. When the order of the polynomial or the number of variables is increased, things can quickly get out of hand for humans. We can't even visualize (at least not easily) what models look like when the number of input variables involved goes beyond two! Thankfully, it's nothing too difficult for computers. In the end, it's really nothing more than calculating distances, albeit distances in higher dimensional spaces.

Unsupervised Machine Learning: K-Means Clustering

K-Means Clustering is an unsupervised machine learning algorithm that can be used to discover similarity groups within a dataset. Consider a small dataset composed of the heights (in centimeters) and weights (in kilograms) of ten different people.

 1: 198 cm, 90 kg
 2: 216 cm, 128 kg
 3: 203 cm, 112 kg
 4: 191 cm, 84 kg
 5: 198 cm, 82 kg
 6: 182 cm, 77 kg
 7: 184 cm, 82 kg
 8: 193 cm, 80 kg
 9: 190 cm, 90 kg
10: 175 cm, 76 kg

This might be visualized as points plotted on a graph (Figure 15.8). Given this data and the number of groups we want (say, two groups), what model best captures the most 'natural' way to group these people based on heights and weights? Once we have this model, we'll be able to classify a new person into one of the two groups. It's easy to see that there are two natural groupings—one in the upper right corner involving the two points at locations (203,112) and (216,128) and the other in the lower left corner involving the other eight points.

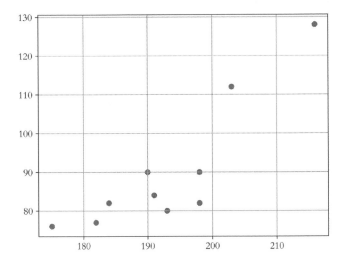

Figure 15.8 Ten people's heights and weights.

The problem, as before, is computers can't 'see' the data the way we do. We need to come up with a way of quantifying good groupings. One way of doing this is, as before, using distances. Here, I will describe the algorithm that is at the foundation of the K–Means Clustering algorithm. Given that we're asking the computer to find two natural groupings, we begin with two random locations (the black and gray X–markers are at two random locations in Figure 15.9).

What we then do is classify each of the data points according to their closeness with either of the random markers. If the data point is closer to the black marker, then it will be classified as black. If the data point is closer to the gray marker, then it will be classified as gray. We now have two groupings based on the two markers (Figure 15.10).

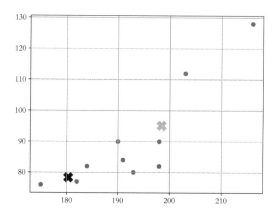

Figure 15.9 Two random locations.

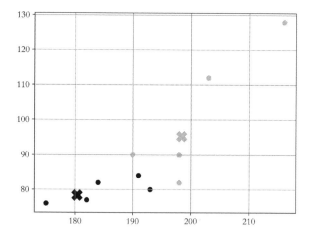

Figure 15.10 Two groupings based on the initial two random locations.

We then find the centroids for each of these two groups. A centroid is the geometric center of all the points in a given group. The centroids of these two groups are not in the same location as the two original randomly chosen locations at the beginning of the algorithm (which are now fainter shades of gray). This can be seen in Figure 15.11.

Using these centroids, we then *recalculate* the groupings of each of the data points based on their closeness with either of these centroids. If the groupings are different, then new centroids are found for these new groupings and the process is repeated.

This process goes on until the groupings stabilize and the centroids stop moving. The end result is shown in Figure 15.12. The groupings found by K–Means Clustering align well with our visual intuitions. While this

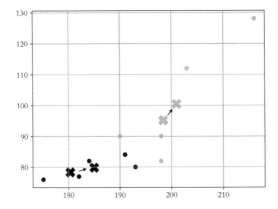

Figure 15.11 The centroids of the two groups are different from the initial two random locations.

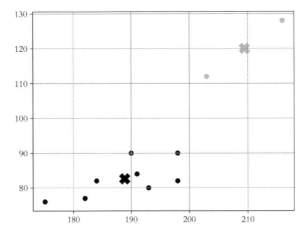

Figure 15.12 Two groups discovered by K-Means Clustering.

example was done in two dimensions, this algorithm can easily run on arbitrarily high dimensional spaces. Again, while we can no longer visualize what's going on in these higher dimensions and can easily get swamped by the sheer number of operations, for a computer it's all just more of the same—calculating distances.

Discussion: Can you think of a dataset where the use of an unsupervised machine learning algorithm might be used to discover latent structure?

Numpy & Sklearn

Hopefully, the conceptual ideas behind Regression and K-Means Clustering are clear. They can be powerful tools for finding and exploiting patterns in data in a variety of contexts.

Given our understanding of these algorithms, we could try to implement them ourselves. Thankfully, others have already developed efficient implementations of these algorithms (along with implementations of many other machine learning algorithms). With a bit more exploration, you'll see that Python has a rich ecosystem of tools that can help us deploy machine learning techniques with relative ease and speed.

For the remainder of this chapter, we will focus on using the numpy and sklearn libraries to exploit existing implementations of machine learning algorithms. numpy is a library for manipulating large two-dimensional list-like structures called arrays. sklearn is a library for machine learning that includes both supervised and unsupervised algorithms. For more on installing libraries, see the Appendix.

The standard way to import numpy into your Python code is with the following statement.

```
import numpy as np
```

Make sure that you can get this to work without generating any errors (if there are errors at this point, chances are you did not install the numpy library). The key object that is made available through this library, as mentioned earlier, is the array. You can create an array by using the np.array() function that takes a structured object as input. For our purposes, the structured object is a list.

```
>>> a1 = np.array([1,2,3,4])
>>> a1
array([1,2,3,4])
```

In many ways, an array is just like a list. It can be indexed, and it can be sliced.

```
>>> a1[1]
2
>>> a1[2:4]
array([3,4])
```

Exercise 15.1: Create an array with the first hundred positive even integers. Do this by first creating a list of the first hundred positive even integers and then converting the list into an array.

An array, however, is different in a couple of important respects. First, the data type of each of the elements in an array must, unlike a list, be the same. You can check what the data type is by checking the dtype attribute.

```
>>> a1.dtype
dtype('int32')
```

In this case, every element in a1 is a 32-bit integer. By ensuring that all of its elements have the same data type, an array is organized as a contiguous chunk of memory and can therefore be processed much faster than a list. Moreover, it is very easy to carry out element-wise operations on an array. We can, for example, add 1 to every element in a1 with the following statement.

```
>>> a1 + 1
array([2,3,4,5])
```

This generates a new array with elements: 2, 3, 4, and 5. The other arithmetic operators work as element-wise operators as well.

```
>>> a1 - 1
array([0,1,2,3])
>>> a1 * 5
array([5,10,15,20])
>>> a1 ** 2
array([1,4,9,16])
```

You can even define functions that can be applied element-wise across an array. Below is a function that takes a number as input and returns the number that is two more than twice its value.

```
>>> def func(x):
        return x * 2 + 2
>>> func(a1)
array([4,6,8,10])
```

Exercise 15.2: Write a function called `area` that takes a number, `r`, as input and returns the area of a circle with radius `r`.

Exercise 15.3: Write a statement that will apply the function `area` element-wise across an `array` with the first hundred positive even integers.

An `array` object really shines, however, when manipulating multi-dimensional structures. Consider the following 3×3 two-dimensional `array` that was created using a two-dimensional `list`.

```
>>> a2 = np.array([[1,2,3],[4,5,6],[7,8,9]])
```

This `array` can be sliced along both axes: rows and columns. If we want, we can select all the data in the first two columns with the following statement.

```
>>> a2[:,:2]
array([[1,2],[4,5],[7,8]])
```

The first slice, `:`, specifies which rows we would like to include. Since there are no numbers given, it includes all rows. The second slice, `:2`, specifies which columns we would like to include. Since there is no number before the `:`, this specifies all the columns from the beginning to (but not including) the column at index 2—which refers to the first two columns. The ability to slice two-dimensional arrays is extremely useful when working with machine learning techniques.

Exercise 15.4: Create a 10×10 two-dimensional `array` of numbers from 1 to 100. You can start by creating a two-dimensional `list`.

Exercise 15.5: Slice the last three rows out of this two-dimensional `array`.

Deploying Regression

Make sure you can successfully import the `sklearn` library before moving on.

```
import sklearn
```

This is critical for trying out the implementations of the Regression and K-Means Clustering algorithms available through the library.

Univariate Linear Regression

Now we have all the pieces we need to utilize the regression tools available through `sklearn`. Let's begin by trying to solve the single variable linear regression problem introduced above. We can first put the data into a two-dimensional array.

```
>>> d =
np.array([[164,61],[171,74],[180,75],[187,77],[192,94]])
```

This array has five rows and two columns. What we want to do is use the first column of data (the heights) to make predictions about the second column of data (the weights). To do this, we will use the `LinearRegression` object.

```
from sklearn.linear_model import LinearRegression
model = LinearRegression()
```

The first line imports the `LinearRegression` class from the `sklearn` library and the second line creates a `LinearRegression` object that will handle regression for us. To use the regression object, we need to organize the data in the right way. The values that will be used to make the predictions (X) must be provided as a two-dimensional structure. The reason why it must be two-dimensional is to allow for multiple variables per data row (e.g., using height *and* age to predict weight) even though we will only be using a single variable in this example (using only height to predict weight). Because of this multivariable possibility, inputs are often called **vectors**.

```
>>> X = d[:, :1]
>>> X
array([[164], [171], [180], [187], [192]])
```

Here, we extract the first column of data from every single row as a two-dimensional array by using `[:, :1]`. Remember, simply using : for the first slice will extract every row, and using :1 for the second slice will extract the set of columns beginning with the column at index 0 and ending at the column with index before 1 (which will extract only the first column).

The values that are being predicted (Y) must be provided as a one-dimensional structure. Let's extract only the second column of data as a one-dimensional `array` by simply using `[:,1]`. As before, the : for the first slice will extract every row. Using 1 (without a colon) will act as an index and extract only the column at index 1.

```
>>> Y = d[:,1]
>>> Y
array([61,74,75,77,94])
```

Discussion: Before going on be sure you understand why the dimensions of the X and Y are what they are. Why is X two-dimensional, and why is Y one-dimensional?

Notice that both arrays have the same number of elements (though the types of these elements are different—X is an array of arrays and Y is an array of numbers). This way there is a one-to-one correspondence between each of their elements in the two lists.

```
[164]  →  61
[171]  →  74
[180]  →  75
[187]  →  77
[192]  →  94
```

To repeat, the first array is two-dimensional because this allows each element in this array to represent one or more variables. For multivariate regression, we will correlate multiple variables with an answer so all of these pieces of data can be organized as a single element, a vector. We'll see how this works after we handle linear regression for a single variable.

Now that we've split the data into inputs (X) and outputs (Y), the rest is actually extremely simple! All we have to do is execute the fit function.

```
model.fit(X,Y)
```

This is often referred to as the 'training' phase of a machine learning algorithm. We are teaching the computer to find a model that best approximates the relationship between heights and weights in the dataset. In essence, this finds a straight line that minimizes the total distance to the various data points—precisely what we discussed on a conceptual level previously.

Now that we have a model trained on the data, we can use this model to make predictions. Maybe I want to know how heavy an average person who is 185 cm tall is. I can use the predict function on this input value to get a prediction based on the trained model.

```
model.predict([[185]])
```

Notice that the input is a two-dimensional list. This allows for multiple predictions and inputs that consist of more than one value. I could have made three predictions by adding more inputs to the list.

```
model.predict([[185],[187],[190]])
```

You may be wondering why I used a list here instead of an array. Both lists and arrays can be used for everything we've learned so far.

Because of the extra functionality and efficiency arrays have (especially when dealing with large amounts of data), we will more often use arrays. However, in this case, since we just want to make a prediction based on a single piece of data, it takes less typing to use a list.

Here's all of the code (in one place) that is needed to train a univariate linear regression model and use it to make a prediction.

```
from sklearn.linear_model import LinearRegression
import numpy as np

d =
np.array([[164,61],[171,74],[180,75],[187,77],[192,94]])
model = LinearRegression()
model.fit(d[:,:1],d[:,1])
print(model.predict([[185]]))
```

That's it! Once you have the data in an array, using the tools available through sklearn can be quite easy.

Exercise 15.6: Try training a univariate linear regression model on the following dataset to find a relationship between the brain weight and body weight of various mammals.

Brain Weight	3.38	0.48	1.35	465.0	36.3	27.6	14.8	1.04
Body Weight	44.5	15.5	8.10	423.0	119.5	115.0	98.2	5.50

An important point here is that in a real-life use of linear regression we would not manually input data into an array. Typically, we would extract this data from a large file—like the CSV files we considered in the previous chapter. A good exercise would be to find a large dataset stored as a CSV file, extract and format this data as an array, and then feed the data to the LinearRegression object in the sklearn library.

An efficient way of extracting data from a CSV file into an array is through the read_csv function in the pandas library. To see how this works, let's examine the gold_prices.csv file that contains annual information on the price of gold from 1950 to 2019. This file can be found on my website (https://danielflim.org/phil-through-cs/resources/). Here are the first five lines of this file:

```
Date,Price
1950,34.72
1951,34.66
1952,34.79
1953,34.85
```

The first line of information in this file is metadata (data about the data in the file)—it includes descriptive names of the columns ('Date' and 'Price'). To extract the relevant data from this file, we can use the read_csv function and then convert the resulting object into a two-dimensional array with the to_numpy function.

```
import pandas as pd
import numpy as np

df = pd.read_csv('gold_prices.csv',sep=',')
a = df.to_numpy()
```

The sep=',' input value makes it so commas are used to distinguish each piece of information in a given row of data. The resulting object that stores the data read from the CSV file is assigned to the variable df. This object is then converted to a two-dimensional array using the to_numpy function. Now, this array can be used to supply your regression model with training data.

Exercise 15.7: Using the gold_prices.csv file as data, can you create a linear regression model? Can you use this model to predict how much gold will be in 2050, 2055, and 2060?

Multivariate Linear Regression

Now let's consider what we might do if our input vectors had more variables. Let's say we also included age data in our dataset. Aside from having additional data, the code for training a linear regression model will be exactly the same.

```
d = np.array([[164,30,61],[171,48,74],[180,32,75],
              [187,33,77],[192,50,94]])
model = LinearRegression()
model.fit(d[:,:2],d[:,2])
model.predict([[185,35]])
```

You'll notice that each row of data now consists of three values: the first two represent the height and age while the third represents the weight. To train the model, we use the first two columns of data in a two-dimensional structure for our input (X), with the third column of data in a one-dimensional structure for our output (Y). We get the following one-to-one correspondence between the inputs and outputs:

```
[164,30] → 61
[171,48] → 74
[180,32] → 75
[187,33] → 77
[192,50] → 94
```

Once the model is trained on this data, we can make predictions. The input must be a two-valued vector, so in the example above, I provided a person who is 185 cm tall and 35 years old as the two-dimensional list: `[[185,35]]`.

Univariate Polynomial Regression

Now, for the final piece, let's see how we can handle regression based on higher-order polynomials. Thankfully, this does not take too much extra work. We need to import an additional object from the `sklearn` library: `PolynomialFeatures`.

```
from sklearn.preprocessing import PolynomialFeatures
```

The `PolynomialFeatures` object is used to convert our first-order vector data into higher-order data. For example, changing our height information into data that can be plugged into a fifth-order polynomial requires a bit of manipulation.

$y = a_1x^1 + a_0x^0$ **first-order polynomial**

$y = a_5x^5 + a_4x^4 + a_3x^3 + a_2x^2 + a_1x^1 + a_0x^0$ **fifth-order polynomial**

Notice that the first-order polynomial (linear equation) only needs to use the height value twice: once for x^0 and once for x^1. For the fifth-order polynomial, however, we need to use the height value several more times: x^0, x^1, x^2, x^3, x^4 and x^5. This expansion of the data is precisely what the `PolynomialFeatures` object handles for us.

```
>>> t = PolynomialFeatures(degree=5)
```

This creates an object that can take a first-order value and transform it into a fifth-order value. In fact, this object can take a first-order value and transform it into any order simply by specifying a value for the `degree` input parameter. Once this is done, first-order values can be transformed into whatever order value you desire.

```
>>> t.fit_transform([[2]])
[[1., 2., 4., 8., 16., 32.]]
```

So if our input data consists of a single element vector `[2]`, the transformer will expand this to cover all the x components in a fifth-order polynomial `[1., 2., 4., 8., 16., 32.]`. Notice that these numbers correspond to x^0 (1), x^1 (2), x^2 (4), x^3 (8), x^4 (16), and x^5 (32), where x is equal to 2.

This is precisely what must be done with *all* of our data in order to train the model. If we go back to our first dataset that correlates heights to weights, we can transform all of our data into data appropriate for a fifth-order polynomial as follows.

```
d =
np.array([[164,61],[171,74],[180,75],[187,77],[192,94]])
t = PolynomialFeatures(degree=5)
t.fit_transform(d[:,:1])
```

Whenever we want to work with higher-order polynomials, we must explicitly transform our input data to fit the order of the polynomial we are hoping to use for the regression. Now we can put all of this together:

```
from sklearn.preprocessing import PolynomialFeatures
from sklearn.linear_model import LinearRegression

d =
np.array([[164,61],[171,74],[180,75],[187,77],[192,94]])
t = PolynomialFeatures(degree=5)
model = LinearRegression()
model.fit(t.fit_transform(d[:,:1]),d[:,1])
model.predict(t.fit_transform([[185]]))
```

Notice that we must use the transformer again when we use the `predict` function since the input vector has to be transformed to handle fifth-order polynomials.

Deploying K-Means Clustering

Given how much we've covered so far, deploying the K-Means Clustering algorithm through the `sklearn` library should be fairly straightforward. We begin with the data.

```
data = np.array([[198,90],[216,148],[203,120],[191,84],
                 [198,82],[182,77],[184,82],[193,80]])
```

With the data in place, we can import the relevant code from the library.

```
from sklearn.cluster import KMeans
```

Now we simply create a `KMeans` object.

```
kmeans = KMeans(init='random',n_clusters=2)
```

Notice that we provided two input values. n_clusters specifies how many groupings we'd like to find in the dataset. Here, it is set to 2 but it could be set to a different integer of your choosing. init specifies how the initial locations should be chosen. In this example, I specified that the initial locations be chosen randomly. Once this is finished, you simply need to call the fit method.

```
kmeans.fit(data)
```

You can find the locations of the centers of the two discovered groups with the following command.

```
kmeans.cluster_centers_
```

This will return a two-dimensional array of center locations. Here is what my execution returns:

```
[[191.    82.5]
 [209.5 134.]]
```

Remember, because the initial locations for the K-Means algorithm are chosen randomly, you may get different numbers or different orderings of the numbers.

These locations can then be used to classify new data points. If the group with center at (191, 82.5) is designated G1 and the group with center at (209.5, 134) is designated G2, then new data points can be classified based on their distances to these two centers. So, for example, to determine which group a new data point at (190, 83) should be classified as, the distances to the centers of G1 and G2 are calculated and compared. Because the distance to the center of G1 (1.118) is shorter than the distance to the center of G2 (54.6), this new data point should be classified as a member of G1.

The distances can be calculated with the following code:

```
import math

G1,G2 = kmeans.cluster_centers_
new_data = np.array([190,83])
dist1 = math.sqrt(np.sum((G1-new_data)**2))
dist2 = math.sqrt(np.sum((G2-new_data)**2))
```

The first line imports the math library. This is so we can use the square root function (math.sqrt) that is needed to calculate the distance between two points. The formula for calculating distances is:

$$d = \sqrt{(x_2 - x_1)^2 + (y_2 - y_1)^2}$$

The second line assigns the values of each of the sublists in kmeans.clus-ter_centers_ to the variables G1 and G2. The new data point is assigned an array with values 190 and 83. An array and not a list is used here to take advantage of element-wise operations that are available through the numpy library. (G1-new_data)**2, for example, will subtract each element in G1 with each corresponding element in new_data and then take each element in the resulting array and square them. Finally, the np_sum function is used to add up all the resulting values in the array.

To end this section, we can put all of this together:

```
import math
from sklearn.cluster import KMeans

data = np.array([[198,90],[216,148],[203,120],[191,84],
                [198,82],[182,77],[184,82],[193,80]])
kmeans = KMeans(init='random',n_clusters=2)
kmeans.fit(data)
G1,G2 = kmeans.cluster_centers_
new_data = np.array([190,83])
dist1 = math.sqrt(np.sum((G1-new_data)**2))
dist2 = math.sqrt(np.sum((G2-new_data)**2))
if dist1 < dist2:
    print('new data should be classified as G1')
else:
    print('new data should be classified as G2')
```

Key Points

- Machine learning algorithms can be divided into supervised and unsupervised algorithms.
- Regression is an example of a supervised machine learning algorithm.
- K-Means Clustering is an example of an unsupervised machine learning algorithm.
- These (and other) machine learning algorithms are efficiently implemented and available through Python libraries.

References

Li, F. F. (2021, January 9). *ImageNet*. Retrieved from ImageNet: http://image-net.org

McCarthy, J., Minsky, M., Rochester, N., & Shannon, C. (1955). *A Proposal for the Dartmouth Summer Research Project on Artificial Intelligence*. Retrieved from Stanford: http://www-formal.stanford.edu/jmc/history/dartmouth/dartmouth.html

Turing, A. (1950). Computing Machinery and Intelligence. *Mind, 59*(236), 433–460.

Varian, H. (2010). Computer Mediated Transactions. *American Economic Review, 100*(2), 1–10.

Chapter 16

Induction

The **philosophy of science** is the branch of philosophy that deals with concepts and issues pertaining to the nature, methods, and implications of science. Some of the central questions in this branch of philosophy include: What is science (or what distinguishes science from non-science)? What is scientific reasoning? How do scientific theories get chosen? Are scientific theories true, or are they merely useful tools for making predictions? It is a fascinating field with questions that connect with issues in many other branches of philosophy.

In this chapter, we will focus primarily on the so-called Problem of Induction. This is an important problem because it cuts to the heart of scientific practice and its venerable result: scientific *knowledge*. Moreover, it overlaps in many ways with issues in machine learning. I am, by no means, the first to point out the similarities between induction and machine learning. In the late 20th century, Paul Thagard argued that:

> [We should] consider from a more integrated perspective the potential benefits of construing machine learning and the parts of philosophy concerned with induction as essentially the same field.
>
> (Thagard, 1990, p. 262)

Thagard makes the striking claim that the parts of philosophy concerned with induction constitute essentially the same field as machine learning. He then makes explicit some insightful benefits of identifying the philosophy of induction with machine learning:

> [The identification] provides a novel vocabulary for investigating inference, concentrating on questions of process and control.
>
> (Thagard, 1990, p. 274)

The task of writing a program requires one to be very explicit about what is expected, and the mere act of designing a program often brings to light interesting philosophical questions. For example, working on

DOI: 10.4324/9781003271284-16

a program for making judgments of explanatory coherence made clear to me several ideas about the simplicity of theories that I would not have otherwise distinguished.

(Thagard, 1990, pp. 274–275)

If Thagard is right, there is a lot to be gained by studying induction through machine learning. Because writing a program (as opposed to thinking more abstractly) forces one to make assumptions explicit, this process not only clarifies vague ideas, but it also helps generate further interesting and novel questions. More recently, Kevin Korb emphasizes the similarities between induction and machine learning.

Machine learning studies inductive strategies as they might be carried out by algorithms. The philosophy of science studies inductive strategies as they appear in scientific practice. Although they have developed to a great extent independently, the two disciplines have much in common.

(Korb, 2004, p. 433)

It's with guidance from thinkers like Thagard and Korb that we embark on an examination of the overlapping conceptual space between the problem of induction and machine learning.

The Problem of Induction

In a discussion concerning statistics under the heading, 'Garbage In Garbage Out (GIGO),' John Guttag writes the following:

The message here is a simple one. If the input data is seriously flawed, no amount of statistical massaging will produce a meaningful result.

(Guttag, 2016, p. 222)

GIGO neatly encapsulates the idea that machine learning algorithms, no matter how sophisticated and powerful, can only be as good as the data they are trained on. Consider data collected from 48 individuals regarding their ages and respective blood pressures visualized in Figure 16.1. How do we know whether this data should be considered 'garbage'?

An important factor in assessing this concerns random sampling from the right population. We might want to know, for example, whether the blood pressure measurements were taken from a sample with a more or less even number of male and female participants. Or, we might want to know whether or not the sample was taken from the right population, say, a population free of relevant diseases. The idea is that a truly random sample from the right population will contain patterns that are identical to the relevant patterns in the entire *healthy* population.

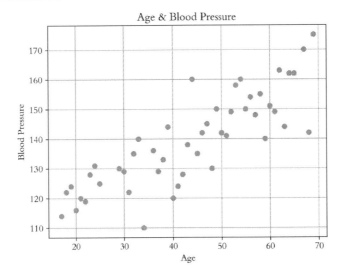

Figure 16.1 **48 people's ages and blood pressures.**

But can we ever ensure that our data sampling is truly random and from the right population? In some circumstances, we can ensure that our sample is sufficiently random, and chosen from the right population. In general, however, there is no guarantee. There is, after all, no logical reason that the unobserved parts of the population will fit the pattern found in the observed parts. Further exploration of the population may very well reveal data points that fail to adequately 'fit' any learned pattern in the sample.

This can be visualized in Figure 16.2. It's possible that subsequent blood pressure measurements involving an older population fail to fit the model trained on the original sample. As this figure suggests, the trend for participants who are 70 years or older may be quadratic, not linear.

One might be tempted to reject the new measurements based on our background knowledge—blood pressure can never go that high (e.g., 800). 'Never,' however, is an extremely strong word. It reaches into the distant (possibly infinite) unobserved universe (that includes all the unobserved humans existing now as well as all the unobserved humans who will exist in the future) and makes a definitive claim. Given the massive space that the unobserved encompasses, how can we ever be certain that our sampling is unbiased?

This brings us to David Hume's so-called Problem of Induction, which focuses on the justification we have for making inferences from past experiences (or more generally, what has been observed) to future experiences (or more generally, what has not been observed). I infer based on past experiences, for example, that I will get wet if it rains. But why think that this way of reasoning, from past experiences to future experiences, is

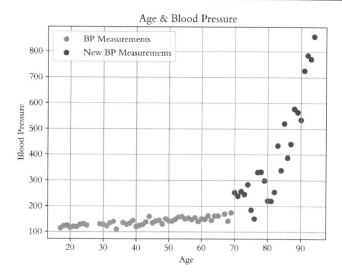

Figure 16.2 The pattern in the original sample does not hold for new data.

justified? What gives us the epistemic right to trust such inferences? Alex Broadbent summarizes the problem as follows:

> I have been out in the rain many times before, and each time, the rain drops have showed no inclination to divert around me… thus they will do so again this time. But how, Hume asks, does that follow? … This is the problem of induction.
>
> (Broadbent, 2016, p. 3)

The force of this philosophical problem is not always obvious to the un-initiated. Inductive practices (e.g., predicting wetness from rain) are so routinely and ubiquitously deployed in everyday life, they seem extremely well justified.

To get a better handle on this, first, let's remind ourselves of the difference between deduction and induction. Here is an example of a deductive argument (from Chapter 4):

Argument A₁

1. If Obama is American, then Obama is human.
2. Obama is American.
3. Therefore, Obama is human.

Remember that deductive arguments aspire to provide premises that entail the conclusion. That is, they aspire to be valid by offering premises that *absolutely guarantee* the truth of the conclusion. This is not to say that the premises are actually true. It is only to say that *if* the premises were true, then the conclusion would have to be true.

Now consider an example of an inductive argument (from Chapter 4):

Argument E₁

1.   If the first 100 marbles drawn from a bag are red, then the 101st marble to be drawn will also be red.
2.   The first 100 marbles drawn from a bag are red.
3.   Therefore, the 101st marble to be drawn will also be red.

Here, the premises do not entail the conclusion. It is possible for the premises to be true and the conclusion false. We think, nevertheless, that the premises give us good reason to believe the conclusion.

Discussion: Consider the things you need to know in order to go about your life from day to day—brushing your teeth, driving to work, reading a book, etc. You need to know, for example, that when you turn the handle on the water faucet in the bathroom that water will come out. Is this knowledge based on a deductive inference or an inductive inference?

Hume's Problem of Induction is targeted at the kind of knowledge that is acquired through inductive inferences. He thinks this kind of knowledge is problematic in a way that knowledge acquired through deductive inferences is not.

To see why let's consider a distinction that is sometimes referred to as Hume's Fork. Here is what Hume writes:

> All the objects of human reason or enquiry may naturally be divided into two kinds, to wit, relations of ideas and matters of fact. Of the first kind are the sciences of geometry, algebra, and arithmetic; and in short, every affirmation which is either intuitively or demonstratively certain... that three times five is equal to the half of thirty, expresses a relation between these numbers. Propositions of this kind are discoverable by the mere operation of thought, without dependence on what is anywhere existent in the universe... Matters of fact, which are the second objects of human reason, are not ascertained in the same manner; nor is our evidence of their truth, however great, of a like nature with the foregoing. The contrary of every matter of fact is still possible; because it can never imply a contradiction, and is conceived by the mind with the same facility and distinctness.
>
> (Hume, 2007, p. 28)

Put another way, the way we justify our knowledge can be divided into two broad categories. Knowledge can be justified based on 'relations of ideas' or based on 'matters of fact.' Examples of the first category include our knowledge that his should be the following mathematical equation: $3 \times 5 = \dfrac{30}{2}$ because we can, based purely on our conceptual understanding (our ideas) of The 'x' and '/' and '=' are mathematical operators 2, 3, 5, 30, ×, /, =, see that the previous equation is true. Despite calling arithmetic a 'science' (which meant something completely different in Hume's time), there was no need to do experiments nor was there a need to make observations of the world in order to verify the truth of $3 \times 5 = \dfrac{30}{2}$. Today, we call this kind of knowledge *a priori* **knowledge**, where '*a priori*' can be translated from Latin as 'from the earlier.' It is knowledge that is acquired (in some sense) *independently* from (or *prior* to, before) empirical evidence or experience. Or, as Hume wrote, it is knowledge acquired "by the mere operation of thought, without dependence on what is anywhere existent in the universe."

Examples of the second category include our knowledge that Hydrogen contains a single proton. This kind of knowledge cannot simply be gained by reflecting on our conceptual understanding of Hydrogen and protons. Unlike our knowledge of $3 \times 5 = \dfrac{30}{2}$, we actually have to do some experiments and make observations in order to discover that Hydrogen contains a single proton. After all, the contrary of this truth—that Hydrogen does not contain a single proton—does not imply a contradiction. Prior to the discovery, one could have easily imagined Hydrogen containing two protons. It could not have been ruled out *a priori*. We can easily imagine Hydrogen containing, say, two protons instead of one. The same, however, cannot be said for $3 \times 5 = \dfrac{30}{2}$. We cannot imagine this being false. After all, if you carry out this calculation, you get the following equation: $15 = 15$. To imagine this failing to hold is to imagine something impossible—a contradiction. Today, we call knowledge based on 'matters of fact' *a posteriori* **knowledge**, where '*a posteriori*' can be translated from Latin as 'from the later.' It is knowledge that *depends* on (or is *posterior to*, comes after) empirical evidence and experience.

Discussion: Do you find Hume's Fork helpful in classifying what you know? Can you think of other examples of *a priori* knowledge and *a posteriori* knowledge? Are these two categories exhaustive in classifying all knowledge?

The distinction at the heart of Hume's Fork nicely mirrors the distinction between the two approaches to AI that emerged after the Dartmouth Conference (introduced in the previous chapter). The Symbolic AI approach attempted to directly simulate the human mind, whereas the learning-based approach attempted to simulate the human mind through a regimen of education. We might say that proponents of Symbolic AI took an *a priori* approach to making intelligent machines. They thought they could simply 'insert' human knowledge into machines as a series of symbols and logical rules. So, the knowledge inside these machines might be characterized as *a priori* in the sense that, for these machines, it is knowledge that is acquired independently of their 'experiences.' On the other hand, we might say that proponents of the learning-based approach took an *a posteriori* approach to making intelligent machines. They thought they could educate machines, through exposure to various examples. So, the knowledge inside these machines might be characterized as *a posteriori* in the sense that, for these machines, knowledge is acquired through their 'experiences.'

The distinction at the heart of Hume's Fork also provides us a way of explaining the difference between deductive and inductive inferences. Deductive inferences are *a priori* because the justification needed to move from premise to conclusion is independent of empirical evidence or experience. We don't have to check if Obama is actually an American or if all Americans are humans in order to check if the argument is valid. We can see that the structure of Argument A_1 is valid. It will remain valid regardless of the way the world turns out to be. Even if it turns out that Obama is *not* American, the reasoning in Argument A_1 will remain valid. In fact, there is *nothing* that can overturn the validity of this argument. This is because denying its validity would lead to a contradiction. In a straightforward sense, it would be nonsensical!

So, it seems we have good reasons to believe in our deductive inferences. But what good reasons do we have to believe in our inductive inferences? Why does the claim that the first 100 marbles drawn from a bag are red give us good reason to believe that the 101st marble to be drawn will also be red? Or why does seeing the sunrise every day give us good reason to believe that the sun will rise tomorrow?

Given Hume's Fork, there are only *two* possible answers. The first possible answer is an *a priori* answer. Do we know, based purely on our conceptual understanding of the sun, what it means to rise, and what tomorrow means that 'the sun will rise tomorrow' is true? It seems not. After all, we can easily imagine its negation—we can easily imagine that the sun will *not* rise tomorrow. There is nothing nonsensical about this proposition, even if it seems unlikely. So it seems we do not have an *a priori* reason to think that the sun will rise tomorrow.

The second possible answer is an *a posteriori* one. The reason I know that the sun will rise tomorrow is based on empirical evidence or experience. For as long as I've been alive, I've gathered (albeit implicitly) empirical evidence for its truth. Every morning I observe the sun rising—not a single day has gone by without the sun's rising. That's at least 15,000 consecutive days! We might even put this reasoning into premise-conclusion form:

Sun Argument

1. The sun has risen 15,000 consecutive times.
2. Therefore, the sun will rise tomorrow.

However, all the empirical evidence that was marshaled in the previous paragraph does not really give us a reason to trust the inference from premise 1 to the conclusion. All it provides us with is a reason to believe in premise 1. In order to address Hume's Problem of Induction, however, we need a reason for believing that the conclusion should be inferred from premise 1. We might be tempted to say that premise 1 entails the conclusion, but this would be a mistake. It's possible, after all, for premise 1 to be true and the conclusion false.

According to Samir Okasha's interpretation of Hume's Problem of Induction, what is needed to provide a reason for the inductive inference from premise 1 to the conclusion is a commitment to the 'uniformity of nature' (UN). He writes:

> In each of these [inductive] cases, our reasoning seems to depend on the assumption that objects we haven't examined will be similar, in the relevant respects, to objects of the same sort that we have examined.
> (Okasha, 2002, p. 24)

Let's make this assumption explicit by revising the Sun Argument:

Revised Sun Argument

3. UN is true.
4. The sun has risen 15,000 consecutive times in the past.
5. Therefore, the sun will rise tomorrow.

Since the sun's rising is part of nature and UN encompasses *all* of nature, it follows that we can extrapolate the following conditional from UN:

> If the sun has risen 15,000 consecutive times in the past, then the sun will rise tomorrow.

We can restate the Revised Sun Argument as follows:

Revised Sun Argument

6. If the sun has risen 15,000 consecutive times in the past, then the sun will rise tomorrow.
7. The sun has risen 15,000 consecutive times in the past.
8. Therefore, the sun will rise tomorrow.

This certainly gives us a good reason to make an inference from premises 6 and 7 to the conclusion. In essence, this would turn the original argument into a deductive one. Because it is valid, denying the inference would lead to a nonsensical result!

But now we can ask: what good reason do we have to believe in premise 6 (UN)? It is clearly not an *a priori* reason. There is nothing in the concept of nature that entails uniformity. After all, there is nothing nonsensical about imagining the falsity of UN. We can easily imagine a universe with a chaotic nature, where every day is completely different from the one before—there is no contradiction here.

Can we come up with a good *a posteriori* reason for believing UN? Do we have empirical evidence for UN? We might think we do. *All* (not merely some) of our *past* experiences provide support for UN. But does this help us? This would limit our empirical evidence to things we've actually observed and would only ground UN for everything that's already been observed. But notice, UN's distinctive claim is that even the *un*observed parts of nature are uniform with the observed parts (e.g., what will happen in the future). What is needed is the inferential connection from the observed to the unobserved to have justification for UN to hold *tomorrow* (and not merely today and in the past). By definition, we cannot observe the unobserved (since observing a previously unobserved object will make that object an observed object), so we cannot ground UN based purely on past experiences.

It seems that we neither have an *a priori* reason nor an *a posteriori* reason for believing UN. The unsettling consequence seems to be that we have no good reason for believing that the sun will rise tomorrow (despite 15,000 consecutive days of experiencing the sun's rising). More generally, Hume concludes that we have no good reason to believe in *any* of our inductive inferences (e.g., that water will come out when we turn the handle on the faucet)!

His argument might be regimented into premise-conclusion form as follows:

Problem of Induction

1. If induction is justified, then it is justified *a priori* or it is justified *a posteriori*.
2. It is not justified *a priori*.
3. It is not justified *a posteriori*.
4. Therefore, it is false that induction is justified.

This is a valid argument because it is structured, as we learned in Chapter 4, in *modus tollens* premise-conclusion form. The negation of the consequent of a conditional will guarantee the negation of the antecedent.

Discussion: What do you think of Hume's argument? Does it show that most of what we think we know is unjustified?

This is an astonishing conclusion! It suggests that we have never had a good reason for believing the results of our inductive inferences. Given how much of our knowledge is grounded in induction, this pretty much affects everything we think we know. Hume is making the radical claim that we have no good reason for believing almost everything we think we know.

Of course, this does not mean that we should stop believing what we've acquired through induction. Hume admits that we cannot stop making inductive inferences. Like a basic instinct flowing out of human nature, we've formed a habit (or custom) for inductive reasoning. Indeed, it's a universal human practice that cannot easily be abandoned. Nevertheless, Hume shows us that this practice is not, as we might have thought, grounded in reason or understanding. Rather, it is grounded in non-rational (but not necessarily *ir*rational) instinctive patterns solidified by habituation.

Falsification and Pragmatism

There have been many notable responses to Hume's Problem of Induction over the years. Here, we will look at two. First, consider Karl Popper's response. He writes:

> My own view is that the various difficulties of inductive logic here sketched are insurmountable. So also, I fear, are those inherent in the doctrine, so widely current today, that inductive inference, although not 'strictly valid', can attain some degree of 'reliability' or of 'probability'... The theory to be developed in the following pages stands directly opposed to all attempts to operate with the ideas of inductive logic. It might be described as the theory of the deductive method of testing, or as the view that a hypothesis can only be empirically tested.
> (Popper, 2002, pp. 6–7)

What is immediately obvious is that Popper concedes Hume's thesis. He acknowledges that the difficulties of inductive logic (chiefly grounded in Hume's Problem of Induction) are insurmountable. His response, however, is that this is totally fine. Though it is commonly assumed that science is based on induction, Popper disagrees. Since science has never needed inductive inferences to make progress, the fact that inductive inferences can't be justified poses no problem for the foundations of scientific practice and knowledge.

Popper offers a different vision of how science works. He writes:

> According to the view that will be put forward here, the method of critically testing theories, and selecting them according to the results of tests, always proceeds on the following lines. From a new idea, put

up tentatively, and not yet justified in any way—an anticipation, a hypothesis, a theoretical system, or what you will—conclusions are drawn by means of logical deduction... [we can then test] to find out how far the new consequences of the theory—whatever may be new in what it asserts—stand up to the demands of practice, whether raised by purely scientific experiments, or by practical technological applications... Next we seek a decision as regards these (and other) derived statements by comparing them with the results of practical applications and experiments. If this decision is positive, that is, if the singular conclusions turn out to be acceptable, or verified, then the theory has, for the time being, passed its test: we have found no reason to discard it. But if the decision is negative, or in other words, if the conclusions have been falsified, then their falsification also falsifies the theory from which they were logically deduced.

(Popper, 2002, pp. 9–10)

Science proceeds by developing theories that make *novel* predictions. That is, they must make claims about what is currently unobserved. Popper sometimes calls these 'bold predictions'—bold because they have not yet been verified. Experiments are then conducted to see if these bold predictions actually hold. If the bold predictions are confirmed by experiment, then the theory passes the test. However, if the bold predictions are disconfirmed by experiment, then the theory is **falsified** and we can confidently reject this theory.

Consider theory T—my claim that Mike is a werewolf. For it to be a theory worth considering, it has to make bold predictions. Since my theory of werewolves includes the claim that werewolves retain human form during the day but turn into wolves at night when subjected to the light of a full moon, there is a bold prediction lurking nearby. Let P be the claim that Mike will turn into a wolf if, at night, I subject him to the light of a full moon. Now I need to devise an experiment to test this prediction. On a clear night with a full moon, I'll lure Mike outside by offering him some exquisite beer. If he comes out to enjoy the exquisite beer with me, is subjected to the light of a full moon, and fails to turn into a wolf then my theory has been falsified.

The logic of scientific inquiry, for Popper, is purely deductive. It is simply an application of the *modus tollens* argument structure. We might regiment Popper's reasoning about my werewolf theory as follows:

Werewolf Argument

1. $T \rightarrow P$ (theory T makes prediction P).
2. $\sim P$ (experiment shows that the prediction is false).
3. $\sim T$ (the theory is falsified).

According to Popper, all we can do, and all we really need, is to deductively try to falsify theories for science to make progress. Science is in the business of producing interesting theories with bold predictions that have the chance of being falsified.

Critically, Popper is extremely modest in his language about the status of a theory when it is *not* falsified. This is very deliberate on his end. When the bold prediction of a theory coincides with experimental results, he makes the rather bland observation that "we have found no reason to discard [the theory]." He does not make the more obvious (and interesting) claim that we have reason to *believe* the theory was confirmed or that the theory is true—which, after all, is how scientists speak and behave. When, for example, Arthur Eddington's 1919 experiments on the deflection of light by the sun's gravitational field confirmed Einstein's predictions based on the theory of relativity, scientists did not merely think there was no reason to discard Einstein's theory. They took it as extremely strong confirmation for the theory's truth! Some took it even further and announced that this was a 'proof' of Einstein's theory.

Popper is clear, however, that these epistemic tendencies would be mistakes:

> It should be noticed that a positive decision can only temporarily support the theory, for subsequent negative decisions may always overthrow it. So long as a theory withstands detailed and severe tests and is not superseded by another theory in the course of scientific progress, we may say that it has 'proved its mettle' or that it is 'corroborated' by past experience.
>
> (Popper, 2002, p. 10)

Here, Popper operates on a different meaning for 'proof.' All it means is that it has withstood all current tests. For Popper, Einstein's theory of relativity is 'only temporarily' supported. The upshot is that scientific practice is only able to falsify theories, it can never confirm them. Because of this, some have been unsatisfied with Popper's response to Hume.

Discussion: Do you agree with Popper that we don't need induction in science? Does Popper's view do justice to our understanding of scientific practice?

Another way of responding to Hume is to get practical. Hans Reichenbach has developed and defended such a pragmatic response. He writes:

> An example will show the logical structure of our reasoning. A man may be suffering from a grave disease; the physician tells us: "I do not know, whether an operation will save the man, but if there is any remedy, it is an operation." In such a case the operation would be justified.

Of course, it would be better to know that the operation will save the man; but, if we do not know this, the knowledge formulated in the statement of the physician is a sufficient justification. If we cannot realize the sufficient conditions of success, we shall at least realize the necessary conditions. If we were able to show that the inductive inference is a necessary condition of success, it would be justified; such a proof would satisfy any demands which may be raised about the justification of induction.

(Reichenbach, 1938, p. 349)

Of course, this example already presupposes induction because the physician's knowledge that an operation is the only possible way of saving the man's life must be inductively grounded. Nevertheless, the structure of the reasoning might be used to vindicate the practice of induction.

To begin, consider the possibilities. These possibilities can be divided into two categories: possibilities where we are in worlds that are ordered and uniform and possibilities where we are in worlds that are disordered and chaotic. If we happen to be in a world that is ordered and uniform, then our inductive practices will be successful. We will predict that the sun will rise tomorrow and this will be correct. If, however, we happen to be in a world that is disordered and chaotic, then our inductive practices will fail. We will predict that the sun will rise tomorrow, but because of its chaotic nature, the prediction will fail to be true. But, then again, *everything* we predict will likely fail to be true in such a world. In fact, any possible strategy for making useful inferences will likely fail in this world. In a chaotic world, inferences would only be useful by sheer luck.

Discussion: Do you agree with the claim that there can be no justified strategy for making useful inferences about the unobserved in a chaotic world?

Reichenbach's claim is that whatever world we find ourselves in, we'll at least have the possibility of succeeding if we practice induction. That is, using induction is a necessary condition for successfully inferring things about the unobserved even if it is not a sufficient condition. According to Reichenbach, that's reason enough to practice induction.

Note, however, this is *not* a solution to Hume's Problem of Induction in the strict sense. It does not provide us with a good reason for induction itself. All it claims is that if anything will work, will be induction.

Prediction, Accommodation, and Overfitting

As we've seen, the Problem of Induction is a serious problem for anyone who believes, for example, that science produces knowledge (that is, *rationally justified* beliefs). Consequently, it's a problem for anyone who believes that we can rationally justify the use of existing data and machine learning techniques to make good predictions. But even if we set aside worries over the Problem of Induction (and GIGO), there are other serious problems that confront machine learning algorithms. In the previous section, finding the best 'fit' for a given dataset was presented as a straightforward matter: simply find the *line* that minimizes the total distance between the model and the dataset. But matters aren't so simple because there are many possible models that can be used to fit the data. For example, differing orders of polynomials can always be used as alternative models.

Consider the use of a 20th-order polynomial to fit the age and blood pressure data introduced earlier. You can see in Figure 16.3 that a 20th-order polynomial fits the existing data pretty well—much better than a first-order linear model would. Indeed, as we saw in the previous chapter, the higher the order of the polynomial, the better the fit.

But something clearly looks wrong with this 20th-order polynomial. Although the model fits the *existing* data well, it will do miserably when making predictions—especially regarding blood pressure measurements for people over the age of 70. The model will shoot straight up on the right edge. The 20th-order polynomial may fit the existing data better than any linear model, but it fits the existing data *too* well. This is known as **overfitting**.

Korb writes:

> With such approaches [like regression] we ignore the complexity of our theories and suppose that the only epistemological criterion of value is 'explanatory power' – how closely the data are represented

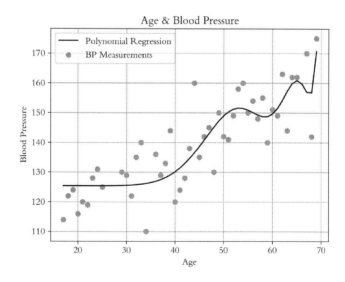

Figure 16.3 20th order polynomial regression.

by the theory. It has been well established in both statistics and in machine learning that the result of such *over-attention* to the *data in hand* is overfitting.

(Korb, 2004, p. 436)

Overfitting occurs when a given model is so tightly tuned to the existing data that its ability to generalize and make good predictions is undermined.

How might one deal with the problem of overfitting? One way is through **validation** techniques. Instead of using the entire set of existing data to train a model, the data can be divided into two separate sets: (i) a *training* set and (ii) a *testing* set. Without exposing the machine learning algorithms to the testing set, a model is fit to the training set. Once the model is trained, it can be validated against the testing set. Models that overfit the training set tend to fare poorly on the testing set.[1]

Here's how Guttag describes validation:

> In such situations, one can simulate a set of experiments by dividing the existing data into a *training set* and a *testing set*. Without looking at the testing set, we build a model that seems to explain the training set. For example, we find a [reasonable] curve... for the training set. We then test that model on the testing set. Most of the time the model will fit the training set more closely than it fits the testing set. But if the model is a good one, it should fit the testing set reasonably well. If it doesn't, the model should probably be discarded.
>
> (Guttag, 2016, p. 221)

But how is one to go about choosing which data points are to be included or excluded from the training set? The natural answer is through randomization. Simply take a random sampling of the data to be the training set. As far as proportions go, there are some who have recommended a 70/30 split (70% for training and 30% for testing).

Data splitting in Python can be done with a single line of code:[2]

```
X_train, X_test, Y_train, Y_test = train_test_split(X, Y)
```

The 70/30 split, however, can feel a bit arbitrary. For those worried that a single 70/30 split might or might not yield reliable results, Guttag goes on to discuss a more comprehensive validation technique:

> A related but slightly different way to check a model is to train on many randomly selected subsets of the original data, and see how similar the models are to one another. If they are quite similar, then we can feel pretty good. This approach is known as *cross validation*.
>
> (Guttag, 2016, p. 221, my emphasis)

Depending on the way the data are divided through the `train_test_split` function, the amount of error of the resulting models will vary. Nevertheless, on average, the 20th-order polynomial model will produce more errors when getting validated on the testing set than the first-order linear model. This confirms our intuition that a 20th-order polynomial model will overfit the data represented in Figure 16.3.

Reflection on the motivation for validation techniques nicely mirrors an interesting debate in the philosophy of science over scientific theory adjudication. It seems natural to think that a scientific theory deserves more inductive support if it accurately *predicts* novel observations than if it merely *accommodates* existing observations. Here's how Peter Lipton summarizes this idea:

> A theory deserves more inductive credit when data are predicted than when they are accommodated, on the grounds that only in the predictive case is the correctness of the theory the best explanation of the fit between theory and evidence.

> (Lipton, 2004, p. 164)

Certain cases of prediction in the history of science (e.g., Mendeleev's prediction of gallium) were more dramatic than mere cases of accommodation. But is our preference for prediction over accommodation merely an artifact of human psychology, or is there something of epistemological significance being registered?

To tie this issue together with validation in machine learning, I will simply defer to others who have already done interesting work in this area. To begin, let me distinguish two positions. The view that prediction lends more inductive support to a theory than accommodation can be called 'predictivism.' The denial of this view can be called 'accommodationism.'

In entering the debate over predictivism and accommodationism, Christopher Hitchcock and Elliott Sober argue for a weak version of predictivism using the notion of overfitting:

> Theorists who aim to accommodate some known set of data run the risk of committing a methodological sin—*overfitting* the data; and overfitting is a sin precisely because it undermines the goal of predictive accuracy. Prediction is at least sometimes better than accommodation, both because it can provide a measure of protection against overfitting, and because successful prediction can provide evidence that overfitting has not occurred.

> (Hitchcock & Sober, 2004, p. 3)

They provide a hypothetical example to develop their case. Consider Penny Predictor and Annie Accommodator. In carrying out their research they get access to a data set, let's call it D. Penny formulates theory T_P based on a portion of the data, let's call it D_1. Penny then uses T_P to make predictions about the remaining data, let's call it D_2. As it turns out, T_P enjoys a high degree of accuracy regarding D_2. Annie, on the other hand, formulates theory T_A based on the *entire* data set. In fleshing out the story, Hitchcock and Sober present the theories in terms of polynomials:

> Penny and Annie each posit a functional relationship between X and Y that is polynomial in form: $Y = a_r X^r + a_{r-1} X^{r-1} + a_{r-2} X^{r-2} + \ldots + a_1 X + a_0$.
>
> (Hitchcock & Sober, 2004, p. 9)

The similarity with the regression-based machine learning example above could not be any more explicit.

According to Hitchcock and Sober, the fact that T_P makes successful predictions about D_2 is evidence that Penny's theory avoids overfitting D_1. If T_P had overfit D_1, we would not have expected as many successful predictions regarding D_2. Of course, with cross-validation on the table, we could've strengthened these expectations by creating and using multiple training/testing sets. Be that as it may, T_P's predictive accuracy also provides evidence that appropriate care was taken to balance simplicity against goodness of fit where simplicity in this case is based on the order of the polynomial used. Lower-order polynomials are considered simpler than higher-order ones. Contrary to Penny's theory, T_A, Annie's theory, does not give us any reason to think that the balancing of simplicity against goodness of fit was embraced and overfitting avoided. Though we know T_A fits the existing data (D) well, we have no evidence that it generalizes to new data.

Key Points

- Machine Learning algorithms are only as good as the data they are run on.
- David Hume concludes, based on the Problem of Induction, that there are no rational grounds for our inductive practices.
- Karl Popper agrees with Hume but argues that we don't need induction.
- Hans Reichenbach agrees with Hume but argues pragmatically that induction is all we can do.
- Validation techniques help avoid overfitting and provide a reason in support of predictivism.

Notes

1   Models can also *underfit* the training set—the model may not be sophisticated enough to capture the actual pattern in the data and, as a result, fare poorly on the testing set.
2   This function defaults to a 75/25 split (training/testing) when the ratio is unspecified.

References

Broadbent, A. (2016). *Philosophy for Graduate Students: Metaphysics and Epistemology.* New York: Routledge.

Guttag, J. (2016). *Introduction to Computation and Programming Using Python.* Cambridge: MIT Press.

Hitchcock, C., & Sober, E. (2004). Prediction Versus Accommodation and the Risk of Overfitting. *British Journal for Philosophy of Science, 55*(1), 1–34.

Hume, D. (2007). *An Enquiry Concerning Human Understanding.* Cambridge: Cambridge University Press.

Korb, K. (2004). Machine Learning as Philosophy of Science. *Minds and Machines, 14*(4), 433–440.

Lipton, P. (2004). *Inference to the Best Explanation* (2nd ed.). New York: Routledge.

Okasha, S. (2002). *Philosophy of Science: A Very Short Introduction.* Oxford: Oxford University Press.

Popper, K. (2002). *The Logic of Scientific Discovery.* New York: Routledge.

Reichenbach, H. (1938). *Experience and Prediction: An Analysis of the Foundations and the Structure of Knolwedge.* Chicago, IL: Chicago University Press.

Thagard, P. (1990). Philosophy and Machine Learning. *Canadian Journal of Philosophy, 20*(2), 261–276.

Chapter 17

AI Ethics

We've now come to the end of this book—congratulations on surviving! Through this brief tour of computer science, we've become better acquainted with a variety of areas of philosophy. As a result, I hope you have a bit more comfort with the Python programming language and have a rudimentary ability to think computationally and translate algorithms into actual code. I also hope you have more confidence in your ability to think philosophically about a variety of issues.

In this final chapter, I would like to discuss some of the ethical issues that have arisen out of recent advances in computation. Not a day goes by without news agencies devoting time and energy to confront the socio-ethical consequences of technologies driven by artificial intelligence (AI). Some worry that the current revolution in AI is going to rob many of us of our jobs. With the rapid development of self-driving cars, for example, jobs that heavily depend on human drivers are potentially at risk. After all, if AI can reliably drive trucks across the country in a cost-effective way, why would human drivers still be needed? And if significant portions of the population are unemployable due to AI, what, on a societal level, is the ethical way forward?

Consider another area that AI is impacting. Reliable image classification was once an intractable task for computer scientists. With recent machine learning techniques based on neural networks, however, remarkable progress has been made. In certain narrow domains, AI-driven image classification is just as reliable as human-driven image classification. Using these techniques, Google made it possible to search its massive database of images. Unfortunately, in 2015, Google's search engine classified an image of a black couple as 'gorillas.' How could such an offensive misclassification occur? As it turns out, no one (not even Google) seems to have a definitive answer. A critical factor, however, is related to the kind of data that was used to train Google's image classification system. It is likely that misclassifications have a higher probability of occurring with darker-skinned subjects because the datasets used to train the system are disproportionately composed of lighter-skinned subjects.[1] There simply

DOI: 10.4324/9781003271284-17

isn't as much data available for the system to learn how to properly classify darker-skinned subjects. The result is a kind of racism. Google's search engine is better at handling queries concerning lighter-skinned subjects than handling queries concerning darker-skinned subjects.

The number of such issues is growing each day as AI makes inroads into more and more of our lives.[2] Because we cannot cover everything, I will be selective and focus only on two. Before we get to these, however, let's take a moment to discuss some theoretical issues about ethics to set the stage.

Ethics

Ethics is the branch of philosophy that deals with concepts and issues pertaining to moral rightness and wrongness. Some of the central questions in this branch of philosophy include: Is a given action morally right? What makes an action morally right or wrong? Is moral rightness culturally relative? Here, we will focus on the second question. Traditionally, there have been two broad approaches to the analysis of moral rightness.[3]

Consequentialism is the view that the moral rightness of an action is determined solely by the action's consequences. While there are a number of nuanced ways consequentialism has been developed, the classic way, known as **utilitarianism**, can be traced back to the 18th century British philosopher, Jeremy Bentham (1961). The claim is that an action is morally right if and only if that action maximizes the net happiness for all.

There are a couple of things to note about this analysis. First is that *net* happiness is what is being maximized. By net happiness, we just mean the total amount of happiness minus the total amount of unhappiness that results from the action. It will not do if we only take increases in happiness into consideration. Increases in unhappiness must also be considered. So, even if an action increases the happiness of some, the action may also increase the unhappiness of many others, resulting in a net loss of happiness. Second, the calculation of net happiness is to be carried indiscriminately over *all* people. There are no favorites: all people are treated as equals.

While Bentham's consequentialism may sound banal and uncontroversial, given its place in history, it was a revolutionary idea. 18th century Europe was dominated by religion, and it was commonplace to ground moral rightness in God. To understand moral rightness without any reference to God was radical. Moreover, consequentialism doesn't rely on abstract rules, commandments, or laws. While some may think that it is 'wrong to steal,' consequentialism has nothing to say about stealing per se. The moral rightness of stealing depends purely on its consequences. Should an act of stealing maximize the net happiness for all, then it may in certain circumstances be a morally right action.

Discussion: What do you think of consequentialism? Do you see any problems with it?

Not everyone has been satisfied with consequentialism. One issue that has been raised against it has to do with the analysis of 'happiness.' Note that consequentialism, as formulated above, doesn't define what happiness even *is*. This is critical if we're supposed to discern the moral rightness of an action based on the net happiness it produces. One traditional way of analyzing 'happiness' is as pleasure—any mental state that feels good. Examples of pleasure are diverse and might include a sense of accomplishment, a soothing sensation when receiving a massage, an emotional release at the resolving climax of a movie, etc.

But is pleasure all that happiness amounts to? Are there things that we value (and therefore bring happiness) other than pleasure? First, some argue that not all pleasures should count toward happiness. Consider the pleasure that a sadist receives from hurting a victim. Or consider the pleasure that a drug addict receives from taking another hit. Should these count as instances of happiness (for assessing the morality of an action)? Second, there seem to be plenty of things we value independently of pleasure. Consider the love a husband has for his wife. Does that love become any less valuable because he receives less pleasure from his wife due to her contracting a life-diminishing disease?

Robert Nozick offers a memorable thought experiment to drive this point home. He writes:

> suppose there were an experience machine that would give you any experience you desired... neuropsychologists could stimulate your brain so that you would think and feel you were writing a great novel, making a friend, or reading an interesting book. All the time you would be floating in a tank, with electrodes attached to your brain... of course, while in the tank you won't know that you're there; you'll think it's all actually happening... Would you plug in?
> (Nozick, 1974, pp. 42–43)

Discussion: Would you plug into the experience machine? Why or why not?

Nozick offers several reasons why one shouldn't plug into the experience machine. First, we want to *actually* do certain things and not merely have the experience of doing them. Second, who we are is very important to us, and someone plugged into the experience machine cannot be a certain way. That person is an 'indeterminate blob' who cannot be courageous or cowardly, for example. Finally, plugging into the experience machine limits one's life to an artificial reality, cutting one off from the possibility of a deeper reality that transcends what humans can construct.

Turning from the issue of happiness and the experience machine, there is another important issue raised against consequentialism: it seems to give the *wrong* verdict when it comes to certain actions. Consider the following case offered by Judith Jarvis Thomson:

> This time you are to imagine yourself to be a surgeon, a truly great surgeon. Among other things you do, you transplant organs, and you are such a great surgeon that the organs you transplant always take. At the moment you have five patients who need organs. Two need one lung each, two need a kidney each, and the fifth needs a heart. If they do not get those organs today, they will all die; if you find organs for them today, you can transplant the organs and they will all live. But where to find the lungs, the kidneys, and the heart? The time is almost up when a report is brought to you that a young man who has just come into your clinic for his yearly check-up has exactly the right blood-type, and is in excellent health. Lo, you have a possible donor. All you need do is cut him up and distribute his parts among the five who need them. You ask, but he says, "Sorry. I deeply sympathize, but no." Would it be morally permissible for you to operate anyway?
>
> (Thomson, 1985)

In this scenario, the consequentialist ought to answer affirmatively. Yes, you should harvest the organs of the young man who came in for his yearly check-up. This will yield some negative consequences—an innocent man will die. But consider the positive consequences: five patients who need organs will live and not die. The positives (five lives saved) outweigh the negatives (one life lost), so it would be right, at least in this scenario, to harvest the young man's organs. The consequences dictate the morality of the action.

But surely this is the wrong conclusion. It is morally wrong to harvest a person's organs against his will. Our judgment about this kind of claim counts as evidence against consequentialism. A correct theory of moral rightness should never come to this conclusion.

Question: Can you use these ideas to offer an argument against consequentialism in premise-conclusion form?

Though consequentialists have offered plausible responses to these worries, many find something fundamentally wrong at the heart of consequentialism. According to them, the moral rightness of actions cannot depend only on their consequences. Sometimes, despite the negatives, we value things like justice and rights. We turn now to another approach to analyzing moral rightness that does this.

Deontology is the view that the moral rightness of an action is determined solely by the intention, or motivation, behind the action. If you found Thomson's counterexample compelling, then you might find de-ontology offers a better analysis of moral rightness than consequentialism. You may think that the killing of an innocent is morally wrong no matter what positive consequences result.

While there are a number of nuanced ways deontological ethics have been developed, the classic way can be traced back to the 18th century German philosopher, Immanuel Kant (2002). He begins by arguing that goodwill is the only thing in this world that is intrinsically good:

> There is nothing it is possible to think of anywhere in the world, or indeed anything at all outside it, that can be held to be good without limitation, excepting only a good will.
>
> (Kant, 2002, p. 9)

This is because the *consequences* of any action are beyond one's control. Positive consequences can arise out of an action that was motivated by a bad will (e.g., a desire to harm an innocent person) and negative consequences can arise out of an action that was motivated by a good will (e.g., a desire to help someone). We shouldn't judge the moral rightness of a person's actions by focusing on things that are outside the person's control. After all, responsibility should only extend as far as one's domain of control, and all that we truly have control over, are our wills.

Discussion: What do you make of Kant's claim that only a good will is intrinsically good? Do you agree or disagree? Why?

When is an act of will good? According to Kant, it is good when one acts out of a duty to follow the moral law. An example of a rule within the moral law might be: do not harm an innocent person. Traditionally, the moral law was intimately connected with God. God, being the source of morality, would issue the moral law to humanity and the intention to obey this law out of duty could be used to discern which actions are morally right. Understanding the moral law in this way would result in a form of deontology known as **divine command theory**. Kant, however, did not take this path. He believed that reliance on God was not necessary for apprehending the moral law. Rather it could be discovered through human reason.

According to Kant, in order to discover the contents of the moral law, one must reflect on the **categorical imperative** (that is, a command without exceptions). While Kant formulated this imperative in several ways, the (arguably) most well-known formulation is:

> I ought never to conduct myself except so that I could also will that my maxim become a universal law.
>
> (Kant, 2002, p. 18)

'Maxim' is just a fancy way of referring to a moral rule. So a maxim might be: "whenever you need a loan, promise to repay it, even if you know you can't." How does one know if this maxim belongs to the moral law and is therefore categorical? One needs to see if it can be universalized by asking the question: would one allow this maxim to be followed by all people at all times? If so, then the maxim is indeed part of the moral law. If not, then the act is forbidden.

How does the maxim above fare? What would happen if all people obeyed this maxim at all times? According to Kant, making this a universal practice would be self-defeating because it would undermine trust—no one would believe such promises. If no one would believe such promises, then the very institution of making promises would fall apart. The result of universalizing this maxim makes the very institution of promises incoherent. So, a rational person would be able to see, using nothing but reason, that this maxim describes an act that is morally wrong.

It might seem that Kant is making a kind of consequentialist argument: the reason why it is wrong to break promises is that it will lead to bad consequences (e.g., we would never trust anyone's promises). But that is not quite Kant's idea. Instead, Kant thinks that, if you reason through what it would mean to want *everyone* to be able to break promises whenever they want, you are actually wanting something incoherent and irrational. By definition, a promise is something that is not supposed to be broken, so wishing that everyone could make *breakable* promises is like wishing everyone could have brown eyes but also not have brown eyes at the same time: you would be wishing for something logically incoherent. For Kant, morality comes from rationality (and reason) and respecting everyone else's ability to be rational (and reason).

Discussion: What do you think of Kant's categorical imperative? Is it true that the rules that belong in the moral law can be discovered through reason alone?

Not everyone has been happy with Kant's analysis of moral rightness or deontological ethics more generally. It seems that there are uncontroversial counterexamples to some of Kant's categorical imperatives. James Rachels offers the following scenario as a response to the imperative against lying:

> Imagine that someone is fleeing from a murderer and tells you that he is going home to hide. Then the murderer comes by and asks you where the man is. You believe that if you tell the truth, you will be aiding in a murder. Furthermore, the killer is already headed the right way, so if you simply remain silent, the worst result is likely. What should you do? … Under these circumstances, most of us believe that you should lie. After all, which is more important: telling the truth or saving someone's life?
>
> (Rachels & Rachels, 2019, p. 139)

Discussion: Is Rachels' counterexample effective? How do you think Kant might have responded to this?

This scenario also points to the potential conflict that may arise between different categorical imperatives. When the imperative against lying is pitted against the imperative to save lives, one of the imperatives must be relinquished. So it seems both of these imperatives cannot be categorical. There is, of course, the possibility that there is only a *single* imperative that is categorical in the moral law (which is what Kant believes), but this may seem overly restrictive to some.

Lethal Autonomous Weapons

Returning now to AI Ethics, the first issue I want to look at is sometimes controversially referred to as 'killer robots.' Though this term is provocative, it may be misleading when compared to its more official counterpart: 'lethal autonomous weapons' (or LAWs). First, the usage of AI in the military are not limited to robots. The term 'robot' is often used to refer to machines with physical human characteristics, like arms and legs. But the lethal uses of AI in the military are legion and can be found in objects as diverse as guns, lasers, and missiles. None of these objects would naturally be referred to as a robot. Moreover, a killer robot need not be autonomous—it could be controlled remotely by a human operator (as drones are). What we are interested in examining here are lethal military weapons (including but not limited to robots) equipped with AI that operate autonomously.

Over the past several years, the development and potential use of LAWs have become a source of concern for the global community. This concern has reached the highest levels of international discussion and is now a regular part of the United Nations' deliberations through the Convention on Conventional Weapons.[4] There is great controversy over how to move forward with LAWs. While there are states, non-governmental organizations, and high-profile experts (e.g., Stephen Hawking and Elon Musk) unified against the development of LAWs, major military states (e.g., China, Russia, and the United States) are intent on maintaining policies that leave space for the development of LAWs.

Discussion: What are your thoughts about LAWs? What are the moral considerations that must be brought to bear in this discussion?

The reasons offered in debates over LAWs can be grouped into two broad categories: consequentialist and deontological reasons. Consequentialist reasons have been raised for and against the development of LAWs while deontological reasons have been raised exclusively against the development of LAWs. Let's begin by considering some consequentialist reasons.

What are the consequences of using LAWs in military conflicts? Some believe that the consequences are, in the long-run, overwhelmingly negative (Amoroso & Tamburrini, 2018). The development of LAWs may lead to a proliferation of these weapons among dangerous non-state actors like oppressive regimes and terrorists. Another alternative is a new arms race among state actors vying for military supremacy. Moreover, replacing human soldiers with LAWs will make it easier to start wars because human casualties may drastically be reduced. Finally, LAWs may be vulnerable to cyberattacks, which can lead to other serious unintended conflicts.

On the other hand, some believe that developing LAWs may lead to positive consequences and, depending on the developmental trajectory of these weapons, even be a moral imperative (Arkin, 2009). Ronald Arkin believes that future LAWs may perform better than their human counterparts for a variety of reasons. Here are a few: (i) LAWs can act conservatively because they don't have to worry about self-preservation, (ii) LAWs may have sensors that make them better equipped for making battlefield observations and decisions, and (iii) LAWs can be designed without emotions to mitigate hostility toward enemy combatants and the committing of war crimes.

Debates on consequentialist grounds will remain hostage to the perceived consequences of the development of LAWs. There is much disagreement over the relative merits of the various potential consequences and, given the current state of technology, debates over these matters can seem more speculative than informed.

Deontological reasons have, by and large, been raised *against* the development of LAWs. No matter how good the overall consequences are, there is something fundamentally wrong with the use of LAWs in war according to this line of thought. Some have argued that LAWs will not be able to conform to International Humanitarian Law (IHL). More specifically, it is argued that LAWs will not be able to conform to the Principle of Proportionality (Van den Boogaard, 2015) which states that attacks on military objectives must be proportional and not excessive in relation to the concrete and direct military advantage anticipated. Making such judgments, however, require interpretations of IHL that are impossible for a machine to carry out. Peter Asaro writes:

> Applying IHL requires multiple levels of interpretation in order to be effective in a given situation. IHL supplements its rules with heuristic guidelines for human agents to follow, explicitly requires combatants to reflexively consider the implications of their actions, and to apply compassion and judgement in an explicit appeal to their humanity.
>
> (Asaro, 2012, p. 700)

Discussion: Do you agree with this sentiment? Is it impossible for AI to make proper judgments of proportionality in war? Why or why not?

Others have argued that even if LAWs could make judgments of proportionality as effectively as competent humans there would still be a problem (Sparrow, 2007). LAWs are subject to error and, being alien to humans, their errors can be highly unpredictable. LAWs, for reasons opaque to us, may end up committing crimes against humanity. Who would be held responsible for such crimes? The use of LAWs will generate, what some have called, a responsibility gap. LAWs cannot be held accountable for such crimes. LAWs are not moral agents and cannot, therefore, make morally responsible decisions. After all, would it make sense to punish a LAW? What could we possibly do to inflict harm on a machine?

It seems that accountability must be traced back to humans in the decision-making chain. But where in this chain should accountability lie? Should accountability lie with the human programmer? This seems problematic because part of the rationale for designing truly *autonomous* weapons is that the weapons will be able to make decisions independently of their designer. The way the weapon is 'trained' on data and learns on the battlefield will have just as much impact on the decisions that the weapon makes as the original AI program. Should accountability lie with the commanding officer? Similarly, the whole point of imbuing weapons with autonomy is that decisions can be made by the weapons themselves. This is precisely one of the strategic advantages LAWs are supposed to bring to the table. As autonomy increases, it becomes harder and harder to hold any single person accountable for decisions made outside his/her intentions.

If the sentiments expressed above are on the right track, then it seems LAWs may engender a situation where accountability for deaths during a war will be absent. This is unacceptable because it seems to violate a fundamental right that combatants have when entering war—that they will *not* be victims of unaccountable killings. Robert Sparrow writes:

> It is a minimal expression of respect due to our enemy—if war is going to be governed by morality at all—that someone should accept responsibility, or be capable of being held responsible, for the decision to take their life. If we fail in this, we treat our enemy like vermin, as though they may be exterminated without moral regard at all. The least we owe our enemies is allowing that their lives are of sufficient worth that someone should accept responsibility for their deaths.
>
> (Sparrow, 2007, p. 67)

These are weighty matters that require more discussion and deliberation. Whether you like it or not, the use of AI in the military is, for many, an inevitability. How much autonomy can be given to weapons is still an area of speculation, but there is no doubt that research is being carried out to test the limits. There are simply too many tantalizing possibilities that promise remarkable battlefield advantages for research to be stalled let alone stopped.

How debates over LAWs play out, however, will be heavily influenced by the public conscience. Currently, there is little to no public awareness of the research that is being carried out to develop LAWs. A critical part of what it will take to move this debate forward is public education.

Surveillance Capitalism

In 1989, Tim Berners-Lee, a British computer scientist, invented the World Wide Web (or web), an information system that made resources, in particular, webpages, available through the internet. In the early 1990s, web browsers (e.g., Mosaic, Netscape, and Internet Explorer) were developed that enhanced the accessibility of webpages. By the late 1990s, what began as a collection of a dozen or so webpages, mushroomed into a sprawling multi-million webpage network. With this exponential proliferation of information, what became glaringly obvious was that users needed an effective way of navigating the web—it was no longer obvious how to find what one was looking for. Search engines were developed to address this need. Among the many search engines that vied for users were Yahoo!, WebCrawler, Excite, and AltaVista. Perhaps surprisingly, Google was a latecomer in this competition. Needless to say, Google eventually won the search engine war.

What made Google's search engine superior to its competitors was its ingenious use of what many considered to be 'useless' data that included, among other things, the number and pattern of search terms, spelling, punctuation, dwell times, click patterns, and geographical location. Shoshana Zuboff explains how these data were then exploited:

> What had been regarded as waste material—"data exhaust" spewed into Google's servers during the combustive action of Search—was quickly reimagined as a critical element in the transformation of Google's search engine into a reflexive process of continuous learning and improvement. At that early stage of Google's development, the feedback loops involved in improving its Search functions produced a balance of power: Search needed people to learn from, and people needed Search to learn from. This symbiosis enabled Google's algorithms to learn and produce ever-more relevant and comprehensive search results. More queries meant more learning; more learning produced more relevance. More relevance meant more searches and more users.
>
> (Zuboff, 2019, p. 70)

Zuboff calls this the behavioral value reinvestment cycle. Millions of people use Google's search engine daily, providing Google with a steady (and massive) stream of behavioral data. These data are then fed into their algorithms to produce more relevant and comprehensive search results. Initially, it was a virtuous cycle—more search queries led to more behavioral data, more behavioral data led to more learning, more learning led to better search results, and better search results led to more users and search queries.

By the turn of the 20th century, powerful venture capital firms were investing millions of dollars into Google. Not only had Google become the gold standard of web search, it now had the finances to do truly remarkable things. But there was a critical financial problem—Google didn't know how to reliably turn investor capital into revenue. While Google boasted fantastic, cutting-edge technologies, it didn't have a business model to exploit them. When the so-called 'dot-com' bubble burst in Silicon Valley, startup companies began folding left and right and Google came under tremendous pressure.

To monetize their vast quantities of behavioral data, Google developed the concept of 'targeted' advertising. Advertisements wouldn't simply be connected with search queries, but with the *individuals* that made them. By leveraging its growing computing power, Google was able to transform the massive amounts of behavioral data it collected into individual user profiles (through advanced machine learning techniques). No longer would ads have to be wasted on large swathes of the population; instead ads could be personalized to every single person. This would guarantee exquisite ad relevance for users and hence reliable value to advertisers. Because Google could also track which ads users clicked on and when they clicked, Google was able to devise a quantitative measure, called a 'click-through rate,' which measured the effectiveness of a given ad.

In essence, Google had developed a sophisticated mechanism that could be used to read individual people's minds and make increasingly accurate predictions about their subsequent behaviors. You might say Google had developed an extremely powerful platform for doing behavioral psychology. Critically, all of this was developed without user awareness. As a user surfed the web using Google's search engine, Google collected, curated, and transformed the wealth of behavioral data the user produced to generate profiles that, with every interaction, increased in accuracy. Zuboff summarizes:

> Google's invention revealed new capabilities to infer and deduce the thoughts, feelings, intentions, and interests of individuals and groups with an automated architecture that operates as a one-way mirror irrespective of a person's awareness, knowledge, and consent, thus enabling privileged secret access to behavioral data.
>
> (Zuboff, 2019, p. 81)

The way to perfect this system was to collect more and more data. So instead of limiting its domain to web search, Google ventured into other forms of user interaction by acquiring companies (e.g., YouTube), exploring different online applications (e.g., Google Maps), and developing wearable devices (e.g., watches). Profiles could now include information about what users like to watch, where users physically go, and how users' physical bodies react (e.g., heart rate). Zuboff unabashedly calls this a form of mass surveillance. Hence, she labels the logic behind Google's innovation: 'surveillance capitalism'—the monetization of data collection on individuals.

Since its discovery, the logic of surveillance capitalism has seeped into other major tech companies (e.g., Facebook) and, it's safe to say, is now a fundamental part of all modern businesses. What are the ethical implications of surveillance capitalism? Zuboff contends that surveillance capitalists have access to an ever-growing pool of what she calls 'instrumentarian power'—the instrumentalization of behavior for the purposes of modification, prediction, monetization, and control.

Discussion: What other companies deploy the logic of surveillance capitalism? What information is vital to their businesses? What might be done with this information?

Some, like Zuboff, believe that the growth of instrumentarian power in the tech industry is a threat to human free will and autonomy. The use of profile information to predict the behavior of individuals can be exploited to manipulate behavior. Consider, for example, what Cambridge Analytica did for the Republican Party during the 2016 U.S. presidential election. The company collected data available through Facebook on over 200 million U.S. citizens. Using these data, they were credited with identifying and then motivating critical potential swing voters to vote. They were allegedly able to target specific voters (using surveillance capitalist techniques) in key swing states and send them personalized messages that catered to their individual personalities. With this form of 'nudging,' the behavior of a critical mass of U.S. citizens was subtly and effectively manipulated. According to Zuboff, this threatens the very core of the democratic process and the individual right to privacy and autonomy that makes democracy possible. As such, those opposed to surveillance capitalist practices have offered deontological reasons against the use of instrumentarian power—that violations of the right to privacy and autonomy can never be condoned.

Others, however, contend that instrumentarian power can be used for good based on consequentialist reasons. Richard Thaler and Cass Sunstein (2008) argue that nudging (of the right sort) can be beneficial for society. They argue that people are by and large inconsistent, ill-informed, and weak-willed. If so, Thaler and Cass go on, perhaps the general population requires some amount of nudging. By carefully engineering a society's 'choice architecture,' better decisions might be made by a greater proportion of the population. Adding the personalized information that surveillance capitalist techniques bring to the table makes it possible for state governance to be micro-targeted and hence more effective.

This is not mere idle speculation. It is no secret that China is developing a social credit system to better regulate citizen behavior. Moreover, the Chinese government is attempting to leverage the latest developments in machine learning technologies to create more accurate and comprehensive profiles of its citizens. Some preliminary studies have shown that a majority of the Chinese public views the social credit system in a positive light (Kostka, 2018). Instead of seeing it as a threat to privacy or autonomy, they see it as a benefit to society. Not only does it support collectivist Chinese moral values, but it also promises to promote honest interactions in society and the economy.

Discussion: Are you familiar with China's social credit system? Is it qualitatively different from what the U.S. government does in terms of monitoring and regulating the behavior of its own citizens?

Though many in the west have raised ethical concerns over surveillance capitalist tactics, the same sentiments might not be as prevalent in China. This shows that ethics requires a critical amount of finessing across sociocultural boundaries. Because of the relative perceived merits of various considerations, a nuanced approach to ethics seems increasingly necessary for the future of our world.

The Future

What can we expect moving forward? There is no doubt that computers and allied technologies will make more and more inroads into our lives. Given the way the web has connected the entire world, we can also expect that the issues that arise out of computing technologies will have global effects. This brings us back to C.P. Snow's worries that we began this book with. He was concerned that the rift between the sciences and the humanities would pose problems for the U.K.'s ability to address world problems. By producing citizens that specialized in either the sciences or the humanities (but not both), the U.K. would be hampered in contributing to the rapidly emerging future.

I hope, in introducing you to the world of philosophy through the world of computer science, this book has played a small part in addressing Snow's worries. More important than the content of any specific philosophical problem discussed, or the intricacies of the Python programming language, the skills of philosophical and computational thinking will be essential for moving fluidly in and contributing positively to our future world. Not only should you have the technical understanding to be aware of the ways computational technologies are transforming the world, but you should also be able to reflect critically on the issues that they raise. And perhaps most importantly, you need the ability to engage in dialogue with those holding divergent beliefs. It takes skill and effort to understand the perspectives of people rooted in different sociocultural contexts. Part of what this requires is suspending your own deeply held beliefs to entertain other possibilities.

Key Points

- Consequentialist ethics assess the morality of an action based on its consequences.
- Deontological ethics assess the morality of an action based on its conformity with a set of rules.
- AI is being used in the military to create smarter, more autonomous weapons.
- AI is being used in the tech industry to analyze, predict, and manipulate human behavior.

Notes

1   See Buolamwini and Gebru (2018) for an evaluation of other commercial image classification systems trained on datasets disproportionately composed of lighter-skinned subjects.
2   See Coeckelbergh (2020) for a wide-ranging discussion of recent issues being raised by AI. See Floridi (1999) for an attempt at providing a philosophical foundation for computer ethics. See Moor (2006) for a brief discussion of the possibility of imbuing machines with ethics.
3   See Rachels and Rachels (2019) for a broad and accessible introduction to ethics.
4   For more information on UN meetings concerning LAWs, visit https://www. un.org/disarmament/the-convention-on-certain-conventional-weapons/ background-on-laws-in-the-ccw/.

References

Amoroso, D., & Tamburrini, G. (2018). The Ethical and Legal Case Against Autonomy in Weapons Systems. *Global Jurist, 18*(1), 1–12.

Arkin, R. (2009). *Governing Lethal Behavior in Autonomous Robots.* London: Chapman & Hall.

Asaro, P. (2012). On Banning Autonomous Weapon Systems: Human Rights, Automation, and the Dehumanization of Lethal Decision-Making. *International Review of the Red Cross, 94*(886), 687–709.

Bentham, J. (1961). *An Introduction to the Principles of Morals and Legislation.* Garden City, NY: Doubleday.

Buolamwini, J., & Gebru, T. (2018). Gender Shades: Intersectional Accuracy Disparities in Commercial Gender Classification. In *1st Conference on Fairness, Accountability, and Transparency* (pp. 77–91).

Coeckelbergh, M. (2020). *AI Ethics*. Cambridge: MIT Press.

Floridi, L. (1999). Information Ethics: On the Philosophical Foundation of Computer Ethics. *Ethics and Information Technology, 1*(1), 33–52.

Kant, I. (2002). *Groundwork of the Metaphysics of Morals*. New Haven, CT: Yale University Press.

Kostka, G. (2018, July 23). China's Social Credit Systems and Public Opinion: Explaining High Levels of Approval. Berlin. Retrieved from: http://dx.doi.org/10.2139/ssrn.3215138

Moor, J. H. (2006). The Nature, Importance, and Difficulty of Machine Ethics. *IEEE Intelligent Systems, 21*(4), 18–21.

Nozick, R. (1974). *Anarchy, State, and Utopia*. New York: Basic Books.

Rachels, J., & Rachels, S. (2019). *The Elements of Moral Philosophy* (9th ed.). New York: McGraw Hill Education.

Sparrow, R. (2007). Killer Robots. *Journal of Applied Philosophy, 24*, 62–77.

Thaler, R., & Sunstein, C. (2008). *Nudge: Improving Decisions about Health, Wealth, and Happiness*. New Haven, CT: Yale University Press.

Thomson, J. J. (1985). The Trolley Problem. *Yale Law Journal, 94*(6), 1395–1415.

Van den Boogaard, J. (2015). Proportionality and Autonomous Weapons Systems. *Journal of International Humanitarian Legal Studies, 6*(2), 247–283.

Zuboff, S. (2019). *The Age of Surveillance Capitalism: The Fight for a Human Future at the New Frontier of Power*. New York: Public Affairs.

Chapter 18

Solutions

Chapter 2

Exercise 2.1

```
type(1)                    # integer
type(1.0)                  # float
type(True)                 # boolean
type(None)                 # nothing
type('Hello World')        # string
```

Exercise 2.2

```
(10 * 5280 / 3.28084) * 100
```

Exercise 2.3

```
365 * 24 > 24 * 60 * 60
```

Exercise 2.4

```
hourly_rate = 30
weekly_rate = hourly_rate * 40
annual_rate = weekly_rate * 52

25 * annual_rate
```

Exercise 2.5

```
radius = 10
volume = (4 / 3) * 3.14 * radius ** 3

print('sphere - radius: '+ radius +', volume: '+ volume)
```

DOI: 10.4324/9781003271284-18

Chapter 3

Exercise 3.1

```
x = 6      # for testing purposes
if x % 2  == 0:
    print('It is even!')
```

Exercise 3.2

```
x must be less than 10.
```

Exercise 3.3

```
x, y = 5,6    # for testing purposes
x % 2 == 1 or y % 2 == 0
```

Exercise 3.4

```
x = 70    # for testing purposes
if x % 2 == 0:
    if x % 10 == 0:
        print('foo')
    if x % 7 == 0:
        print('bar')
else:
    print('baz')
```

Exercise 3.5

```
coin1,coin2,coin3 = 1,1,1    # for testing purposes

if coin1 == coin2:
    if coin1 == coin3:
        print('there are no counterfeit coins')
    elif coin1 > coin3:
        print('coin3 is counterfeit and lighter')
    else:
        print('coin3 is counterfeit and heavier')
elif coin1 > coin2:
    if coin1 == coin3:
        print('coin2 is counterfeit and lighter')
    else:
        print('coin1 is counterfeit and heavier')
else:
    if coin1 == coin3:
```

```
        print('coin2 is counterfeit and heavier')
    else:
        print('coin1 is counterfeit and lighter')
```

Chapter 4

Exercise 4.1

Argument E_1 is unsound because premise 1 is (probably) false—money is not a guarantee for happiness. Nevertheless, the reasoning is perfect so the argument is valid.

Argument E_2 is unsound and invalid because the premises do not entail the conclusion. Nevertheless, the premises and the conclusion are all true.

Chapter 5

Exercise 5.1

```
x = 1

while x <= 10:
    print(x * 3)
    x += 1
```

Exercise 5.2

```
x = 1000

while x <= 2000:
    if x % 11 == 0:
        print(x)
    x += 1
```

Exercise 5.3

```
name1 = 'George Boole'
print('Mr. ' + name1[7:] + ', pleasure to meet you.')
```

Exercise 5.4

```
name1 = 'Barack Hussein Obama'   # for testing purposes
number_of_vowels = 0
x = 0

while x < len(name1):
    if name1[x] in 'aeiouAEIOU':
        number_of_vowels += 1
    x += 1

print(number_of_vowels)
```

Exercise 5.5

```
result = []
x = 1
while x <= 10:
    result.append(2 ** x)
    x += 1
print(result)
```

Exercise 5.6

```
for x in range(1,11):
    print(3 * x)
```

Exercise 5.7

```
L2 = [1,2,3,4,5]
sum = 0
x = 0
while x < len(L2):
    sum += L2[x]
    x += 1
print(sum)
```

Exercise 5.8

```
L2 = [3,4,1,5,2]    # for testing purposes
largest_so_far = L2[0]

for x in L2:
    if x > largest_so_far:
        largest_so_far = x
print(largest_so_far)
```

Exercise 5.9

```
x = 97    # for testing purposes
prime = True
if x <= 1:
    prime = False
else:
    for divisor in range(2,x):
        if x % divisor == 0:
```

```
            prime = False
            break
print(prime)
```

Chapter 6

Exercise 6.1

```
grid = [[1,2,3], [4,5,6], [7,8,9]] # for testing purposes
print(grid[2])
```

Exercise 6.2

```
grid = [[1,2,3], [4,5,6], [7,8,9]] # for testing purposes
print(grid[0][2])
print(grid[1][0])
print(grid[2][1])
```

Exercise 6.3

```
data = [[1,2,3,4],[5,6,7,8]]    # for testing purposes
for row in range(2):
    for column in range(4):
        print(data[row][column])
```

Exercise 6.4

```
purple: (255,0,255)
yellow: (255,255,0)
```

Exercise 6.5

Turquoise: an equal mix of green and blue.

Exercise 6.6

```
from graphics import *
win = GraphWin('Exercise 6.6',250,250)
img = Image(Point(125,125),250,250)
for x in range(250):
    for y in range(250):
        img.setPixel(x,y,color_rgb(0,0,255))
img.draw(win)
img.save('blue.png')
```

Exercise 6.7

```
from graphics import *

new_img = Image(Point(125,125),250,250)
inc = 256/250

for y in range(250):
    R = 0
    G = int(255-inc*y)
    B = int(inc*y)
    for x in range(250):
        new_img.setPixel(x,y,color_rgb(R,G,B))

new_img.save('green-blue-gradient.png')
```

Chapter 8

Exercise 8.1

```
def respond(n):
    print('Hi ' + n + ', doing well, thanks!')

respond('Hubert')
```

Exercise 8.2

```
def volume(r):
    return (4 / 3) * 3.14 * r ** 3

print(volume(10))
```

Exercise 8.3

```
def average(L):
    total = 0

    for num in L:
        total += num

return total / len(L)

print(average([1,2,3,4,5]))
```

Exercise 8.4

```
def largest(L):
    largest_so_far = L[0]
    for num in L:
        if num > largest_so_far:
```

```
              largest_so_far = num
      return largest_so_far
print(largest([1,2,3,4,5]))
```

Exercise 8.5

```
def ccp_7():
    if coin6 == coin7:
        ccp_5()
    elif coin6 > coin7:
        outcome_imbalance(coin6, 'coin7', 'coin6')
    else:
        outcome_imbalance(coin7, 'coin6', 'coin7')
```

Chapter 9

Exercise 9.1

```
def multiply_3(x,y):
    result = 0
    i = 1

    while i <= y:
        result += x
        i += 1
    return result

print(multiply_3(5,4))
```

Chapter 10

Exercise 10.1

```
step1 = [['*','*','*',' ',' '],
         ['*',' ','*','*',' '],
         ['*',' ','*',' ',' '],
         [' ','*','*',' ',' '],
         [' ',' ',' ','*',' ']]
print(step1)
```

Exercise 10.2

```
def create_row(n):
    row = []
    for i in range(n):
```

```
        row.append(' ')
    return row

print(create_row(10))
```

Exercise 10.3

```
def create_grid(rows, cols):
    grid = []

    for r in range(rows):
        grid.append(create_row(cols))

    return grid

print(create_grid(3,3))
```

Exercise 10.4

```
import random

def flip():
    if random.random() <= 0.5:
        print('heads')
    else:
        print('tails')

flip()
```

Exercise 10.5

```
import random

def roll():
    val = random.random()

    for i in range(1,7):
        if val <= i / 6:
            return i

print(roll())
```

Exercise 10.6

```
import random

def populate(grid, prob):
    rows = len(grid)
    cols = len(grid[0])
```

```
    for r in range(rows):
        for c in range(cols):
            if random.random() <= prob:
                grid[r][c] = '*'
            else:
                grid[r][c] = ' '
```

Exercise 10.7

```
def neighbors(grid, row, column):
    total = 0

    height = len(grid)
    width = len(grid[0])

    for x in range(row-1,row+2):
        for y in range(column-1,column+2):
            # if x or y are out of bounds
            if x < 0 or x >= height or y < 0 or y >= width:
                continue
            # if x and y specify the cell itself
            if x == row and y == column:
                continue
            if grid[x][y] == '*':
                total += 1
    return total
```

Exercise 10.8

```
def visualize(grid):
    rows = len(grid)
    cols = len(grid[0])

    separator = ''
    for i in range(cols * 2 + 1):
        separator += '-'

    print(separator)

    for r in range(rows):
        line = '|'
        for c in range(cols):
            line += grid[r][c] + '|'
        print(line)
        print(separator)
```

Exercise 10.9

```
def evolve(grid):
```

```
    rows = len(grid)
    cols = len(grid[0])

    new_grid = create_grid(rows,cols)

    for r in range(rows):
        for c in range(cols):
            n = neighbors(grid,r,c)
            if grid[r][c] == '*':
                if n == 2 or n == 3:
                    new_grid[r][c] = '*'
                else:
                    new_grid[r][c] = ' '
            else:
                if n == 3:
                    new_grid[r][c] = '*'
                else:
                    new_grid[r][c] = ' '
    return new_grid
```

Exercise 10.10

```
from graphics import *

win = GraphWin('Face',500,500)

eye1 = Rectangle(Point(100,100),Point(150,150))
eye1.setFill(color_rgb(0,0,255))
eye1.setOutline(color_rgb(0,0,0))
eye1.draw(win)

eye2 = Rectangle(Point(350,100),Point(400,150))
eye2.setFill(color_rgb(0,0,255))
eye2.setOutline(color_rgb(0,0,0))
eye2.draw(win)

nose = Rectangle(Point(225,200),Point(275,325))
nose.setFill(color_rgb(0,150,0))
nose.setOutline(color_rgb(0,0,0))
nose.draw(win)

mouth = Rectangle(Point(100,400),Point(400,450))
mouth.setFill(color_rgb(255,0,0))
mouth.setOutline(color_rgb(0,0,0))
mouth.draw(win)
```

Exercise 10.11

```
from graphics import *
```

```
def create_grid_visual(rows, cols, window):
    grid_visual = create_grid(rows,cols)

    p_w = window.getWidth() // cols    # pixel width
    p_h = window.getHeight() // rows   # pixel height

    for r in range(rows):
        for c in range(cols):
            grid_visual[r][c] = Rectangle(Point(c*p_w,r*p_h),
                              Point((c+1)*p_w,(r+1)*p_h))
            grid_visual[r][c].setFill(color_rgb(0,0,0))
            grid_visual[r][c].setOutline(color_rgb(50,50,50))
            grid_visual[r][c].draw(window)

    return grid_visual
```

Exercise 10.12

```
def mirror(grid, grid_visual):
    rows = len(grid)
    cols = len(grid[0])

    for r in range(rows):
        for c in range(cols):
            if grid[r][c] == '*':
                        grid_visual[r][c].
                        setFill(color_rgb(0,255,0))
            else:
                        grid_visual[r][c].
                        setFill(color_rgb(0,0,0))
```

Chapter 12

Exercise 12.1

```
def summation(n):
    if n == 1:                    # base case
        return 1
    return n + summation(n-1)  # recursive case

print(summation(10))
```

Exercise 12.2

```
def exponent(x,y):
    if y == 0:                    # base case
        return 1
```

```
    return x * exponent(x,y-1)   # recursive case
print(exponent(5,2))
```

Exercise 12.3

```
def sum_list(L):
    if len(L) == 0:                              # base case
        return 0
    if type(L[0]) == int or type(L[0]) == float: # recursive case
        return L[0] + sum_list(L[1:])
    else:                                        # recursive case
        return sum_list(L[1:])
print(sum_list([1,2,3,4,5]))
```

Exercise 12.4

```
def count(L, n):
    if len(L) == 0:                # base case
        return 0
    if L[0] < n:                   # recursive case
        return 1 + count(L[1:],n)
    else:                          # recursive case
        return count(L[1:],n)
print(count([1,2,3,2,1],3))
```

Exercise 12.5

```
def palindrome(S):
    if len(S) <= 1:                # base case
        return True
    if S[0] != S[-1]:              # base case
        return False
    else:                          # recursive case
        return palindrome(S[1:-1])
print(palindrome('racecar'))
print(palindrome('racecas'))
```

Chapter 14

Exercise 14.1

```
f = open('filename.txt','r')
print(f.read())
```

```
f.close()
```

Exercise 14.2

```
f = open('test.txt','w')
for x in range(1,1001):
    f.write(str(x) + '\n')

f.close()
```

Exercise 14.3

```
f = open('test.txt','r')

for x in range(1,1001):
    line = f.readline()

    if x % 5 == 0:
        print(line[:-1])

f.close()
```

Exercise 14.4

```
def word(sentence, n):
    return sentence.split(' ')[n-1]

print(word('Hi, how are you?',2))
```

Exercise 14.5

```
def team_ELO(code, year):
    ratings = []
    f = open('nbaallelo.csv','r')
    lines = f.readlines()

    for line in lines[1:]:
        data = line.split(',')

        if data[8] == code and data[4] == str(year):
            ratings.append(data[12])
    return ratings

print(team_ELO('LAL',2003))
```

Exercise 14.6

```
LAL_ELOS = []

f = open('nbaallelo.csv','r')
lines = f.readlines()
```

```
for line in lines[1:]:
    data = line.split(',')
    if data[8] == 'LAL' and data[4] == '2009' and data[7] == '0':
    LAL_ELOS.append(float(data[12]))

print(LAL_ELOS)
```

Exercise 14.7

```
import matplotlib.pyplot as plt
GSW_ELOS = []

f = open('nbaallelo.csv','r')
lines = f.readlines()

for line in lines[1:]:
    data = line.split(',')

    if data[8] == 'GSW' and
        data[4] == '2009' and
        data[7] == '0':
        GSW_ELOS.append(float(data[12]))

X = []

for i in range(len(GSW_ELOS)):
    X.append(i)

plt.plot(X, LAL_ELOS, label='Lakers')
plt.plot(X, GSW_ELOS, label='Warriors')
plt.legend()
plt.grid()
plt.show()
```

Chapter 15

Exercise 15.1

```
import numpy as np

L = []
for i in range(1,101):
    L.append(i * 2)

A = np.array(L)

print(A)
```

Exercise 15.2

```
def area(r):
    return 3.14 * r ** 2
```

```
print(area(10))
```

Exercise 15.3

```
area(A)   # assuming A is already defined as in Exercise 15.1
```

Exercise 15.4

```
import numpy as np

L2D = []

for r in range(10):
    row = []
    for c in range(1,11):
        row.append(10 * r + c)
    L2D.append(row)
A2D = np.array(L2D)

print(A2D)
```

Exercise 15.5

```
A2D[7:10,:]
```

Exercise 15.6

```
from sklearn.linear_model import LinearRegression
import numpy as np

d = np.array([[3.38,44.5],[0.48,15.5],[1.35,8.10],
              [465.0,423.0],[36.3,119.5],[27.6,115.0],
              [14.8,98.2],[1.04,5.50]])
model = LinearRegression()
model.fit(d[:,:1],d[:,1])
print(model.predict([[15]]))
```

Exercise 15.7

```
from sklearn.linear_model import LinearRegression
import pandas as pd
import numpy as np

df = pd.read_csv('gold_prices.csv',sep=',')
a = df.to_numpy()

model = LinearRegression()
model.fit(a[:,:1],a[:,1])

print(model.predict([[2050],[2055],[2060]]))
```

Appendix

Downloading Files

In Chapter 6, reference is made to John Zelle's graphics library using the following URL: https://mcsp.wartburg.edu/zelle/python/graphics.py. Depending on your web browser, this URL will be treated in different ways.

Apple's Safari (version 14.0.3): the URL goes to a webpage that displays the contents of the file. To then download this file to your computer, <CTRL> + click anywhere on the webpage and choose the 'Save Page As' option. The default value for the file format is 'Web Archive.' This should be changed to 'Page Source' so that the file can be saved without a '.webarchive' extension.

Google's Chrome (version 95.0.4638.54): the URL goes to a webpage that displays the contents of the file. To then download this file to your computer, right-click anywhere on the webpage and choose the 'Save as' option.

Microsoft's Internet Explorer (version 1909): the URL goes immediately to download the file.

Mozilla's Firefox (version 93.0): the URL goes immediately to download the file.

File Paths

When opening a file in Python using the open function, all of the examples in this book have assumed that the relevant file, say info.txt, is in the same directory (or folder) as the Python file, say exercise.py, you are running. But what if info.txt is *not* in the same directory? It can still be opened, but additional information about the file's location in the overall directory structure must be supplied. This additional information is called the file's **path**.

Paths can be expressed in two different ways: (i) absolute and (ii) relative paths. Let's begin with absolute paths. These paths locate a file in a directory structure regardless of what directory you are currently in (or what directory the Python file trying to access this file is in). For those of you using Windows, you can find the absolute path of a file by finding the file, right-clicking on the file, and checking its Properties. Within Properties, you should be able to see the Location attribute under the General tab. This should specify the directory that the file is in. The info.txt file is located in the following directory on my computer:

```
C:\Users\dl288\Documents\Publications\Book
```

The backslash characters are used to demarcate directory names. We can see that info.txt is in the Book directory, which is in the Publications directory, which is in the Documents directory, and so on. I can use this information to open info.txt as follows:

```
open('C:\Users\dl288\Documents\Publications\Book\info.
txt')
```

Notice, the path and the name of the file (info.txt) are combined with a backslash in between.

This, unfortunately, generates an error. This is because the backslash is an escape character in Python and is used to signal that the character immediately following the backslash will be used to represent a non-standard character. For example, '\n' is used to represent a newline character instead of the letter n. So in order to treat the backslash as the character '\' and not an escape character, we have to use an additional backslash. The correct statement is:

```
open('C:\\Users\\dl288\\Documents\\Publications\\Book\\
info.txt')
```

The nice thing about absolute paths is that, unlike using only the file name, it will specify the relevant file regardless of where you execute the open function. When this function was first introduced, it was required that exercise.py (the file that the open function is in) and info.txt both be in the same directory. When using absolute paths, this no longer holds. The exercise.py and info.txt can be different directories and there will be no issues.

A relative path locates a file in a directory structure based on the directory that you are currently in (or the directory the Python file trying to access this file is in). When you open info.txt using only its name, you are providing a relative path. You are assuming that info.txt is in the same directory as exercise.py. But what if exercise.py is in a different directory? Perhaps its absolute path is:

```
C:\Users\dl288\Documents\Publications\Book\Python
```

This means that exercise.py is in the Python directory, which is in the Book directory. So we can say that info.txt is in the 'parent' directory of exercise.py (because info.txt is in the Book directory). The relative path from the directory that exercise.py is in to the directory that info.txt is in can be expressed as follows:

```
..\info.txt
```

This can be used with the open function as follows:

```
open('..\\info.txt')
```

The ' . . ' represents the parent directory of the current location. Because exercise.py is located in the Python directory, the ' . . ' represents the Book directory. The usefulness of ' . . ' is that actual directory names are not important. All that matters is the relationship of the current location to the desired location within the directory structure.

Everything discussed here is applicable to those of you who use MAC OS. The only difference is that the character used to demarcate directory names in a path is a forward slash instead of a backslash. So the following use of the open function should work:

```
open('C:/Users/dl288/Documents/Publications/Book/info.
txt')
```

Installing Libraries

An important skill in expanding your ability to leverage Python is to install libraries (also referred to as modules as well). The **numpy** Library is a library for manipulating two-dimensional list-like structures. The standard distribution of Python does not include this library. Installing these libraries, like numpy, should be fairly straightforward given the standard package manager for Python called pip.

Depending on what kind of operating system you are running, you will have to learn two different ways of using pip. For those of you using Windows, you will need to access the 'Command Prompt.' Some people also call this the 'Command Line Window' or the 'Powershell.' There are several ways to access the command prompt. One way is to press <Windows>+X. This should open up a menu of options where you should be able to find one of the terms mentioned above. Another way is to type in any of the terms in the Start Menu Search box. Finally, if you open the Start Menu, you can scroll down the list of applications until you see 'Windows Powershell' or under the 'Windows System' folder, you will find 'Command Prompt.' Hopefully one of these will work for you.

For those of you using a Mac, you will need access to the 'Terminal.' You can find this application in the 'Utilities' folder. You can also press Command-Spacebar to launch Spotlight. You can simply type 'Terminal' in the resulting search bar to access the application.

Once you have access to the Command Prompt on Windows or the Terminal on a Mac, you can run the following install command:

```
pip install numpy
```

Hopefully, this will do the trick and you will now be able to import the relevant code so that you can work with array objects. To check that it was installed correctly, make sure the following statement doesn't generate any error messages in your Python interpreter.

```
import numpy
```

List Comprehensions

A list comprehension is a way of creating a new list based on the values of an existing sequence. The syntax looks like this:

```
new_list = [ expression for var in sequence ]
```

The for loop portion of a list comprehension is exactly the same as a normal for loop. A variable name and a sequence (e.g., a string, a list) must be provided. Then, for each iteration of this loop, the expression will be evaluated. The results from the evaluations of each expression will become the elements of the new list. The following list comprehension will create a new list of ten 0s.

```
[ 0 for i in range(10) ]
```

The sequence in this list comprehension is range(10) and the variable is i. So the for loop will iterate ten times. Notice that i is never used in the expression. This is totally fine if you want to repeat the same value again and again. Changing the 0 to i will generate a list of integers from 0 to 9.

```
[ i for i in range(10) ]
```

List comprehensions are extremely useful when creating certain kinds of lists and can save you many keystrokes (and time).

randint

What if we wanted to model the rolling of a die? When a fair die is rolled, we expect the six different numbers (from 1 to 6) to occur with equal frequency. A 1 should be rolled with 1/6 probability, a 2 should also be rolled with 1/6 probability, and so on. Can you think of a way to model the rolling of a fair die using the random function?

We might model the rolling of a die with the following code exploiting the fact that we can divide the range of numbers between 0 and 1 into six equal parts.

```
num = random.random()
roll = 0
if num <= 1/6:
    roll = 1
elif num <= 2/6:
    roll = 2
elif num <= 3/6:
    roll = 3
elif num <= 4/6:
    roll = 4
elif num <= 5/6:
    roll = 5
else:
    roll = 6
print(roll)
```

Make sure you understand what's happening here before moving on. Note that a multi-clause conditional with an else clause was used to ensure that one and only one of the clauses will be executed.

An easier way of modeling the rolling of a die is by using the randint function. To use it, you must supply it with two integer values that specify the range of integers to randomly select from. The first integer specifies the lower bound and the second integer specifies the upper bound of the range.

```
>>> random.randint(1,6)
2
```

This will generate a random *integer* between 1 and 6 (inclusive). If you wanted to model a die with more sides, like an eight-sided die or a 20-sided die, you could simply change the 6 to an 8 or a 20.

Index

Made in the USA
Middletown, DE
12 November 2023

42555403R00159